YOUR DATA WILL BE USED AGAINST YOU

Your Data Will Be Used Against You

Policing in the Age of Self-Surveillance

Andrew Guthrie Ferguson

New York

NEW YORK UNIVERSITY PRESS
New York
www.nyupress.org

Library of Congress Cataloging-in-Publication Data
Names: Ferguson, Andrew G. author
Title: Your data will be used against you : policing in the age of self-surveillance / Andrew Guthrie Ferguson.
Description: New York : New York University Press, 2026. | Includes bibliographical references and index. | Summary: "This book is a stark warning about how smart devices and digital self-surveillance will be turned against us by police, prosecutors, and political whims"-- Provided by publisher.
Identifiers: LCCN 2025021773 (print) | LCCN 2025021774 (ebook) | ISBN 9781479838288 hardback | ISBN 9781479838295 ebook | ISBN 9781479838301 ebook other
Subjects: LCSH: Privacy, Right of--United States | Electronic surveillance--Law and legislation--United States | Wiretapping--Law and legislation--United States | Eavesdropping--Law and legislation--United States
Classification: LCC KF1263.C65 F47 2026 (print) | LCC KF1263.C65 (ebook) | DDC 342.7308/58--dc23/eng/20250506
LC record available at https://lccn.loc.gov/2025021773
LC ebook record available at https://lccn.loc.gov/2025021774

This book is printed on acid-free paper, and its binding materials are chosen for strength and durability. We strive to use environmentally responsible suppliers and materials to the greatest extent possible in publishing our books.

The manufacturer's authorized representative in the EU for product safety is Mare Nostrum Group B.V., Mauritskade 21D, 1091 GC Amsterdam, The Netherlands.
Email: gpsr@mare-nostrum.co.uk.

Manufactured in the United States of America

10 9 8 7 6 5 4 3 2 1

Also available as an ebook

Thank you to Alissa, Cole, and Lexa for your love and support.

Thank you to Emma Berry for your excellent edits. Thank you to Jazzmen Fobbs and Maliha Sammo for excellent editing and cite checking.

Thank you to Clara Platter and the entire team at New York University Press for always believing in my books.

CONTENTS

Introduction

You Are a Warrant Away from Incrimination

I start the class with a question:

"How many of you have used a physical, paper map to travel anywhere in the past year?"

In this group of bright, young law students, no one raises their hand.

"How many of you have printed or written down directions from the Internet?"

No hands.

"How many of you have asked a fellow human being for directions in the past year?"

Still no hands.

"How many of you use your phones, or the digital maps in your car, for directions?"

This time, everyone raises their hand.

"How many of you know that the same mapping technologies built into your smartphones and cars are available to police and can be used against you in a criminal case?"

A sheepish hand or two.

"How many of you know that a record of every place you have traveled with that phone is available to police with a warrant?"

Sad looks all around.

"Are any of you going to give up Google or Apple Maps? Or the navigation system in your car?"

Heads shake no. Hands stay down.

So begins a class I teach in law school. The students, like all of us, are trapped by surveillance technology of our own making. We have given data companies—and thus the government—access to our inner lives, and we don't know what to do about it.

* * *

This book is about power. It is about how the digital trails we leave behind undermine our privacy and freedom, leaving our most personal information open to police discovery. This book is also about people—because it's the choices we've made to embrace digital convenience and personal security that have created this web of self-surveillance. Every time we step outside our home with a smartphone, or ask a smart speaker to play us a song, or Google anything, we create data, and that data reveals who we are.

In a world where everything is data, everything is evidence.

This book is a warning about how the rise of sensor-driven digital technology can be weaponized against democratic values and personal freedoms. This book is not an anti-technology screed. The innovative wonders that put a computer in your pocket or a digital pacemaker in your heart are deserving of respect and consumer attention. But the costs of that innovation are real. We are transforming our physical world and our personal lifestyles with "smart" devices that provide useful data to improve our lives but also reveal them completely. The question is when, if ever, should that smart digital pacemaker in your heart be used as evidence against you in a criminal case. And, it has been.[1]

The simple truth is that digital innovation comes at the cost of digital surveillance. The sensor on your wrist provides personal insights by monitoring you, but that data can be accessed by police and prosecutors looking to find incriminating information.[2] Americans have also bought into the belief that surveillance makes us safer. So, cities invest in networks of cameras instead of community-centered after-school programs.[3] This too is self-surveillance, just mediated by a democratically elected government.

This book explains how you are—at best—a warrant away from having your most intimate personal details revealed to a government agent looking to incarcerate, embarrass, or intimidate you. When your data can be used against you, the government gains power over you and your family in ways that are deeply uncomfortable. All the police need is a judge's signature and everything—from your smart bed to your most embarrassing Google search—becomes evidence.[4] And, even if the government does not make the request, the threat of exposing that data remains ever present.

Two transformations of modern society are just starting to generate the necessary attention and concern. First, this book catalogs the transformation of the built environment—homes, cars, things, and people—into digital tracking devices. The shift is part of an attempt to sell "surveillance as a service" to consumers whereby insights, efficiencies, and patterns become quantified and commodified.[5] Second, this book explores the rise of policing technologies that democratically elected governments are building into cities as affirmative methods of surveillance. The rise of what I have called "big data policing" combines new sensor technologies and old pathologies of surveillance into a new form of social control.[6] This book explores how police and prosecutors are starting to use these two types of data in criminal cases. The intersections are accelerating and will only increase as the digital web of patterns and habits reveal more of our lives and activities.

This book is grounded in constitutional law and aims to highlight the gaps in legal rules that govern access to the personal data collected by smart devices and public surveillance systems. But in writing it, I also have a higher ambition: to convince you that a world in which you are a warrant away from total digital exposure is not a world you want to live in. No matter how law-abiding or upstanding you consider yourself, the safeguards built into our legal system—search warrants, judicial oversight, concepts like probable cause—are too weak to protect us from the self-surveillance systems we are building. Worse, the commodification of "surveillance as a service"—a billion-dollar industry—provides us a false sense of security, when in fact, it opens our lives to greater intrusion. After all, that digital camera on your door keeping the bad guys away, is also watching you.

Let me begin by telling a story—a modern-day Romeo and Juliet—where two star-crossed lovers find themselves pregnant and living in a state that has criminalized abortion.[7] The couple—privileged, educated, students at a major university—decide to obtain an abortion in a world of digital tracking and sensor surveillance. The tale begins with a Google search outside a sorority house: "Abortion services?" It next involves the car's computer navigation system tracking them travelling from one state to another. (Like my students, using a paper map is not even contemplated.) In addition, the couple's smartphones, and dozens of location-tracking apps all follow the car from the sorority house to a medical facility in a nearby state. Cell site location data reveals precisely how long the couple stayed at the facility. Multiple surveillance cameras, license plate readers, toll records, and a host of other sensors memorialize the trip as well. One need not even add the young woman's smartwatch that is monitoring her vital signs, her Amazon Echo, her period-tracking App, or the texts she sent her worried mother, or even any of her mobile purchases at the drugstore to realize that the web of digital clues about her actions are available to uncover.

If prosecutors discover the couple's intent, investigators can easily scoop up the digital clues. They are investigating a "crime." Many of those pieces of incriminating data do not even require a warrant, but even those that might—a Google search, geolocation data—is just a piece of paper away from being obtained.[8] The couple will be convicted based on the almost inescapable digital clues of their lives. Everyone she communicated with or assisted her is now an accomplice and the subject of criminal investigation with their own digital trails exposed. And, while we might realize in the abstract that digital conveniences come at the cost of digital tracking, we might not realize how easy it is for police to obtain the information once that young couple becomes the target of a criminal investigation.

The story is happening somewhere in the United States today. And, if it is not making headlines, that is only because of the relative affluence and privilege of the parties which affords them protection from prosecution. Not everyone will be so lucky. The law is not on their side, and the ease of searching digitally available evidence is rapidly shifting the balance of power toward the government.

That same pregnancy story, of course, has happened many times before.[9] In the era before *Roe v. Wade*, illegal abortions were common. Information about practitioners was shared via word of mouth, which meant that marginalized people often had a more difficult time accessing safe, competent care. But it also meant that most people could, and did, end their pregnancies quietly, without leaving a record. There would be no search history, no digital map for looking up directions to a clandestine provider, no geolocation to pinpoint the precise time of the procedure, no texts to a worried mother, no vital signs recorded on a smartwatch. Sure, a police officer could have followed the pregnant person in a car or on foot, but that would require time, effort, and information (knowing the time and date of the procedure, for example), which would have limited the utility of this method of investigation.

What has changed is not just the ease of accessing digital evidence, but also the scale, scope, and ubiquity of existing digital trails.[10] Prosecutors can now search for anyone who has queried a search engine about abortion services and begin an investigation. Police can now geolocate any building that they believe correlates with people seeking abortion services.[11] The existence of digital clues and the growth of surveillance capabilities casts a wider net on who becomes a target.

The lessons from this story extend to other circumstances in which people might find themselves on the wrong side of those in power: A journalist uncovering political corruption, an employee blowing the whistle on corporate malfeasance, a gun owner buying a new weapon, an undocumented worker, a citizen protesting police brutality, or anyone criticizing the government itself. Digital policing is a godsend for authoritarianism, and in an era where federal and local policing has been weaponized for partisan purposes, the threat of targeted surveillance is all too real. Every perceived political enemy is vulnerable to digital exposure.

Of course, as has long been the reality in the United States, the primary focus of policing will be on the poor and those who commit crimes driven by poverty, addiction, trauma, mental illness, structural inequality, or those lacking education and opportunities to pursue a different path.[12] While crime occurs across socio-economic strata, and many violent acts cannot be excused by poverty, vast parts of the criminal legal system are focused on policing poverty and ensuring a form of social control over those with lesser economic means. Such has been the history of policing in the United States—with a good bit of overt, implicit, and structural racism thrown in—and such is the future of technology-enhanced, sensor-driven policing.[13] My aim here is not to debate policing. There are many excellent critiques of policing already written.[14] The point is to show how the web of surveillance exploited by the police changes the balance of power between the government and the people—including you.

In the face of this growing digital web, "the law"—the subject I study and teach—has remained decidedly analog. My goal with this book is to alert readers to the danger of that legal stagnation. The lack of legal responses to growing digital privacy threats is a failure of imagination, but also a reflection of other structural inequities in the legal process. Probable cause warrants—the constitutional protection that the Supreme Court has spent countless pages writing about—are weak protections of personal data.[15] Judges are not technologists. Some magistrate judges (who sign probable cause warrants) are not even lawyers.[16] Probable cause is a low standard of proof.[17] And police control all the information in the warrant, making the judge's role even more limited. It's not that warrants are not important, but they are better thought of as keys to access information, rather than barriers to prevent access.

While old-fashioned law stagnates, technology speeds ahead. This book focuses on four major changes in how ever-present sensor surveillance impacts American society. First, the ease and affordability of digitizing everything has reordered our lives without generating new laws or protective rules. Old, "dumb" things like cars and clocks have become "smart" devices that record our personal patterns and yet the law—statutory and constitutional—remains decidedly analog.[18] This reality presents a problem because courts must follow existing laws, even when they do not respond to the moment. Whether we are talking about the Internet of Things, or a smart car, or the geolocation metadata on a saved photograph, digital clues are becoming the building blocks of criminal prosecution.[19]

Second, the book catches us up to the present reality where a world of big data policing filled with predictive analytics, facial recognition, and citywide camera systems create a new surveillance trap.[20] Sensors are not just inside our homes, but also built into our streetlights, listening for gunshots, or automatically reporting on suspicious behaviors.[21] Big cities are erecting AI-assisted surveillance systems capable of long-term, aggregated, pervasive tracking capabilities.[22] Smaller jurisdictions are investing in centralized command centers that seamlessly link license plate readers, video analytics, and suspect lists together.[23] Police body cameras, 911 calls, and private neighborhood social media accounts are used to identify and prosecute individuals.[24] As I will discuss, there are few laws and little regulation around this architecture of structural surveillance.

Combined, the prevalence of private self-surveillance tools and the expansion of public surveillance systems creates a world where targeted individuals can find little place to escape. If you cannot claim privacy inside your home or outside of it, you—we—have created a world of enhanced and largely discretionary police power. And, as I will discuss, this power remains unchecked by legal protections and undermined by consumer habits. We live in precarious times when all that stands in the way of digital exposure is a magistrate judge's signature on a piece of paper.

Third, the book examines the costs and consequences of digital self-surveillance. The costs include shifts in power, privacy, and privatization, as well as practical problems. When everything is evidence, the government gains power to prosecute, and people also lose a measure of security, autonomy, and community. A federal government with access to unlimited personal data is a recipe for authoritarian abuse. In addition, this surveillance growth strengthens corporate power—*vis á vis* police—as private platforms distort public safety priorities and community engagement. "Policing as a platform" is not only a marketing pitch, but also a threat to democratic governance. The result is a half-step away from a form of tyranny where those who possess the data can control the citizenry. "Tyranny" is a rhetorically loaded word, but the fear of an all-controlling, ever-observing digital power is not too far a stretch in an era of politized prosecution.[25] Finally, self-surveillance comes with a host of practical problems including how data is used, misused, and just gets things wrong. For every program that seeks to turn data into usable intelligence, there are a dozen scandals about how the data is wrong, conflates causation and correlation, or is racially biased against certain communities.[26]

Lastly, the book offers solutions to a world where everything is evidence that will be used against you. Perhaps not surprisingly, the response also takes everything into account. Constitutional limitations require a judicial response that expands Fourth Amendment understandings to suit the digital age. Legal limitations require federal, state, and local legislative responses to fill the gaps around consumer data and police use of new surveillance technologies. Impacted communities must be given a voice through the creation of local mechanisms of community control. We must heed abolitionist warnings about the foreseeable abuses from technologies of social control. And, finally, individuals must be empowered to reshape consumer demand for self-surveillance technologies that put data controls and destruction in the hands of the users and not with the companies. There is no reason why surveillance data must be retained, or accessible by anyone but the user. Technology must pass what I call "the tyrant test," and if it fails, it should not be sold or used.[27]

Today, criminal prosecutions look pretty similar to the court practice of the past century. Prosecutors rely on human witnesses and physical evidence. Cell phones and social media posts make an appearance. Forensic evidence—most obviously DNA—has become a routine part of many serious cases.[28] But digital forensics—proving a case with the digital clues of life—is only just becoming common enough to generate concern.[29] In the near future, this will change, and criminal courtrooms will be filled with digital evidence generated by our smart things and the surveillance world around us. This book explores how we should understand that change and adapt to it. It also seeks to warn about what might happen if we ignore the growing surveillance systems increasingly integrating into our lives.

The overarching goal of this book is to contribute to the national conversation around surveillance, privacy, power, and law. But I also hope you'll find it relevant to you personally. If you think about all the data you put out into the world—data that reveals your interests, desires, habits, and connections in intimate detail—you will see that these issues directly affect your life and the lives of your loved ones. While this book is filled with stories about criminal wrongdoers getting caught because of their digital trails, the surveillance net captures everyone. Who is deemed "criminal" is a contested and changeable reality.[30] Politicians can easily demonize individuals and groups, turning surveillance against citizens. Technologies developed to thwart violent crime can be repurposed for political repression. American history—from revolutionaries, to abolitionists, to draft avoiders, to dissenting religious, cultural, and political voices—is filled with stories about people who were convicted based on hatred, ignorance, or prejudice.[31] And to put a finer point on it—all of those people would have been far easier to prosecute with the digital evidence now available.

All that said, police are using our data to catch people who have done truly awful things. Depending on how you view police power, you may read this book's various vignettes of dumb criminals and smart data as evidence that these technologies are a great gift to criminal justice. Murderers are caught. Innocent people are exonerated. Data proves the truth, or at least eventually gets to the right result.

The uncomfortable reality is that the national conversation is not one-sided. Both the promise of new technologies and their dangers are very real. Part I offers a window into how criminal prosecution is changing in response to digital technologies of self-surveillance. Part II examines the consequences of this shift, focusing on changes in power, privacy, and criminal justice practice. Part III offers solutions to the problems raised in the book, with a focus on what judges, legislatures, and individuals can do to respond to the risks.

Despite its complexity, the debate over new policing technologies is an urgent conversation to begin. We all need to engage in the debate so that we can get the rules right when it comes to surveillance power. Especially now, as federal power expands and politicized prosecutions grow more common, the danger of doing nothing becomes intolerable. The laws governing digital evidence are still unwritten. And for every minute we spend waiting, the net of self-surveillance we've trapped ourselves in grows tighter. How or whether we escape that net will be up to us. I hope this book helps point the way out.

PART I

Our World Digitally Transformed

1

Our Homes

In Hallandale Beach, Florida, police responded to a bizarre 911 call.[1] Silvia Galva had been impaled by a twelve-inch spear through her chest. Her boyfriend reported that a verbal argument had turned into a physical struggle, during which Silvia fell off their bed, landing on the spear blade, which had served as decor.[2] The girlfriend was dead. The suspect had a story. Who could be an objective witness? Enter the two Amazon Echo Dots, programmed to record voice queries and provide answers, the couple had kept in their bedroom.[3] Both the police and the defense sought access to the Echo Dot voice recordings around the time of the fight. Both sides wanted to call "Alexa" as a witness in their case.[4]

In a quiet Maryland neighborhood, five gunshots rang out.[5] A woman was found dead in her bedroom. Suspicion of her husband turned into proof once police realized that a Google Nest surveillance camera had been recording all night.[6] The playback is chilling. At approximately 11:23 p.m., Ricardo Muscolino let the dog out, poured himself a glass of cold water, walked upstairs to the bedroom, closed the door, and shot his wife, Lara, five times, killing her.[7] The Google Nest home security camera recorded it all and saved it to the cloud. Audio captured Lara's screams and each of the five shots. Video captured Ricardo leaving the bedroom and exiting the house. Investigating officers viewed the footage through a shared password and later obtained a warrant for the cloud recordings to be used as evidence at trial.[8]

Our homes are getting smarter, even if people keep doing dumb things.[9] More than 60 million American homes have a smart speaker, television, stove, thermostat—or one of the dozens of other such devices on the market. (Worldwide, that number is in the billions.)[10] "Smart," in this case, means digitally connected and digitally recording. Appliances that once sat idly in our kitchens or bedrooms are now constantly collecting information from around our homes, surveilling our most personal activities and saving the details to the cloud—where police can and do retrieve them. In the not-too-distant past, much of this information would have been impossible for police to obtain.[11] Today, however, our homes are filled with spies. And we're the ones who invited them in.[12]

This chapter explores the transformation of our homes into sources of digital evidence.[13] That smart video doorbell that alerts you when someone is on your front porch is also an evidence collection machine, capturing when you leave and with whom, and when you come home drunk at 2:00 a.m. That Wi-Fi system streaming the world of entertainment to your couch also monitors what room you are in while you're watching and offers clues about what you are doing there. If you find yourself under criminal investigation or on the wrong side of a politicized government, these digital footprints can become evidence to be used against you.

Our Homes Transformed

Our homes used to be spaces of relative privacy. Whether we lived on a farmstead or in a suburban tract house, a mansion or a studio apartment, our home's physical structure ensured the exclusion of others.[14] Only those allowed within our four walls could see, hear, sense, or understand what happened there. From Fourth Amendment principles to criminal trespass and burglary statutes, our laws have respected these physical and psychological markers of privacy, creating norms—constitutional and otherwise—that kept outsiders, including the police, outside.[15]

Smart home technology erases those physical limitations.[16] In addition to Amazon Echo speakers and Google Nest security cameras, you can buy a smart refrigerator that orders milk when you run out, or an energy-efficient lighting system that turns bulbs on and off as you walk from room to room.[17] Brochures for luxury smart homes advertise remote artificial intelligence that will adapt to your preferred temperature and light patterns, anticipate your arrival, and sense your moods and needs.[18] Some of the technology will be built into the walls (like temperature control tablets), and some will respond to the physical environment (like window shades that react to the sun and lights that turn off when they no longer sense motion).[19]

Even in less futuristic homes, alarm systems note when you come and go, entertainment systems record when music is played in different rooms, and smart energy systems monitor electricity usage for various appliances. With the right interface, you can see at a glance that one child is listening to Spotify instead of doing her homework and the other is watching YouTube videos instead of doing his chores. Of course, if you can spy on your children, others can spy on you.[20] This is the trap of the digital world.

For police, the digital patterns captured by our smart devices can provide clues that might become extremely relevant to a criminal investigation.[21] In 2017, New Hampshire detectives sought information about a double murder.[22] Two women had been found brutally stabbed to death, their bodies wrapped in tarps and hidden under the front porch of the house where one of them had lived. There was no direct evidence of who had committed the crime. There was no direct evidence to indicate exactly when the stabbings occurred. The homeowner—an alleged drug dealer who found the bodies—had an alibi: He was in Florida with one of his two girlfriends (the other was one of the victims). Fortunately for investigators, the home was wired with seven cameras, along with smart Amazon speakers. Police were able to discover that a man named Timothy Verrill—a friend of one of the women—was the only person who had been with the victims the day they were killed.[23] The cameras captured him going in and out of the house at the approximate time of the killing. And the smart speaker overheard the women joking with him as they asked Amazon's "Alexa" questions and instructed it to play songs.[24]

If this kind of data collection feels invasive, just wait: Smart homes get creepy fast. Smart televisions record every show or movie you watch, at what time, and note how quickly you change the channel.[25] This data is then sold to advertisers interested in your preferences. Smart TVs even came with microphones originally until it was revealed the companies were eavesdropping on your TV room conversations.[26] Those who want to relive their childhood nightmares can buy Google Nest's "Sleep Sensing," a device that watches you sleep.[27] The service tracks your body movements via radar, listens to your nighttime sounds, monitors your body temperature, and senses light levels. Advertised as a way to improve your sleep patterns, Sleep Sensing might also provide good evidence of your whereabouts on a particular night.

The list of smart-home devices is long, ranging from rather helpful items, like smart sprinklers that know when to water your neglected lawn, to rather unnecessary items, like smart cups that monitor your daily water intake. But regardless of their utility (or absurdity), all these smart devices do one thing: They collect personal data. Was the suspect asleep when the murder occurred? Does their alibi check out? Instead of trying to parse conflicting statements from humans (or simply facing a black box mystery), law enforcement can turn to digital records of our movements, actions, and daily routines. The creepy guy watching us from the shadows is real—and willing to testify.

The Law of the Home

In the hierarchy of Fourth Amendment rights, the home stands as our most protected space, and it has long had a special primacy in U.S. constitutional law.[28] As Justice Antonin Scalia once stated, "When it comes to the Fourth Amendment, the home is first among equals."[29] He meant that homes are a place of refuge for family and personal freedom.

This protection is both physical and legal—bounded by property rights, but guarded by liberty interests. As the Supreme Court reflected, "The Fourth Amendment protects the individual's privacy in a variety of settings. In none is the zone of privacy more clearly defined than when bounded by the unambiguous physical dimensions of an individual's home—a zone that finds its roots in clear and specific constitutional terms: 'The right of the people to be secure in their . . . houses . . . shall not be violated.'"[30] It makes sense to carve out a space free from government observation. The choices we make by ourselves or with our families, the conversations we have, the experiments we undertake, and the activities we engage in—all are essential to human development and help make life worth living. Done under the constant watch of the government, they would be irrevocably altered. And so the home has remained a refuge.

Legal scholars have observed that there is almost a home "exceptionalism"[31] in Supreme Court cases, which regularly upholds protections at the threshold of the home. Police are required to obtain a warrant to enter a home, for example, and the Court has looked down upon attempts to use technology to circumvent those restrictions. Even a "crude" thermal imaging device, deployed from outside someone's home, could reveal "intimate" details such as "at what hour each night the lady of the house takes her daily sauna and bath," wrote Scalia, prohibiting prosecutors from using evidence collected by such devices without a warrant. As the Supreme Court has long stated, "the Fourth Amendment stands [for] the right of a [person] to retreat into his own home and there be free from unreasonable governmental intrusion."[32] Your home is your castle—or it was, until your castle got Wi-Fi and started sharing data with Google and Amazon and other third parties.

The Third-Party Problem

Smart homes have become popular because they promise to use our data to improve our lives. Your smart dishwasher notices when you're running low on detergent and adds it to your online shopping cart, saving you from an emergency trip to the store. Your robot vacuum uses cloud-connected cameras to map out an efficient cleaning route and avoid obstacles. (Then again, it might also upload a picture of you on the toilet.)[33] Our digital conveniences work by sharing information with private third-party companies, which use it to optimize and commodify those efficiencies.[34] Your Google Nest thermostat is not simply informing you of your patterns of energy use; it is also sharing the data with Google. This creates a significant privacy problem, because the rules designed to protect private activities inside the four walls of your home have not necessarily adapted to cover the digital clues that escape outside those walls. If your smart security system connects with a company's central cloud server, your private information exists both inside the home and outside the home at the same time.[35] Unfortunately, traditional law protects only half the data (the half that's physically inside your home.) The other half, in the hands of a third-party company, receives no such protection.[36]

Imagine that police suspect your home's high energy consumption is consistent with growing marijuana in your basement using high-powered grow lights.[37] Under the traditional law of the home, police cannot barge into your house to search the horticulturally suspicious basement without a warrant. As we've seen, they'd also need a warrant to use a fancy thermal imaging device to read the basement's heat levels.[38] But the police have another way to confirm their suspicions. The third party that controls your smart thermostat has the data about your excessive energy use because you gave it to them.[39] If the police want that data, all they have to do is ask the company to provide it. This is the third-party problem.[40]

People intuitively understand this third-party problem, even if they largely ignore it. The question you just asked your smart speaker does not stay in your bedroom; it goes to Amazon, where it is stored along with millions of other queries. Because it is digital, it can be searched for, recovered, and connected back to your house and to you. Even the fact of the query itself—independent of the content—could be evidence in a case. As the suspect who joked with Alexa in the New Hampshire murder case learned, proof of presence at a crime scene can be incriminating in and of itself.[41]

Information shared with others doesn't receive the same Fourth Amendment protection as information you keep to yourself. In constitutional law, this is known as the "third-party doctrine."[42] Although the issue is not completely settled as a matter of law, in general, the Supreme Court has determined that data you share with private third parties loses an expectation of privacy, allowing police to gain access to it without a warrant. The original third-party doctrine cases arose from police accessing bank records and landline telephone records.[43] Essentially, the Supreme Court determined that people could not claim any expectation of privacy when it came to their bank records because they knew the bank had access to the information and they had chosen to share it.[44] (After all, we expect the bank to keep accurate records of the money we give it to hold.) It would be hard to claim the bank records were private, and if the records were not private, then the police could obtain them without a warrant.

This logic expanded to other data shared with third parties, under the theory that we are voluntarily sharing information and thus relinquishing any expectation of privacy. This seems logical. If you asked a friend a question—"Hey, Jimmy, what is the best way to dispose of a dead body?"—and Jimmy told police investigators you had asked this incriminating question, you would have little right to complain that your privacy had been violated. You're the one who asked Jimmy. You undermined your own privacy. Why would it be different if you asked Siri or an AI-agent? You knew the information was going somewhere, and you knew it wasn't private. As a matter of Fourth Amendment law, whether you're telling your secrets to a friend at a bar or a smart speaker in your bedroom, you lose the expectation of privacy (and thus Fourth Amendment protection).

Even if the Supreme Court wanted to expand Fourth Amendment protections for data collected in homes—something I have advocated for—the Court would still permit police to collect that information with a judicial warrant. Almost all efforts to protect the home from government intrusion have focused solely on the requirement to obtain a warrant before conducting a search.[45] With a warrant, police can obtain any evidence relevant to a possible crime. Meaning that all those digital secrets are available for the government to view. All of them. Including the most intimate. Data from smart beds, bathtubs, medical devices, and even sex toys—are all fair game with a judicial warrant.

Essentially, if the data exists, there is a legal process for obtaining it. While getting a warrant from a judge is not as easy as asking a company to turn over its data voluntarily, this legal reality means that even if the smart home data stays inside the home—a step that has been promoted by privacy-focused companies—it is still accessible by the police. This is what makes digital homes so different. In a traditional home, the things that happen just happen—they don't produce a record. If James Madison had murdered someone in his home, eighteenth-century investigators who entered that home with a warrant might have found a weapon or piece of the victim's property, but little else. In a twenty-first-century smart home, that same warrant would provide access to a treasure trove of data. All the captured digital clues of life could be pieced back together. Patterns, actions, omissions—all might be valuable information for investigators.

In one of the first cases to involve Amazon Echo recordings, police had a hot tub murder mystery to solve.[46] Four men in Arkansas spent the night drinking and watching a Razorbacks college football game. In the morning, one of the men was dead, lying face up in a hot tub.[47] Blood stains were discovered outside the hot tub, and investigators observed damage consistent with signs of a struggle, including broken bottles, a broken shot glass, and various knobs broken off the tub.[48] The deceased had a bloody eye, and his cracked eyeglasses were found at the bottom of the hot tub. The homeowner said he had gone to bed and did not know what happened until he found the body in the morning. The other men claimed to have left before anything went down. The coroner ruled the case a homicide—but who did it, and when? Enter smart data.

Turns out the Arkansas home was smart and wired. The home had a Nest thermometer, a Honeywell alarm system with motion detection, outdoor remote lighting sensors, and an Amazon Echo, all controllable from a smartphone.[49] Police sought the Echo data to see if anything changed in the middle of the night: Did the lights turn on? Did the streaming music stop? The home also had a smart water meter, which had recorded an increase in water usage in the middle of the night, that officers believed was consistent with someone cleaning up blood.[50] Each of the four men denied involvement, and no other witnesses came forward. All the police had was the data. Of course, data does not always clarify things. In this case, the data and inconsistent witness stories proved unhelpful, and eventually prosecutors had to drop the case against the accused.[51] Such an ending provides a lesson for defense lawyers. In a world where everything creates data, too much data can create doubt. But note how easy it was for police to access the information. Had the home been wired with any other smart home accessories, that data would have been accessible via a probable cause warrant, too. Warrants open the door to our digital lives. The only way to truly avoid giving the government open access to our home's data is to avoid producing it in the first place—but most of us are moving in the opposite direction.

From the Outside In

So far, I've been focusing on data collected inside smart homes by private third-party services. But digital surveillance can also happen from the outside, as police monitor homes for clues about what is happening inside. This isn't entirely new—human stakeouts have been an investigative tactic for years. But new digital camera systems allow this kind of surveillance to take place on a scale that would have once been unimaginable. Cameras don't need to eat or sleep or take a cigarette break. They don't draw a salary. They can sit watching the same house for months and months—and, increasingly, they're doing just that.

Daphne Moore was a lawyer who worked in a Springfield, Massachusetts, courthouse.[52] She lived with her daughter, who was suspected of drug dealing. To collect evidence against her, police set up a digital pole camera to record the comings and goings around the family home.[53] A digital pole camera is exactly what it sounds like: a smart camera mounted on a pole (or otherwise elevated) that can record for long periods at a time.[54] Without getting a warrant, police recorded every moment in and around the Moore home for eight months. The evidence was later used in criminal cases against both mother and daughter. Daphne Moore moved to suppress the digital recordings as a violation of her Fourth Amendment rights.[55] She argued that this warrantless collection of information about her home violated her reasonable expectation of privacy.

Travis Tuggle lived in Mattoon, Illinois, in a quiet rural neighborhood where he ran a midsized methamphetamine distribution business.[56] To build a case against him, police installed three digital pole cameras outside his home and recorded his activities for eighteen months, all without a warrant.[57] Every person, friend, family member, delivery person, and fellow drug dealer who visited the home was captured in footage that went directly back to the FBI office in Springfield. The stored footage could be searched at any time and was connected to other data sources, which allowed investigators to identify people and cars. Over one hundred video clips were used to convict Tuggle.[58] He challenged the use of the warrantless video clips as a violation of his Fourth Amendment rights.[59]

Both digital pole camera cases raised the same issue: Do people have any expectation of privacy from long-term government surveillance of their homes? If so, the police need a warrant. If not, the police can surveil any house (including yours), for any length of time, for whatever reason they wish.

The question puts two legal principles in tension. The first principle is the protection of the home. As I've discussed, the home has long been protected by the Fourth Amendment. At least when it comes to physical trespass (police walking on someone's porch), courts have afforded the home and the area just around the home (the curtilage)[60] with equivalent protection.[61] "Curtilage" is an old-fashioned word that refers to the area around the house that is considered private.[62] In the olden days, this area might have been physically marked out with a "curtilage wall," but it need not be fenced in to be protected. As the Supreme Court stated, "The protection afforded the curtilage is essentially a protection of families and personal privacy in an area intimately linked to the home, both physically and psychologically, where privacy expectations are most heightened."[63] This ruling makes some sense because during the Founding era, before the rise of indoor plumbing, the curtilage was where you did a lot of very personal activities, like use the outhouse or take a bath. To respect that reality, the courts, including the Supreme Court, have protected the curtilage from physical intrusion by investigating officers. But cameras are not physically walking on the property; they are just watching from a distance.

This raises the second important legal principle: The Supreme Court has long been leery of granting people too much privacy in public. The general rule is that the police can pretty much see what anyone else can see without running into a Fourth Amendment problem.[64] If you choose to stand on your front lawn selling cocaine, it seems silly to prevent the police from observing alongside the rest of your neighbors. In legal terms, you do not have a reasonable expectation of privacy if the rest of the world can easily watch you.

The long-term pole camera cases raise the question of whether we should be able to claim privacy in the curtilage around our homes free from governmental visual surveillance. Should we focus on the privacy that comes with curtilage, or the public nature of the activities around the home? Does it matter that a police officer theoretically could gather the same information via an old-school stakeout, even though it's very unlikely that police could watch for eighteen months without being detected?[65] Is digital surveillance different?[66]

In most of the cases where this issue has come up, district and circuit courts have allowed long-term police surveillance to take place without a warrant. In making these rulings, they cite earlier Supreme Court cases that held that people cannot claim a reasonable expectation of privacy in public. According to the Supreme Court, police are allowed to fly planes over your backyard and take photographs.[67] They are allowed to fly helicopters 400 feet over your home to see what you are growing in your backyard.[68] They can track you as long as they stay in public spaces.[69] Again, the rationale for these rulings is that by being in public, you forfeit an expectation of privacy against government surveillance—including in the area just around your home.

These older, analog technology cases are still controlling precedent for digital cases. Despite there being a world of difference between a single photo from an airplane and eighteen months of continuous digital surveillance, the Supreme Court has not yet upgraded its thinking to account for the digital age.[70] Information about what you do outside your home is arguably fair game for police investigators to collect even without probable cause or evidence of wrongdoing. And it will continue to be unless the Supreme Court changes the rules.

As a final point, it is also important to remember that the legal battle over this type of digital surveillance has focused on whether the police need a warrant. With a warrant, such long-term monitoring would be perfectly constitutional. And the barrier to obtain a warrant is low, especially in cases like Travis Tuggle's, where the evidence of large-scale drug distribution was strong, thus giving investigators probable cause to continue a more intensive investigation. So even if the courts do eventually require a warrant for such long-term searches, police will still have the power to watch a home like Tuggle's for years.

Inescapable Eyes

As with many things in American life, wealth buys privilege and privacy. The typical single-family home, with its four walls signaling exclusion, can be enhanced with picket fences, large hedges, or a metaphorical moat of manicured lawns keeping its inhabitants safe from prying eyes. Many people, of course, do not live in such private homes (although most Supreme Court justices do). Many people rent apartments, live in public housing, or live a more itinerant life, shuttling between short-term rentals and periods of being without a home.

Surveillance routinely comes standard with these lower-cost housing options. Landlords now recognize that in addition to deterring package theft, smart sensors and cameras have the added benefit of coercing better behavior from their tenants.[71] A smart surveillance camera acts as an added level of security, helping preserve the landlord's investment, but it also provides a window into tenants' habits: Who is throwing large parties? Who is writing graffiti in the elevator? Public housing authorities use camera systems to monitor hallway access and public spaces.[72] Pole cameras allow police to conduct virtual patrols of entire housing complexes. Some public housing authorities have contracted with private surveillance systems, making this housing "public" in more ways than one.[73] Although they are not equipped with the latest smart technology, these systems of surveillance are monitoring residents every single day. Does a boyfriend stay over too long? Is there an extra family member living in the apartment who is not on the lease? The presence of digital surveillance devices gives a newfound power to property owners and landlords. It also provides plenty of potential evidence to police.

To be clear, the Fourth Amendment protects rental properties, and even short-term hotel stays equal to the largest mansion.[74] One does not need to have a mortgage to claim an expectation of privacy. But landlords' increased capability to conduct private surveillance and the ease with which police can obtain data combine to create a weaker privacy picture for those who rent or share.

One day in 2019, residents of the Atlantic Plaza Towers, a 700-unit complex of rent-stabilized apartments in Ocean Hill, Brooklyn, woke up to learn that facial recognition technology would be installed in their building.[75] The system was billed by the management company as a way for residents to securely and "frictionlessly" access the building—the promise of convenience through technology.[76] But the residents were not pleased. The technology would be inescapable. To enter the building, people would need to be recognized by the scanners.

Residents had a host of reasons for not liking the plan, in addition to it seeming creepy. However, because rent-stabilized apartments are in short supply in Brooklyn, those who objected to the proposal had limited power to negotiate, and they risked retaliation if they protested.[77] Most of the residents were working class and couldn't just move to avoid the cameras. The residents, primarily Black and Brown women and their children, took the risk of pushing back against the facial recognition plan.[78] After their protests spurred national media attention, the landlord decided to rethink the cameras.[79] Atlantic Plaza Towers could easily have started a trend of landlords installing facial recognition technology in similar buildings. Instead, the residents' protest spurred legislation in New York that aimed to stop landlords from ever doing it.

At the other end of the economic spectrum, an apartment complex in downtown Philadelphia, advertises the convenience of its contactless facial recognition system, one of many smart features of this high-end building. When you walk into the elevator at the Residences at 2100 Hamilton, it instantly recognizes you and takes you directly to your million-dollar apartment.[80] It's a built-in service, offering what Professor

Chris Guillard has termed "luxury surveillance."[81] Whereas the residents of Atlantic Towers Plaza objected to having facial recognition technology thrust upon them, many of the hyper-wealthy are choosing to impose it on themselves.[82]

In both cases, these camera systems function like private long-term pole cameras for landlords. The same comings and goings, the same patterns, and the same revealing or embarrassing behaviors are captured, mined, and available as evidence. While we are likely to see more camera footage from public housing than from private luxury buildings introduced in criminal cases, the footage is available for both. The truth is that perks sold as security are only as secure as whoever controls the information, and we do not control the information.

The Smart Home Panopticon

Police and landlords do their fair share of surveillance, but the primary driver of the smart home surveillance phenomenon is consumers. It's not police officers installing cameras in our bedrooms or smart security systems on our doors—it's us. The question is, why? Why are we creating a market for "surveillance as a service"?[83] The answer is complex, and yet not entirely surprising. There has always been a market for home alarm systems, security guards, and even gated communities. Today's digital technology is just democratizing "private security" by making it cheaper and easier to obtain. In a dangerous world, digital surveillance systems allow us to buy a sense of security.

Our desire for personal security is both organic and manufactured. The fears that motivate people to invest millions of dollars in these home security systems are honestly held. But fear resonates because local news and national media amplify crime stories that they know will sell.[84] As civil rights advocate Alec Karakatsanis has demonstrated, news organizations spend a disproportionate amount of time covering property crimes at the expense of large-scale community harms like environmental pollution, wage theft, and other less obvious corporate crimes.[85] In fact, as Karakatsanis has argued, what we consider "crime" is largely a creation of the media's focus on the human consequences of structural economic and social inequalities in society, rather than their causes.[86] We focus attention on a destitute woman shoplifting food from a grocery store, but not the corporation shorting the wages of the cashiers at that same store.

Selling surveillance as a service taps into this manufactured fear. Amazon has aggressively entered this space, targeting consumers with its Ring cameras and Neighbors app.[87] The company sold 10 million Ring cameras in less than a decade,[88] and almost 10 million Americans are active Ring users.[89] Amazon also sells a smart robot named Astro that can patrol your home, as well as flying mini-drone cameras to video it when you are gone.[90] And, of course, the Amazon Echo is listening in the living room. Together, these products make up a private digital net of surveillance to protect against possible home invasions and other dangers.

Many companies—including Google, SimpliSafe, ADT, SkyBell, and Vivint—are competing to enter the smart home security space, advertising advanced AI technologies like facial recognition and predictive analytics that will alert you to anomalies in the ordinary patterns of your life.[91] Sneak downstairs to get a glass of water in the middle of the night and your smart alarm will notify you of an unusual movement. Shatter a glass in the kitchen and the glass break notification will sound. The smart sensors are always there and always monitoring. One start-up company even offers an AI face-detecting robot named Eve that shoots paintballs to ward off intruders.[92]

Amazon, however, is the undisputed leader when it comes to consumer surveillance. Ring doorbells are advertised as ways to deter package thieves and to watch for suspicious persons.[93] The cameras offer motion detection up to thirty feet away, which turns on a live feed with audio capture up to twenty feet away. Footage can be seen in real time and stored for sixty days (if you pay for the service).[94] The company's Neighbors app has been described as a way to share local safety tips and alerts, but it's no coincidence that much of the chatter on the app involves identifying suspicious persons captured on Ring cameras.[95] The service was originally touted as a "Neighborhood Watch for the Digital Age."[96]

The popularity of these devices and apps has resulted in the radical acceleration of consumer self-surveillance.[97] Imagine if tomorrow the federal government installed cameras on all of our doors, wiretapped our homes, and organized a network of snitches to report the goings-on in our neighborhoods. Most people would rebel against this dystopian-sounding project. Yet this is exactly what we buy when we buy Amazon's

Ring, Echo, and Neighbors services (in addition to giving the company information about what we buy online, what books we read on Kindle, and which health problems we experience.) It's #DystopiaPrime that we pay for as a convenience.

The evidentiary trove of digital details available from Amazon alone should be concerning. Even more concerning is that this growth isn't happening organically. Local police departments have been actively involved in selling home surveillance technologies.[98] In 2023, more than 2,350 police departments partnered with Amazon[99] on promotions ranging from working with Ring marketing employees to send out solicitations to running public advertisements touting Ring as a preferred smart-home device.[100] Ring even offered cities subsidies for purchasing cameras, gave free devices to certain police departments, and coordinated advertising that blurred the distinction between private surveillance and public safety.[101] Local governments have also gotten into the act, offering discounts and rebates to homeowners willing to install cameras and share that video data with police officers investigating crimes. In the span of just a few years, a private network of cameras has sprung up to monitor neighborhoods with few rules and little oversight.

Imagine you are suspected of a crime. The police want to know if you left your house on a particular day. Your doorbell camera holds the evidence. The camera is running and collecting images of you and anyone else up to fifty feet in front of the camera. Under Ring's old policy, police could solicit anyone linked in the Neighbors Public Safety Service for images of you. You might be out of luck if your neighbor's Ring camera caught you on tape.

Under Ring's new policy, circa 2024, the company will no longer allow police such easy access to the footage on their servers.[102] Previously, police could get the recordings simply by clicking the "Request for Assistance" link in the Neighbors app. Now, they essentially must get a warrant.[103] You're not obligated to volunteer the footage from your camera, even when police detectives knock on your door and "nicely" ask you for a copy.[104] But any protection runs out when police get that warrant (or bypass the requirement by claiming an emergency.)[105] With a warrant, Amazon will comply with the request and turn over your footage. Even though it is your own camera that is going to put you behind bars, there is little you can do about it.[106]

For some homeowners, this police/private partnership has had frightening and invasive consequences. Michael Larkin owned Ring doorbell cameras that monitored his home and business.[107] One day, he received a notice that police wanted footage from his cameras to identify possible drug dealing outside a neighbor's home. Apparently, Larkin had six cameras in and around his house recording the surroundings. Police asked for footage from a specific two-hour time period, and Larkin handed over the video.[108] Later, the police returned and asked for a full day of video footage. Larkin ignored the request because it was difficult to upload the requested video. Then he learned that a judge had signed a warrant to obtain all the footage from all of his cameras from that day, including one that recorded inside his home. Remember, Larkin was an innocent neighbor, not the suspect. His personal data was taken regardless—or would have been, had the home camera not fortuitously been unplugged during the relevant time.[109]

The development of private networks of smart cameras has dramatically shifted the balance of power in favor of the police. Systems ostensibly purchased for personal security have a collective impact on community privacy.[110] When you go outside, it is not just one nosy neighbor keeping tabs on you, but a host of cameras uploading their findings to the Neighbors app.[111] And, of course, the collective suspicions broadcast in the app reinforce the need to buy more security.[112] The Neighbors Public Safety Service offers customers timelines of crimes, incident maps, and a weekly "safety report" to keep the fear of crime ever present, encouraging customers to purchase even more security.[113] It is a self-perpetuating cycle of fear and surveillance.

Other companies have gotten in on the act. One such company is Citizen which offers a smartphone app that turns 911 dispatches from police, fire, and EMS into digital alerts for subscribers.[114] Citizen users can see a visual map of crime reports and incidents, including video. They can also upload their own videos of a crime scene.[115] Though the company originally branded itself as "Vigilante,"[116] its goal is not to encourage vigilantism, per se—although there have been a few instances where an innocent suspect was wrongly reported to the community and police.[117] Like Neighbors, the app aims to keep you in a heightened state of alert by sending scores of criminal incidents to your phone. Conveniently, Citizen also offers the cure for this fear, for a fee—private virtual security services that can monitor you as you walk home or otherwise protect you from threats via smartphone.[118] It's the inevitable evolution of "surveillance as a service."[119]

Citizen won't actually send a person to walk home with you, of course. Nor will a Ring doorbell physically prevent someone from walking off with your package. The "security" these apps provide is the ability to identify those who seem like a threat. Homeowners are trying to keep safe from some frightening "Other" (with all the race and class prejudice that implies) who might invade their home or neighborhood.

And sometimes those homeowners band together, using technology to create a virtual gated community. Alder Meadow is an affluent neighborhood in the Seattle suburbs.[120] In an effort to protect against property crimes, the Alder Meadow homeowners' association partnered with Flock Security to install an automated license plate reader to record all the cars entering the neighborhood.[121] Should a property crime occur, the license plates can be studied to figure who "doesn't belong."[122] Like the Neighbors app, this system is a digital gatekeeper, taking note of unfamiliar cars and making the information available to police. In some areas, there are hundreds of cameras acting as virtual sentries, ready to identify outsiders.

Dangers of Glass Houses

The lens of consumer security points outward toward this "Other." We buy surveillance technologies to keep others out of our homes and communities.[123] But, of course, the camera lens does not just catch the "Other." It catches us as well. The bet of selling "surveillance as a service" is that we care more about the scary "Other" than we do about the government. It's a dangerous bet.

Dangerous, first, because the targets of police interest can change. One day the government does not care about your child's gender identity, and the next day they are criminalizing trans youth.[124] One day it might be fine to protest police brutality, and the next day they are charging conspiracies for public protests. If you become the target of a wrathful or petty government official, the power to surveil your life with long-term pole cameras or third-party requests is almost unlimited. Your home would expose you to a government wanting to harm you and your family.

Dangerous, second, because the line between corporate data collection and government access to that data is never set. If it becomes in the corporate interest to partner with government or another third party (for example, by selling data after a company's bankruptcy or because of financial interests in lucrative government contracts), there is no way for users to prevent their information from being shared.[125] The few privacy protections mentioned in this chapter came from company policy, not law, and corporate interests can change on a billionaire's whim (or to protect millions in government deals). All the data behind what I have called #DystopiaPrime could be handed to the government if the price was right.

Dangerous, finally, because even data that stays in the smart home and never escapes to the cloud still exists—and is a warrant away from recovery. If you become the target—and the government identifies a crime—there is nothing secret in your smart home. The castle vanishes and everything is visible.

As will be discussed in Part I and Part II, when we fill our homes with smart devices, physical or practical barriers to information gathering are simply less protective. Data about our intimate lives is freely shared with third-party providers, who will do with it what they like—including sharing it with police, who can use it to uncover family or personal secrets. This is a new and dangerous power, and we may need to develop responsive legal protections to rebalance that power.

In the meantime, new forms of digital self-surveillance are being created every day and sold as innovations worth the upgrade. Whether we imagine smart home devices designed to optimize some element of our daily routine or security systems built to manage our fear, they emerge into a legal system that has no clear rules about how to protect the personal data they collect. We do not yet live in the proverbial glass house, where all our private acts are visible to the public. But our smart beds, smart lights, security cameras, and always-on sensors provide enough clues to allow anyone who's looking to see quite a bit more of our daily life than we bargained for. And once we've traded away our privacy, it's hard to get it back, especially when the data is in the hands of the government.

2

Our Things

A man walked into a bank in Midlothian, Virginia, his black bucket hat pulled low over dark sunglasses.[1] He handed a note to the teller, brandished a gun, and walked away with $195,000. Police had no leads—but they knew that the robber had been holding a smartphone when he entered the bank.[2] Guessing that the smartphone, like most smartphones, had some Google-enabled service running, police ordered Google to turn over information about all the phones near the bank at the time of the robbery.[3] In response to a series of warrants, Google produced information about nineteen phones that had been active near the bank at the time of the robbery.[4] Further investigation directed the police to Okelle Chatrie, who was ultimately charged with the crime. Chatrie brought a Fourth Amendment challenge to the search of his cell phone signals.[5]

Cathy Bernstein had a tough time explaining why her own car reported an accident to police.[6] Bernstein had been driving a Ford equipped with 911 Assist, which was automatically enabled, when she struck another vehicle.[7] Rather than stick around to trade insurance information, she sped away. But her smart car had registered the bump—and called the police dispatcher, leading to a fairly awkward conversation:[8]

COMPUTER-GENERATED VOICE Attention, a crash has occurred. Line open.

911 OPERATOR Hello. Can anyone hear me?

UNIDENTIFIED WOMAN Yes, yes.

911 OPERATOR OK. This is 911. You've been involved in an accident.

UNIDENTIFIED WOMAN No.

911 OPERATOR Well, your car called in to us because it said you'd been involved in an accident. Are you sure everything's OK?

UNIDENTIFIED WOMAN Everything's OK.

911 OPERATOR OK. Are you broke down?
UNIDENTIFIED WOMAN No, I'm fine. The guy that hit me—he did not turn.
911 OPERATOR OK, so you have been involved in an accident.
UNIDENTIFIED WOMAN No, I haven't.
911 OPERATOR Did you hit a car?
UNIDENTIFIED WOMAN No, I didn't.
911 OPERATOR Did you leave the scene of an accident?
UNIDENTIFIED WOMAN No. I would never do anything like that.

Apparently, Bernstein did do something "like that." She was soon caught and cited for leaving the scene of the accident. Her own car provided evidence of her guilt.[9]

"Sensorveillance"

Once upon a time, our things were just things. A coffeemaker was a tool for making coffee. A bike was a tool for biking. It got you from one location to another, but it didn't "know" more about your travels than any other inanimate object did. It was dumb in a comforting way, and we used it as intended. Today, a top-of-the-line bike can track your route and calculate your average speed along the way. Hop on an e-bike from a commercial bikeshare, and it will collect data for your trip, plus the trips of everyone else who used it that month.[10]

These "smart" objects belong to what technologist Kevin Ashton named the "Internet of Things."[11] Ashton proposed adding radio-frequency identification (RFID) tags and sensors to everyday objects, allowing them to collect data that could be fed into networked systems without human intervention.[12] A sensor in a river could monitor the cleanliness of the water. A tag on a bottle of shampoo (Ashton had worked for Procter & Gamble) could trace its journey throughout the supply chain. Add enough sensors to enough objects and you can model the health of an entire ecosystem—or learn whether you're sending too much of your inventory to Massachusetts and too little to Texas.

Ashton first theorized the Internet of Things (IoT) in the late 1990s. Today, it goes well beyond his initial vision, including not only RFID tags but also Wi-Fi, Bluetooth, cellular, and GPS connections.[13] These small, low-cost sensors record data about movement, heat, pressure, or location and can engage in two-way communication, unlike Ashton's passive sensors. It has fulfilled the prediction author Jeremy Rifkin made in 2014: "The Internet of Things will connect every thing with everyone in an integrated global network. People, machines, natural resources, production lines, logistics networks, consumption habits, recycling flows, and virtually every other aspect of economic and social life will be linked via sensors and software to the IoT platform, continually feeding Big Data to every node—businesses, homes, vehicles—moment to moment, in real time."[14] Of course, such a system is also, by necessity, a system of surveillance. "Sensorveillance"—a term I created to highlight the intersection of sensors and surveillance—is slowly becoming the default across the developed world.[15] This chapter focuses on two of our smartest and thus most revealing things: smartphones and cars.

Most adults in the United States have a smartphone with them at all times.[16] Yours is probably within a few feet of you right now. You might even be using it to read this book. Smartphones are such a pervasive and insistent part of daily life that Chief Justice John Roberts once observed that "the proverbial visitor from Mars might conclude they were an important feature of human anatomy."[17] Even bank robbers struggle to leave them at home—and for good reason; it's hard to navigate life today, socially or practically, without a smartphone. Activities that used to be analog—hailing a cab, ordering at a restaurant, attending a concert—now all-but-require scanning a QR code or downloading an app. This means that we spend most of our days walking around with a device that tracks our every move.

Cars, too, are central to most Americans' daily lives—and a terrific source of information for investigators.[18] Navigational systems and emergency services are tremendously useful for drivers (at least those drivers who aren't trying to get away with a hit-and-run), but they necessarily require GPS tracking.[19] The reason you can push a button on your dashboard and be rescued on a deserted road is that the car knows where you are at all times. Location data is just the beginning. Cars now come equipped with cameras and recording devices, keeping a perfect record not only of where you have travelled but also how fast you drove to get there, and how many stop signs you blew through on the way.[20] If you drove to the scene of the crime or the site of the protest, your car knows it. When Mozilla conducted a privacy report on modern cars, it found that nearly every new car on the market collected an unnecessary amount of information—so much that they called cars "the worst product category [they'd] ever reviewed for privacy."[21] But if you need a car to get to work, it's hard to opt out of driving one.

Surveillance Networks

Let's start with phones. You're probably not surprised that your cell phone company tracks your location; that's how cell phones work.[22] Both smartphones and "dumb" mobile phones use local cell towers, owned by cell phone companies, to connect you to your friends and family, which means those companies know which towers you are near at all times. As the Supreme Court recognized in *Carpenter v. United States*: "Cell phones continuously scan their environment looking for the best signal, which generally comes from the closest cell site. Most modern devices, such as smartphones, tap into the wireless network several times a minute whenever their signal is on, even if the owner is not using one of the phone's features. Each time the phone connects to a cell site, it generates a time-stamped record known as cell-site location information (CSLI)."[23] If you carry your phone with you all the time, your phone's whereabouts—determined by CSLI—reveal yours.

The case's namesake, Timothy Carpenter, found this out the hard way after he and a group of associates set out to rob a series of electronics stores.[24] Carpenter was the alleged ringleader, but he didn't enter the stores himself. He served as the lookout, waiting in the car while his associates stuffed merchandise into bags. It might have been hard for investigators to tie him to the crimes—if not for the fact that every minute he kept watch, his cell phone was pinging a local tower, logging his location. Using that information, the FBI was able to determine that he had been near each store during the exact moment of each robbery.[25] Carpenter was prosecuted, and the CSLI—which had been collected without a warrant—became a critical and damning piece of evidence against him.[26]

Cell signals are the tip of the proverbial data iceberg. If you have a smartphone, you're almost certainly using something created by Google.[27] Google makes money off advertising. The more Google knows about users, the better it can target ads to them—and the more Google can make from those ads.[28] Google's location services are on all Android phones, which use the company's operating system, but they're also on Google apps, including Google Maps and Gmail.[29] For years, all that location information ended up in what the company called "the Sensorvault." The Sensorvault, as the name suggests, combined data from GPS, Bluetooth, cell towers, IP addresses, and Wi-Fi signals to create a powerful tracking system that could identify a phone's location with great precision. Almost everyone with a phone had data in the Sensorvault.[30] As you might imagine, police saw it as a digital evidence miracle.[31] In 2020, Google received more than 11,500 warrants from law enforcement seeking information from the Sensorvault.[32]

In 2024, Google announced that it would no longer retain all of this data in the cloud.[33] Instead, the geolocation information would be stored on individual devices, requiring police to get a warrant for a specific device.[34] The demise of the Sensorvault came about through a change in corporate policy, which could be reversed. But at least for now, Google has made it significantly harder for police to access its data. Still, while the Sensorvault was the biggest source of geolocational evidence, it is far from the only one. Even apps that have nothing to do with maps or navigation might nonetheless be collecting your location data. In one Pennsylvania case, prosecutors learned that a burglar used an iPhone flashlight app to search through a home and they used the data from the app to prove he was in the home at the time of the break-in.[35] These apps might be advertised as "free," but they come with a hidden cost. Remember *Angry Birds*? Those pig-toppling projectiles turn out to have been very effective spies, too.[36] The ad companies buy your data only to sell you out.

Cars, increasingly, are just as sophisticated as phones—and collect almost as much information. Mobile extraction devices can collect digital forensics about a car's speed, when its airbags deployed, when its brakes were engaged, and where it was when all that happened. If you connect your phone to play Spotify or to read out your texts, then your call logs, contact lists, social media accounts, and entertainment selections can be downloaded directly from your vehicle.[37] Because cars are involved in so many crimes (either as the instrument of the crime or as transportation), searches of this data are becoming more commonplace. One detective sergeant with the Michigan State Police Computer Crimes Unit told *NBC News* in 2020 that he and his colleagues pull data from cars for "everyday felonies" two to three times a week.[38]

Courts are split on whether police need a warrant to obtain this car data directly from the car itself. Take, for example, the tragic Georgia accident that centers *Mobley v. State*.[39] In that case, Victor Mobley crashed his Dodge Charger into a Chevrolet Corvette that had been pulling out of a driveway.[40] The two passengers in the Corvette were killed, and Mobley was charged with vehicular homicide.[41] The evidence against Mobley came from data downloaded from the airbag control modules (ACMs) on the Charger and Corvette.[42] The data showed Mobley driving 97 mph right before impact. In this case, the Supreme Court of Georgia held that such data downloads do require a warrant.[43] At the same time, had the investigators simply impounded the car (it was basically totaled in the crash) and searched it later, they could have collected any information they wanted under what is known as the "inventory search doctrine," which allows searches of impounded cars.[44]

Even without physically extracting information from the car, police have other ways to get the data. After all, the car's built-in telemetric system is sharing information with third parties. In addition to the usual personal information one gives up when buying a car (name, address, phone number, email, social security number, driver's license number), Stellantis collects how often you use the car, your speed, and instances of acceleration or braking.[45] Nissan asserts the right to collect information about "sexual activity, health diagnosis data, and genetic [data]" in addition to "preferences, characteristics, psychological trends, predispositions, behavior, attitudes, intelligence, abilities, and aptitudes."[46] Nissan's privacy policy specifically reserves the right to provide this information to both data brokers and law enforcement.[47]

Beyond location data built into turn-by-turn navigation and emergency systems, some modern cars have 360-degree cameras to assist with parking, prevent theft, or perform some autonomous driving capabilities (like slowing down when the car senses you're too close to the vehicle in front of you.) These cameras, of course, are also recording the world around you. Geoffrey Fowler is a technology reporter for the *Washington Post* who has written some of the most interesting stories about how tech impacts our lives. He also featured in a story himself when his Tesla was hit by a bus.[48] Turns out Tesla's anti-theft cameras also capture moments when another vehicle comes too close to yours (by, say, hitting it.) Tesla's "sentry mode" recorded the entire accident and gave him an insight into the surveillance device he was driving.[49]

Of course, not all videos taken by Teslas are so useful. *Reuters* reported on a mini-scandal that erupted when Tesla employees were caught sharing embarrassing photos uploaded from Tesla cameras, including a naked man walking to his car and photos and videos taken inside various garages.[50] The cameras even captured a horrible incident of a Tesla hitting a child on a bike. Tesla, of course, is not alone in putting cameras everywhere on its cars. Most newer cars have advanced drivers' assist capabilities with cameras and sensors that scan and record the surrounding environment for dangers.[51] If that bike crash had turned into a homicide investigation, it would have been easy for police to obtain a warrant for the footage. And then, of course, there is the creepy fact that the sensors in your car are watching you.[52] If—hypothetically—I should turn around and tell my kids to stop squabbling in the backseat of our Subaru, an alert will flash reminding me to keep my eyes on the road. As I watch the road (or fail to), my car is watching me.

The Investigative Power of Tracking

The ever-denser network of cell phone towers, combined with the increasing number of GPS devices on cars and in pockets, has given police the ability to identify suspects and track them down with a stunning degree of precision. One September afternoon in Wisconsin, police responded to a house fire and made a horrifying discovery—someone had tried to burn the bodies of Courtney Bradford and her ten-year-old daughter, who had both been beaten to death.[53] Suspicion immediately fell on Courtney's boyfriend, Christian Nunez, who had disappeared along with Courtney's car. But no one truly disappears in the digital age. Investigators issued a court order to the driver assistance service OnStar to reveal the GPS location of Courtney's missing car.[54] The car was quickly located at Des Moines International Airport in Iowa.[55] Police then sought cell phone data about Christian Nunez's whereabouts. Verizon provided information revealing that Nunez was currently at Chicago O'Hare Airport and had recently called a hotel in El Paso, Texas. As it turned out, Nunez had booked a flight from Des Moines to El Paso with a stopover at O'Hare. Police followed the digital trail and arrested Nunez at the El Paso hotel. He was tracked down in under eighteen hours.[56] While the Nunez case provides a compelling and positive example of digital tracking, the reality is that the same technologies could find almost anyone in the United States.

Historically, some people have attempted to evade this kind of surveillance by purchasing so-called burner phones disconnected from their main lines. But even those phones can be tracked. In another Wisconsin case, a suspect vanished after shooting a man in the back of the head.[57] Detectives learned that the suspect had just purchased a prepaid phone from a local food market, and it became the central clue.[58] First, detectives sought a court order to find the phone somewhere in the city of Milwaukee—an area of one hundred square miles, with half a million residents. Using cell tower data, police were able to narrow the phone's location to a particular neighborhood. Then, police used a "Stingray"[59] device that mimicked a cell tower, thus tricking the phone to connect with it. With the Stingray, police could narrow the phone's location to a particular part of a particular apartment building.[60] Police found the suspect, Bobby Tate, sleeping at his mother's apartment with the prepaid phone and a pair of bloody tennis shoes lying next to him.[61] Out of the entire city of Milwaukee, police tracked a mystery man to a couch in just a few hours.

Even the absence of cell phone location data can be used as evidence. In a high-profile Idaho case involving the murders of four college students, investigators were able to use Bryan Kohberger's phone to track him to the students' house in the days prior to the murders.[62] But equally damaging was that Kohberger allegedly turned off his phone from 2:47 am to 4:48 am on the night of the murders.[63] The inference was that it is awfully suspicious to always keep your phone on all day, every day—except during the four hours when you are suspected of stabbing people to death. Although the phone could not be tracked to the house on the night of the murders, the fact that it was turned off was almost as incriminating. Whether we power our phones on or off, the digital trails that exist reshape governmental power. Every protest, party, or plan can be tracked back to you. The open question is how to use the tracking power for good, and prevent potential misuse.

The Law of Smart Things

The fact that government agents can glean so much information from our things does not mean that they should be able to do so at any time or for any reason. The same technology that helps a detective nab a murderer before he leaves the country could also allow that detective to spy on his ex-wife or a vindictive FBI director to target a political opponent. Without legal limitations on the gathering and use of location information, police are limited only by the technology itself—which is improving rapidly—and the restrictions imposed by tech companies, which can change just as quickly.

The text of the Fourth Amendment—drafted in an era without electricity, let alone global satellite capabilities[64]—protects "persons, houses, papers, and effects" but is naturally silent on the question of location data. At the same time, the Founders were deeply concerned about the possibility of arbitrary government surveillance.[65] They knew that abuses of police power could undermine privacy, autonomy, and free expression and they wrote the Bill of Rights with those abuses in mind. That context is critical for understanding how the Fourth Amendment applies to the data emanating from our "smart" things.

The first question is whether the data from our smart things should be constitutionally protected from police. If police believe that a smartwatch holds a clue to a crime, can they search it? In the language of the constitutional text, the smart device itself is an "effect"—a movable piece of personal property. But what about the data collected by the effect? Is the location data collected by your smartwatch considered part of the watch, or part of the person wearing the watch? Neither? Both? The answers to these questions are consequential, informing which Fourth Amendment protections apply to our data (and which do not.) But so far, the Supreme Court has yet to rule on them.

The second Fourth Amendment issue involves the tracking of smart things. What constitutional protections, if any, prevent the government from using our devices to track our location? To its credit, the Supreme

Court has addressed some of the hard questions around digital tracking. In two cases, the first involving GPS tracking of a car[66] and the second involving the cell site location information (CSLI) tracking of Timothy Carpenter's cell phone,[67] the Court has placed limits on the government's ability to collect location data over the long term.

Antoine Jones owned a nightclub in Washington, D.C.[68] He also sold cocaine and found himself under criminal investigation for a large-scale drug distribution scheme. Federal agents sought to connect Jones to a particular house in Fort Washington, Maryland, where significant amounts of drugs and cash were recovered. To prove Jones's connection to "the stash house," police placed a GPS device on his wife's Jeep Cherokee.[69] This was before GPS came standard in cars, so the device was physically attached to the undercarriage of the vehicle. Data about Jones's travels was recorded for twenty-eight days, during which he visited the stash house multiple times. The prosecutors introduced the GPS data at trial, and Jones was found guilty.[70] Jones appealed his conviction, arguing that the warrantless use of a GPS device to track his car violated his Fourth Amendment rights. The constitutional question for the Court was whether police needed a warrant to virtually follow Jones around the city via the GPS device attached to his car.

In *United States v. Jones*, the Supreme Court held that a warrant was required for two separate reasons. First, in the majority opinion, Justice Antonin Scalia reasoned that the physical placement of the GPS device on the Jeep was itself a Fourth Amendment search requiring a warrant.[71] Scalia's logic makes some sense, as the police were using the GPS device to search for information about the vehicle and had to physically intrude on the vehicle to obtain that information. But what if police had been able to track Jones's car without placing a physical device—say, for example, because the car was already equipped with GPS?

Scalia's majority opinion sidestepped this Fourth Amendment question, but five other Justices tackled it in concurring opinions. These concurring Justices reasoned that long-term tracking of a car violated a reasonable expectation of privacy and thus required a judicial warrant.[72] Writing for herself, Justice Sonia Sotomayor agreed with Justice Scalia about the physical search but went further, discussing the harms of long-term GPS tracking. First, she described the kind of private personal information that electronic monitoring could reveal: "GPS monitoring generates a precise, comprehensive record of a person's public movements that reflects a wealth of detail about her familial, political, professional, religious, and sexual associations. . . . . And because GPS monitoring is cheap in comparison to conventional surveillance techniques and, by design, proceeds surreptitiously, it evades the ordinary checks that constrain abusive law enforcement practices: 'limited police resources and community hostility.'"[73] She also explained how this type of indiscriminate monitoring can impact entire communities: "Awareness that the government may be watching chills associational and expressive freedoms. And the government's unrestrained power to assemble data that reveal private aspects of identity is susceptible to abuse. The net result is that GPS monitoring—by making available at a relatively low cost such a substantial quantum of intimate information about any person whom the government, in its unfettered discretion, chooses to track—may "alter the relationship between citizen and government in a way that is inimical to democratic society."[74] The recognition that public movements reveal personal details represented a critical shift in how the Court thought about expectations of privacy in public. Suddenly, the Fourth Amendment seemed to protect location data.

Timothy Carpenter's ill-fated robbery spree gave the Supreme Court another chance to address the constitutional harms of long-term tracking.[75] In their attempts to connect Carpenter to the six electronics stores that had been robbed, federal investigators requested 127 days of location data from two mobile phone carriers (although only seven days' worth of data were ultimately at issue in the case). Carpenter's CSLI data placed him near the scene of each crime, providing evidence of his guilt.

The problem for the police, however, was that they had obtained the information on Carpenter without a judicial warrant. Carpenter challenged the FBI's acquisition of his cell site location data (or cell site location information, CSLI), claiming that it violated his reasonable expectation of privacy.[76] The question for the Court was whether the FBI's collection of this data constituted a search under the Fourth Amendment. If so, police needed a warrant; if not, they didn't. The search question turned on whether cell phone users have a reasonable expectation of privacy when it comes to our digital trails. It was not an easy question to answer. On the one hand, in *Jones*, five Justices had suggested that long-term tracking was indeed a violation of a reasonable expectation of privacy. On the other hand, the Supreme Court had previously held that people generally do not have an expectation of privacy in public, or in data we share with third parties (such as cell phone providers). Cell data about activities done in public and shared with commercial third parties could arguably fall outside of Fourth Amendment protection.

In a 5–4 opinion, the Supreme Court determined that the acquisition of seven days of CSLI was a Fourth Amendment search.[77] In other words, the Court held that Carpenter (and all of us) have a constitutional interest in our location data. If police want to obtain it, they need a warrant. Chief Justice Roberts wrote about the Court's concern with granting police the ability to indiscriminately collect location data that reveal everywhere we go and what we do there.[78] As the Court stated:

> A cell phone faithfully follows its owner beyond public thoroughfares and into private residences, doctor's offices, political headquarters, and other potentially revealing locales. . . . [W]hen the Government tracks the location of a cell phone it achieves near perfect surveillance, as if it had attached an ankle monitor to the phone's user.
>
> . . . Yet this case is not about "using a phone" or a person's movement at a particular time. It is about a detailed chronicle of a person's physical presence compiled every day, every moment, over several years.[79]

The Fourth Amendment harms arose from the cumulative nature of the collected data and the ability to aggregate those clues to reveal private facts from our lives.

> Moreover, the retrospective quality of the data here gives police access to a category of information otherwise unknowable. In the past, attempts to reconstruct a person's movements were limited by a dearth of records and the frailties of recollection. With access to CSLI [Cell-Site Location Information], the Government can now travel back in time to retrace a person's whereabouts, subject only to the retention policies of the wireless carriers, which currently maintain records for up to five years.[80]

This holding makes good sense. After all, if the Court did not require a warrant for this kind of data, police could track anyone's location, including the Justices', for any reason at all. With a warrant, at least a judge would have to weigh in on whether the police had good reason—probable cause—that the information they sought was related to a crime.

Jones and *Carpenter* are helpful for setting out the boundaries of location-based searches. But, in truth, the cases generate a lot more questions than answers. What about surveillance that is not long-term? At what point does the aggregation of details about a person's location violate their reasonable expectation of privacy? It's also unclear whether and how the ruling applies to other forms of surveillance, such as video and audio surveillance, or to sensors like the smart accelerometers found in modern cars. Finally, the cases do not resolve the question of whether there is any limit on collecting this kind of data with a warrant. Investigators in both *Jones* and *Carpenter* had enough evidence linking the suspects to the crime that they likely wouldn't have had trouble getting a judge to sign off on a valid warrant. What would have happened if they'd done so?

The Warrant According to David

The *Chatrie* case, in which police used Google's location data to identify a mystery bank robber, offers a stark warning about the limits of Fourth Amendment protections under these circumstances.[81] *Chatrie* is a terrific example of why "geofence" warrants, which request information within a certain geographic boundary, are appealing to police. From surveillance footage, detectives could see that the suspect had a phone to his ear when he walked into the bank.[82] A geofence could identify who the suspect was, and likely where he came from and where he went. Google held the answer in its virtual vault. A warrant gave investigators the key.

The police cast a broad net. The geofence warrant asked for data on all the cell phones within a 150-meter radius, an area, as the court described it, "about three and a half times the *footprint* of a New York city block."[83] In addition to the bank, the area within the geofence included two busy streets and a number of other buildings, including a restaurant, a hotel, a church, and a senior living facility. After receiving the police's initial request for information on all the phones in the area, Google returned nineteen anonymized numbers. Over the course of a three-step warrant process, the company narrowed those nineteen phones down to three and then to one, which it revealed as belonging to Okelle Chatrie.[84]

The three-step warrant process is a unique innovation in the digital evidence space. Google's lawyers developed a procedure whereby detectives seeking targeted geolocation data had to file three separate requests, first requesting identifying numbers in an area, then narrowing the request based on other information, and finally obtaining an order to unmask the anonymous number (or numbers) by providing a name.[85] To be clear, Google—a private company—required the government to jump through these hoops because Google considered it important to protect its customers' data. It was the company's lawyers—not the courts or the government—who demanded these warrants.

Richard Salgado was Google's head lawyer in charge of coordinating law enforcement requests for many years. He explained to me that the three-step warrant process was a pragmatic compromise.[86] It has never been clear whether law enforcement actually needs a warrant to get access to targeted geolocation data, but fighting Google on that point would mean fighting Google's lawyers and risking the integrity of a criminal investigation. From the investigators' perspective, getting a warrant was easier and safer, and thus the three-step compromise was born. The three-step process was iterative, requiring narrower requests at each step, but allowing police to ultimately get the information they wanted.[87]

When the case went to trial, Judge Hannah Lauck took issue with the broad, unparticularized nature of the first warrant. The warrant was overinclusive, encompassed many innocent people, and required the capture of personal data on those innocent people without probable cause.[88] In striking down the warrant on those grounds, the trial court offered a legal path to limit these types of warrants. But whatever comfort one might take from Judge Lauck's decision should be tempered. This was a case involving one of the most powerful tracking systems ever created, and the only reason it was struck down was because the warrant was poorly drafted. A more targeted and particularized warrant might have led to a different result. Even more uncertain, the *Chatrie* decision has been reversed on appeal (and ultimately resolved in a way to avoid the hard legal issue). Other appellate courts have also addressed geofences in different cases with different results, including holding geofence warrants to be akin to the dreaded "general warrants" so despised by the Founding Fathers. The current law is unclear and conflicting, and yet a terribly important puzzle to solve.

As a Fourth Amendment matter, the three-step process feels untethered from any constitutional principle. After all, that first request involves searching through all of Google's data (including yours) to identify phones within the geofence—which is about as broad a search as ever attempted in the history of the world. The second step is also overbroad. There was no indication that Chatrie had been working with anyone else when he robbed the bank, which means that of the nineteen people whose information was revealed to police, eighteen were innocent. Police had no probable cause to search their data. And yet, by the third step, the search seems more reasonable, as the targeting gets more focused. What to do?

You might think that this difficult question of law and technology would be vetted by our greatest subject-matter experts and legal minds, whose insights would inform the decisions made by judges as they consider the weighty constitutional responsibility of issuing a probable cause judicial warrant. And in certain respects, you would be right. Google's top lawyers do know their stuff. But in our exalted legal system, the ultimate gatekeeper between detectives and all of Google's most revealing geolocational data about you is the person signing the warrant. In this case: a guy named David.

David Bishop is not a lawyer.[89] David Bishop is not a technologist. In fact, David had only graduated from the Florida Pentecostal Christian College three years before being presented with the warrant in the *Chatrie* case.[90] Under Virginia law, the only requirements for becoming a magistrate judge are a bachelor's degree and a court training period, which David had completed three months earlier.[91] I don't mean to cast aspersions on Judge Bishop, or the many other magistrate judges who decide warrant applications every day. Senior judges with decades on the bench and the finest legal credentials also regularly sign such requests. But it is sobering to recognize that all the data discussed in this book is available to the police if they can convince a guy like David to sign the warrant.

In fact, because warrants for digital data are so easy to obtain, they may even legitimize the regular use of this type of evidence. A lesser-known case out of Virginia proves the point.[92] Police knew that someone was stealing industrial equipment off the lots of various tractor and heavy equipment dealers. Surveillance footage had caught the thieves loading four-wheel skid steers (used to haul dirt and other materials) onto stolen pickup trucks and driving away.[93] Similar crimes had taken place in three different counties in rural Virginia. Thieves would steal a pickup truck, load a skid steer onto it, and finally abandon the pickup truck but keep the heavy machinery. After the third incident, police went to Google and, as they had in *Chatrie*, they proceeded through the company's three-step warrant process. Investigators first sought details of any phones that were at all three lots where the thefts occurred.[94] Such a "coincidence" would identify the likely thief. Two phones popped up as having been at each of the three locations. Police then requested a second warrant, asking Google to unmask the two suspicious numbers. Melvin Thomas was identified as owning one of the two phones.

To strengthen their case, the Virginia investigators asked Google for more digital information about Thomas.[95] The trove of digital evidence was damning. By examining Thomas's phone data, investigators learned that on the day of the first theft, Thomas had searched the Internet for the value of a particular brand of skid steer and for the locations of heavy equipment dealers in the area, including the lot that was eventually broken into.[96] Minutes before the theft, Thomas searched for directions to that lot. His Google Maps data showed him driving into and out of the lot at times that lined up with surveillance footage of the theft. Similar searches directed him to one of the other lots in question. Photos and videos of Thomas with large sums of cash and heavy machinery were also recovered in the search. But all of that was just icing on the cake compared to the phone location data that tracked him minute by minute along his route to each crime scene. Thomas was quickly convicted of the thefts.[97]

In Thomas's case, police at least had probable cause that a crime had been committed, even if it wasn't initially clear that Thomas was the person responsible. In another Virginia case, the bar for getting a warrant was lower still. After Scott Durvin's friend died of a heroin overdose, Durvin's voice was found on voicemails in the friend's phone.[98] Based solely on the voicemails, detectives obtained a warrant allowing them to track Durvin's whereabouts through his phone. Durvin was not involved in the overdose or suspected of using or selling drugs, but a warrant was issued anyway, based on the claim that "users of narcotics will associate with other users and suppliers of narcotics in the drug trade." Detectives were able to track Durvin's location for a month. According to journalist Ned Oliver, who broke the story, similar warrants were used to track down petty thefts from restaurants and to identify possible informants. Virginia police conducted over 7,000 hours of this type of warrant-based phone tracking in 2020.[99]

Buying Data

Warrants may not be all that protective, but they offer at least some procedural barrier to data collection by police. If government agencies want to avoid that minor hassle, they can simply buy the data instead.[100] By contracting with data location services, several federal agencies have already done so.[101] As discussed in chapter 1, the logic for this Fourth Amendment loophole is straightforward: You gave your data to a third-party company, and the company can use it as they wish. If you own a car that is smart enough to collect driving analytics, you clicked some agreement saying the car company could use the data—study it, analyze it, and, if they wish, to sell it.[102] If you don't want to give them data in the first place, that is okay (although it will likely result in less optimal functionality), but you cannot rightly complain when they use the data you gave them in ways that benefit them. If the police wish to buy the data, just like an insurer or marketing firm might, how can you object? It's not your data. Senator Ron Wyden has proposed "the Fourth Amendment is Not for Sale Act" which would limit the ability of police to buy data in this way, but as of 2025, the bill has not passed into law.[103]

So far, Congress has not acted to restrict collection or limit access to this data by police, or anyone else. State laws that have taken some steps to regulate the collection of consumers' personal data have excluded law enforcement from those regulations. In 2018, California passed the California Consumer Protection Act (CCPA) and then the California Privacy Rights Act (CPRA).[104] Colorado,[105] Connecticut,[106] Utah,[107] and Virginia[108] have passed similar, albeit weaker, consumer privacy laws. All of these laws include exemptions for law enforcement use,[109] either sidestepping the issue or allowing police to access the data with a subpoena or warrant.[110] In short, there are no federal or state laws that prohibit modern forms of digital policing in a direct way. While the Federal Trade Commission (FTC) had taken some steps to rein in unbridled consumer data collection—even in cars—any data that does get collected is fair game for police.[111]

Who Is to Blame?

Justice Sotomayor wrote her opinion in the *Jones* case in 2012. Since then, her fears about the amount of personal information that could be revealed with long-term GPS surveillance have become reality. Today, police don't need to plant a device to track your movements—they can rely on your car or phone to do it for them.

Companies sold convenience and consumers bought it. So, it might be tempting to blame ourselves. We're the ones buying this technology. If we don't want to be tracked, we can always go back to using paper maps and writing down directions by hand. If few of us are willing to make that trade, that's on us.

But it's not that easy. You may still be able to choose a dumb bike over a smart one, but a car that tracks you will soon be the only type of car you can buy. And while cars and data can, in theory, be separated, that's not true for all our smart things. Without cell-signal tracking capabilities, a cell phone is just a paperweight. And in today's world, living without a phone or a car is simply not practical for many people.

There are technological steps we can take toward protecting privacy. Companies can localize the data the sensors generate within the devices themselves, rather than in a central location like the Sensorvault. Similarly, the information that allows you to unlock your Apple iPhone via facial recognition stays localized on the phone. These are technological fixes, and positive ones. But even localized data is available to police with a warrant.

This is the puzzle of the digital age. We can't—or don't want to—avoid creating data, but that data, once created, becomes available for carceral ends. The power to track every person is the perfect tool for authoritarianism. For every wonderous story about catching a criminal there will be a terrifying story of tracking a political enemy or suppressing dissent. Such immense power can and will be abused. It will be weaponized for political ends. In Part II, we will examine this reality and its profound ramifications for power, privacy, and the role of private platforms in shaping our lives.

Beyond Cars and Phones

This chapter focused on cars and phones as two prime examples of how our smart things can turn into tracking devices. But, of course, the Internet of Things isn't limited to those two vectors of sensorveillance. Companies from Yves Saint Laurent to Levi Strauss have begun experimenting with "conductive fabric" and selling "smart" clothing and backpacks equipped with chips that "enable[] wearers to perform a variety of functions, such as answering calls and playing music, simply by touching the sleeve of the jacket."[112] For users of products like Tile and AirTags, the tracking itself is the service, rather than an unfortunate byproduct. You can buy tracking devices for luggage, clothing, and even children.[113] Some of those devices share cell phone signal systems similar to smartphones, while others use Wi-Fi or Bluetooth technologies.

For all the potential downsides of having your clothes spy on you, these devices can be very helpful. On a recent trip, my family and I landed at our local airport tired, hungry, and ready to head home. Two of our three bags arrived in the luggage carousel as expected, but not the third. We waited. The carousel stopped. The few families still waiting for their bags looked at each other with that discomfiting feeling that things were going to get very frustrating. Customer service made a few feints at phone calls and announced that the bags were missing (we know!) and would be located (we hope!). Then a father of one of the other families looked at his phone and said, "Our bag is seventy feet away, behind that wall to the right." The Apple AirTag had pinpointed the exact location of his son's bag—and our bags too. After some negotiating, our bags were rescued from right behind the wall. Tracking had saved the day.

Phones, cars, clothes, and tags are just the tip of the tracking revolution. The rise of cheap, ubiquitous chips will make it easier to find our missing keys—or our missing kid. And they'll reveal us in ways we are only starting to comprehend. Still, as hard as it is to get around without a car or phone, we can, in theory, leave all those trackers behind, at least occasionally. That's not the case for another growing category of smart devices: Those connected to our bodies. These devices are the subject of the next chapter.

3

Our Bodies

First responders arrived at the scene of a house fire. When police officers asked what had happened, the homeowner, Ross Compton, told a breathless story of escaping the flames with several suitcases of personal belongings.[1] He described running around, saving his most treasured possessions as his home burned. It was a good story until detectives—suspicious of Compton's timeline—learned that Compton had a smart pacemaker that communicated data to his cardiologist. The biometric data collected by the pacemaker and obtained by detectives told a story that was at odds with the one Compton had told police. He wasn't running around collecting his things at the time of the fire. The fire was premeditated arson committed for the purpose of insurance fraud. Compton was betrayed by his own digital heartbeat.[2]

One Friday night, Douglass Detrie and his girlfriend Nicole VanderHeyden went to a local bar for drinks.[3] They got into an argument and left the bar separately. Detrie went home. VanderHeyden disappeared, only to be found dead in a field the next morning. Her blood-stained clothes were found on a freeway on-ramp. Because of the fight, Detrie became the prime suspect. Except he had an exculpatory witness—his Fitbit, which had recorded only twelve steps during the nighttime hours when VanderHeyden was murdered.[4] Police soon focused on another suspect, George Burch. Burch had made the mistake of trying to cooperate with police investigating an unrelated hit-and-run by giving detectives access to his smartphone—including his Google location data, which placed him at the bar, the field, and the on-ramp. Burch defended against the accusation by testifying that he and VanderHeyden had met at the bar and become intimate, and then they had been attacked by her jealous, gun-wielding boyfriend, Detrie. Burch claimed Detrie had forced him to move VanderHeyden's body before he was able to escape. Two stories, two truths, but one fixed datapoint. As the prosecution was able to convince the jury, Detrie couldn't have participated in the crime.[5] He was asleep with a Fitbit on. Burch's lies were disproved by the data.

Know Thy Quantified Self

Know thyself. It's an old adage that has new resonance in the digital age. Today, you can buy smart devices that monitor your heartbeat, blood pressure, exercise habits, water intake, sleep, mood, menstrual cycle, sexual activity, and meditation patterns, not to mention your poop.[6] The Internet of Things has turned into what Professor Andrea Matwyshyn has termed the "Internet of Bodies"[7] with the promise of selling you insights about your "quantified self."[8] The desire for self-awareness is not new, but these data offer a different twist on enlightenment. Millions of Americans live with a smartwatch that reminds them to stand, breathe, and take a few more steps to meet their daily exercise goals.[9] This helpful (and healthful) algorithmic prompt only works, of course, because your smart device is tracking your bodily activity. It literally knows you are breathing, which can be helpful to police if for some reason you stop.

This chapter considers how the data we produce—from our step count to our DNA—is increasingly coming under surveillance. Not all of this surveillance is unwelcome. Many medical professionals have embraced digital tracking to help their patients. Smart pacemakers measure heartbeats.[10] Digital pills record when someone last took their medication.[11] Smart bandages can warn of early infection.[12] These innovations offer the potential to improve medical outcomes by linking data in and on our bodies to our digital health records. They rely on small sensors that can be placed in watches or implanted in medical devices, allowing you to monitor your own vital signs or to check on friends and family members with health issues. Of course, there are potential downsides to making medical data so available. Health meters like the one that provided an alibi for Douglass Detrie also generate inculpatory data.[13] The digital pill might inform your doctor (or parole officer) that you've stopped taking your psychiatric medication; it's no coincidence that the first such pill approved by the FDA treats schizophrenia and other mental health disorders.[14] And in addition to helping with your marathon training, the data from your smartwatch can identify times when you are using cocaine or having sex.[15]

Recent laws criminalizing abortion raise the stakes of collecting this kind of information.[16] Almost a third of women use period trackers to monitor their reproductive health.[17] Many of these apps—such as Flo, used by 48 million women—collect information about the user's mood, body temperature, symptoms, ovulation, and sexual partners, as well as their location.[18] Even if a user kept the result of her pregnancy test off the app, her missed period, combined with weeks of recorded nausea, would offer a pretty good clue as to her condition.[19] In states that have restricted abortion access, prosecutors could use this data as evidence of a crime.[20]

In states where abortion remains legal, reproductive information might find its way into the hands of marketers instead. In 2023, the Federal Trade Commission fined the "femtech" company Premom for selling data to third parties, including Google and companies in China.[21] Premom, like Flo, which also settled a complaint by the FTC,[22] did not disclose the fact that it was sharing this personal data—which, in the case of Premom, included information about "sexual and reproductive health, parental and pregnancy status, as well as other information about an individuals' physical health conditions and status."[23] Some femtech companies have tried to protect personal data by limiting the amount they collect and localizing it on the device, refusing to log IP addresses, or creating an anonymous mode, but companies and users are still at the mercy of court orders.[24] U.S. companies are bound by U.S. laws, and when abortion is criminalized in a state, data that could provide evidence of an abortion is subject to warrant requests by investigating agents.[25] The only way to avoid turning over the data is by not collecting it, which is difficult for a business predicated on collecting data.

The rise of mental health apps and online therapy has exposed another vector of self-surveillance. The online therapy company BetterHelp has over 2 million users who benefit from their online and mobile mental health services.[26] You can sign up and answer questions about your mental health issues (such as problems with depression, intimacy, or medications), and they provide connections, advice, and resources to help. Then, they turn around and sell your personal data to Facebook and other targeted advertising companies—or at least they did until 2022, when the FTC brought a complaint against BetterHelp and its subsidiaries to stop the practice[27] and ultimately imposed $7.8 million in fines.[28] BetterHelp was not alone in marketing information about its users' mental health. As the Mozilla Foundation reported after an in-depth investigation into the industry, many mental health apps are lax on privacy.[29] Most failed privacy audits, failing to secure (or even outright profiting from) personal mental health data.[30] Even online suicide prevention services turned out to be providing data to Facebook, through automated pixel capture technologies.[31] While there might be nuanced arguments to make about anonymity when it comes to suicide prevention, it's hard to make the case that advertisers should get access to people in crisis for commercial gain. And of course, if data is available for sale, it is also available to law enforcement and the government. Just imagine how mental health data could be used to establish motive in a crime or embarrass a political opponent.

Government Body Snatchers

Police are intensely interested in the secrets our bodies can reveal. The FBI has invested billions of dollars in its Next Generation Information (NGI) biometrics database, billed as the largest such database in the world. Through this system, the FBI collects "voice profiles, palm prints, faceprints, iris scans, tattoos, and, of course, fingerprints,"[32] with the goal of using this information to identify suspects (and victims). The system also pulls in genetic information from CODIS—the agency's Combined DNA Index System—which contains 21.7 million DNA profiles of offenders and arrestees (almost seven percent of the U.S. population).[33] Many states have built their own similar databases using samples from arrestees, victims, and other sources, which are sometimes collected in ethically dubious ways.[34] The district attorney's office in Orange County, California, for example, had a program where they would dismiss misdemeanor violations in return for a DNA sample.[35] That "spit and acquit" sample, of course, could later be used to match suspects in future prosecutions.[36]

New Jersey police went one step further. Under state law, all newborn babies are required to provide a blood sample to be screened for certain life-threatening genetic disorders. The blood sample goes to the Newborn Screening Laboratory operated by the New Jersey Department of Health, which shares the results with parents as needed.[37] After the testing is completed, (and unbeknownst to many parents), the lab retains the DNA for twenty-three years. The result is a rich trove of genetic information that has uses far beyond disease screening—including as evidence in criminal cases.[38] In one instance, state police subpoenaed the laboratory for the DNA of a newborn in order to link the baby's father to a fifteen-year-old crime.[39] In turning over the infant's DNA, the laboratory provided a critical biological link to identify a suspect. The New Jersey public defender's office sued to challenge this DNA matching and the laboratory's lack of transparency, and state lawmakers are working to limit the retention of genetic data to two years. The case—and others like it—demonstrates the danger of large-scale biometric collection.[40] If available, DNA samples will be used for prosecution.

Soon, blood samples may not even be necessary. Next-generation DNA matching can snatch genetic material from the physical environment to test it. Since we all leave our DNA everywhere we go, this will make collection both easier and largely inescapable.[41] New technologies are also allowing DNA to be processed much more quickly. Developed for military use (to identify human remains of U.S. soldiers on the battlefield),[42] these technologies can help identify or exclude suspects and victims in minutes rather than months, offering police valuable clues early in the investigation of a crime.[43]

Biometrics are not new, of course. Police have relied on DNA for decades, and fingerprints longer than that. Digitization at scale, however, has changed the game. More powerful computers can search through massive databases with relative ease, combining DNA evidence with location information and other personal data. To understand the gravity of these shifts, consider your fingerprints. It has long been technically possible for investigators to lift fingerprints off various surfaces, upload those fingerprints to the national NGI database, and create a map of identified people. But doing so would be difficult, time-consuming, and perhaps not very revealing. New DNA technology gives police more information with significantly less effort. So does another growing area of biometric collection: facial recognition.[44]

The potential of facial recognition for law enforcement can be seen in a run-of-the-mill theft case in Manhattan. On an ordinary day in September, Luis Reyes strolled into an apartment building on West 113th Street, entered the mail room, and stole a few packages.[45] His crime would have gone unsolved but for security footage that recorded the theft. Detectives converted the surveillance video into still photographs and ran those photos through the NYPD's facial recognition system. The system alerted to a match, and the detective obtained the police file associated with the suspect. The detective could see that the photo in the police file indeed matched the photo captured from the video. An arrest was made. Case closed.[46] Note, however, that everyone else in the building could also be identified using the same technology. Whether it is a mailroom or a medical waiting room, facial recognition removes anonymity and enhances surveillance power.

Across the river in New Jersey, a much less promising—if not outright terrifying—case unfolded. A man named Nijeer Parks was falsely arrested for shoplifting after police ran a photo identification card collected at the scene through their facial recognition system.[47] Parks was completely innocent—he'd been thirty miles away when the crime occurred—but he spent ten days in jail before his lawyers could prove the mistake.[48] The case is troubling on multiple levels. First, police accepted what turned out to be a fake identification card as a real photograph of the suspect. Second, they sought a warrant to arrest Parks based solely on a facial recognition match to the fake photo. Third, a judge signed off on that arrest warrant without demanding more evidence. Finally, Parks had to spend $5,000 on a lawyer to convince the legal system that they had the wrong man. Unfortunately, Parks is not alone. Several other men have been falsely arrested based on erroneous facial recognition matches, and there are likely more cases we don't know about.[49]

Notably, in both the New York and New Jersey cases, humans were "in the loop" when it came to identifying the suspect, but the algorithmic identification drove the suspicion.[50] In addition, neither case involved a terribly serious crime. If this recently adopted technology is already being used to prosecute low-level offenses, it's easy to imagine it becoming the default investigative tool in future years, particularly given that, as we'll see in the next chapter, more and more of our public life is lived under video surveillance.[51] This is troubling, because as the Georgetown Law Center for Privacy and Technology has reported, face-matching systems are rife with error, in terms of both the quality of input photos and the accuracy of image matching.[52] A NYPD investigator once substituted the actor Woody Harrelson's face for a suspect's because they looked similar, and claimed a match.[53] And because the early AI models were largely trained on white male datasets, they are even more inaccurate when identifying women and people of color.[54] Age and hairstyle can throw off the system, too. Yet, facial recognition matching has been used in many high-profile cases, including the prosecutions of the January 6th rioters at the U.S. Capitol[55] and in deportation investigations.

Biometric databases are just the beginning. In addition to real-time facial recognition, which can identify members of a crowd on sight, there are technologies that can identify a person by their gait, or even by their perceived emotional affect. The latter are being sold to police as tools for preventing crime.[56] The pitch is that by analyzing someone's facial expressions or mannerisms, the algorithm could identify would-be mass shooters and alert police, who could intervene before the violent act. Of course, maybe the person flagged was just having a bad day—which is now about to get a whole lot worse.

Biometrics and the Law

Our ability to control our own bodies is core to human autonomy and identity. You might think, then, that our bodies and the data they produce—from our sleep patterns to our DNA—would receive significant constitutional protection. You would be wrong.

Part of the problem, as we've seen, is that we live our lives in public. Whenever we go to work, the grocery store, the gym, or the bar, we are exposing our faces to the world, sharing our outward-facing identity with everyone present. We shed DNA every time we touch or eat anything or sit anywhere. If we do these things while wearing a smart device, our location maps onto our digital health and biometric trails. Under most theories of the Fourth Amendment, anything that happens in public is free for others, including police, to watch. This is so even if we aren't purposely exposing our bodies' intimate secrets in public—we just can't help doing so.

The law has not quite figured out what to do with this conundrum. As a matter of constitutional law, the Fourth Amendment has not spoken to large-scale biometric surveillance in public.[57] As a matter of statutory law, the federal government has not agreed on a response.[58] The same is largely true when it comes to genetic surveillance through shed DNA and the digital trails created by our smart health devices. This is a significant problem, because evidence from facial recognition systems, shed DNA, and smart devices is already being introduced into criminal cases. Courts will need to grapple with these issues sooner rather than later.

Facial Recognition

Traditionally, the Fourth Amendment has not protected publicly exposed human attributes from police observation. In a 1973 case, the Supreme Court wrote: "Like a man's facial characteristics, or handwriting, his voice is repeatedly produced for others to hear. No person can have a reasonable expectation that others will not know the sound of his voice, *any more than he can reasonably expect that his face will be a mystery to the world*."[59] Extending that logic, if a police officer can identify a suspect on the street without violating that person's expectation of privacy, why shouldn't a facial recognition camera be able to do the same?[60]

This might have been a reasonable stance in 1973, when cameras were expensive and produced grainy images on film. It's far less reasonable in 2026, when police can deploy tens of thousands of high-definition cameras, networked together and equipped with sophisticated facial recognition algorithms.[61] If, as the Supreme Court has said in *Carpenter* and *Jones*, long-term tracking by cell signal or GPS is a search for Fourth Amendment purposes, one might think long-term tracking via facial recognition is also a search.[62] Both use some unique identifier to track a person's location over time. Facial recognition camera systems might, in fact, reveal much more than the systems at issue in *Carpenter* and *Jones*. After all, in addition to location, cameras can also capture video of what you were doing at the location. Yet, as it currently stands, there is no clear Fourth Amendment protection from having your face scanned in public or matched against some facial recognition system.

DNA

Your genetic code is about as sensitive as it gets, revealing clues about your health and biological makeup. Genetic code is also stored within a person—and "persons" are explicitly protected under the text of the Fourth Amendment.[63] In a predigital age, the Supreme Court held in

Schmerber v. California that the police could not forcibly withdraw blood from a suspect to test their blood-alcohol content, stating that "[t]he overriding function of the Fourth Amendment is to protect personal privacy and dignity against unwarranted intrusion by the State."[64] In subsequent cases that involved breathalyzers, the Court also considered forced exhalations to be searches.[65] Roadside sobriety tests, which involve collection of biological material, are permissible, but they retain some Fourth Amendment protections.[66] Urine drug screening, too, has been deemed to be a Fourth Amendment search, requiring the government to offer some justification for the collection and testing.[67]

At the core of these constitutional protections is the recognition that the government should not compel people to reveal their biological secrets without a warrant—though there are some caveats. The Supreme Court has largely allowed the government to require drug testing of federal employees and others whose jobs affect public safety, such as airline pilots.[68] In *Maryland v. King*, the Supreme Court allowed Maryland police to collect DNA through cheek swabs from anyone arrested for a felony in the state, reasoning that this was analogous to fingerprinting a suspect when they are taken into police custody.[69] And, of course, with a warrant police can compel suspects to produce any of these biological products (blood, breath, urine).

While DNA *inside* the "person" is protected, DNA abandoned by that person is essentially up for grabs. Courts have allowed police to collect "abandoned DNA," meaning the DNA from skin or hair or saliva that humans necessarily shed as they go about their lives.[70] As you might imagine, since everyone sheds DNA every day, this is a large loophole for police. It might make sense that a person who breaks into your home to steal your stuff would not have an expectation of privacy for the DNA they leave behind there. But the same logic holds for the DNA in your office bathroom, or on the coffee cup you just tossed into a trashcan on the sidewalk. Police can collect and test that biological material without having to show probable cause that it is connected to a crime.

Medical Devices

When it comes to the data revealed by our devices, the legal issues are trickier still.[71] Remember, the Fourth Amendment protects personal property—the objects we possess—as "effects."[72] But what happens when the data collected by our effects is derived from our person? When our smartwatch tracks our heartbeat, it's our heart health, not the watch, that we are concerned about revealing. If considered part of the person, this data would likely require a warrant. If not—or if it was voluntarily shared with a third party—the Fourth Amendment question becomes more difficult.

The closest case on tracking physical bodies was decided on rather narrow grounds. In *Grady v. North Carolina*, the Supreme Court was asked to determine whether strapping a GPS device onto a convicted sex offender permanently as a condition of supervised release violated his Fourth Amendment rights.[73] The Court stated that it did, but on the grounds that the physical placement of the device on Grady constituted a search. Following the narrow logic of *Jones*, the Court stated that "it follows that a State also conducts a search when it attaches a device to a person's body, without consent, for the purpose of tracking that individual's movements."[74] Left open was the harder question of whether the interception of data from a similar tracking device (say, from a smart pacemaker or a Fitbit) would be a search for Fourth Amendment purposes.[75]

All of this is to say that the short answer to whether our biological information and data are available for police collection is yes. *Without a warrant*, there are open questions about whether faceprints and medical data shared with third parties should be considered abandoned like shed DNA and thus accessible for collection (or not). *With a warrant*, all biological material is available for criminal investigation.

Even more concerning is that the scale and scope of digital surveillance technologies continue to advance. Whereas a human police officer can observe a few hundred people a day, an AI-assisted facial recognition system can identify millions of faces in the same period. While DNA from a crime scene can identify the few people who were present there, an investigator looking for DNA in the FBI's databases can identify millions of biometric samples. The power of police to search and surveil more people is growing far faster than any constitutional protection.

Who Is at Fault?

The story of our bodies evolving into sources of biometric evidence is a familiar one in the digital age. It is in part a story of our own choice to share our personal biometric data, and in part a story of the companies that have commercialized that data. It is also a story of government collection, digitization, and centralization of police data. As in many of the examples in this book, the scale of the problem has been supercharged by technological change, which in some cases we've welcomed freely and in other cases have found imposed on us.

Let's begin with our culpability. Over 30 million Americans have voluntarily given their DNA to a for-profit, private corporation, ostensibly to gain insight into their genetics and heritage.[76] For a small fee and their genetic code, they can learn about their ancestors and family medical history, and, on occasion, discover family secrets. The problem, of course, is that giving up your genetic data to a company means giving up control of what happens to that information. If police want to link you to a crime, a for-profit company with legal obligations to law enforcement now has DNA evidence that can help them do so.[77]

As for facial recognition, almost every adult in the United States has uploaded a picture online. Your LinkedIn page links your best professional photo to your name and work history. The pictures and videos you uploaded to Facebook, Instagram, Snapchat, X (formerly Twitter), Threads, Bluesky, TikTok, or YouTube put your face out there on the web, where they also connect you to other people, places, and events.[78] When Hoan Ton-That set out to design a new facial recognition system, he turned to those billions of images, scraping them from the Internet and using them to train the artificial intelligence that became Clearview AI.[79] The accuracy of the technology's matching ability was impressive. Perhaps the only thing scarier than a facial recognition system that gets things wrong is one that gets it right. As Kashmir Hill reported in her book *Your Face Belongs to Us*, licenses for the technology were given free to law enforcement.[80] After an early spike in interest, many (but not all) local police departments have backed away from using the service because of the ethical concerns it raises—both about the possibility of police misusing the technology and the fact that it was trained on some copyrighted images taken without permission.[81] But, of course, initial reluctance of police use can easily shift with the political winds and federal authorities have been known to use it and equivalent services.[82] At the same time, the growth of private facial recognition services in other areas of our lives has only increased.

Imagine accompanying your daughter to the Rockettes' famed "Christmas Spectacular" at Radio City Music Hall in Manhattan, only to be summarily kicked out by facial recognition technology.[83] That is what happened to a lawyer named Kelly Conlon in 2022. Conlon's law firm was involved in a lawsuit against MSG Entertainment, which owns several large event venues, including Radio City and Madison Square Garden. Apparently, the company's executives decreed that any lawyer working for any law firm involved in ongoing litigation against the company should be barred from attending any event—from Knicks games to pop concerts and iconic Christmas celebrations. When Conlon entered Radio City with her daughter's Girl Scout troop, facial recognition technology matched her face to her picture on the firm's website, and security blocked her entry. The ban covered almost ninety law firms and thousands of lawyers, whether or not they personally had anything to do with the cases against MSG Entertainment.[84] Facial recognition was used to bounce lawyers just doing their jobs from attending events they had paid to attend.

This story is not just about one petty litigant. Many other event venues use facial recognition for security purposes. Visitors to stadiums in Cleveland, Atlanta, San Diego, and Miami can opt into facial recognition to avoid long security lines and get to their seats more quickly.[85] Some venues envision using your face not only as your entry ticket but also for concessions, linking your bar tab to your face (and wallet).[86] Of course, those cameras will also know who has been overserved with alcohol or gotten into a brawl; it's all potential evidence to be used against you.

Some of the most sophisticated video surveillance systems in the world come from big-box stores like Target and Walmart.[87] Investigators can read the time on your wristwatch as you attempt to steal a different one. The technology is that good. Many of these stores use facial recognition to guard against theft, keeping a most-wanted list of suspected shoplifters who can be identified and making the footage available to law enforcement interested in following up with prosecution.[88] Again, sometimes such technology gets things wrong. RiteAid has been banned from using facial recognition for five years because the FTC found that the company's flawed system erroneously targeted innocent women and people of color for suspicion.[89]

All of these companies, from Clearview AI to 23andMe, are in the data extraction business—they take data that is either given to them freely or taken from another source and monetize it. The services they provide add value, but they come with real costs to privacy and anonymity. Once commodified, biometric data becomes just another thing to be bought, sold, or used by third parties, including the government.

Parallel to the rise of private monitoring systems are governmental face verification systems. Facial recognition kiosks now guard international borders, collecting data from all who pass.[90] Government buildings and other secure facilities use facial recognition to limit access.[91] The logic is that these systems are essentially just replacing a security guard asking you to sign a logbook after cursorily looking at your ID. Because the person must be present to verify their identity in this way, the matching technology does not reveal much more than a human guard would naturally observe. This is true as far as it goes. But while these systems may have begun as a way to speed up the line at customs, their ability to expand into new areas of life is limited only by money and political will. Those checkpoints are training and improving AI facial recognitions systems that can eventually be placed pretty much anywhere. Think about how many places you sign into each month, from schools to hospitals to office buildings. Sure, it's all a form of "security theater" (making you feel safe without actually making you safe) but it will soon be replaced by "surveillance theater" or worse. It could easily lead to bans if the government wanted to weaponize the same power by banning certain people from federal buildings or restricting travel through airports or trains stations.

The architecture of facial recognition surveillance is being built with few limits on its use. A 2022 Government Accountability Office (GAO) report found that eighteen different federal agencies used facial recognition technology.[92] The Departments of Justice, Homeland Security, Treasury, and Interior used facial recognition for domestic law enforcement, and the Departments of Agriculture and Commerce, and the Environmental Protection Agency (EPA) used facial recognition for digital access.[93] Ten of the eighteen agencies are expected to expand access to facial recognition in the coming years as part of an identity management system.[94] And, of course, a government that wanted to control its citizens could use the existing technology to restrict protest, limit travel, and monitor dissent.

Collective Costs

Facial recognition is a good example of surveillance that generates broad and diffuse privacy harms. Police see facial recognition as a tool for catching the lone bad guy. But everyone else is captured in the net.[95] After all, to capture a single face on video, you need a camera system that scans everyone. That means even though only the suspect will experience the tangible cost of surveillance (getting caught), everyone else loses that much more of their privacy. This collateral, collective harm is a community harm, and not one that is easily addressed under existing law.

The same is true when it comes to DNA databases. When you upload your DNA to a private database like GEDmatch, you are also uploading clues about close family members, whether they want their DNA in the government's hands or not.[96] Several high-profile cases (including the Idaho college murders) have relied on this familial DNA evidence.[97]

The science behind DNA evidence is complicated, but it works something like this: Traditional forensic DNA techniques rely on short tandem repeats (STRs), units of genetic material that repeat a different number of times in different people, allowing similar DNA samples to be matched.[98] Under most protocols, analysts are looking for between sixteen to twenty-seven matching STRs, which provides a very high degree of certainty that the two samples were taken from the same person (or their identical twin).[99] In one North Carolina sexual assault trial, the expert testified that "the probability of randomly selecting an unrelated individual with a DNA profile that matches the DNA profile obtained from [the sample] . . . is approximately one in 28.0 thousand trillion in the North Carolina Caucasian population, one in 398 trillion in the North Carolina black population, one in 6.00 thousand trillion in the North Carolina Lumbee Indian population, and one in 330 thousand trillion in the North Carolina Hispanic population."[100] Such evidence is highly convincing to a jury, and the typical kind of DNA evidence that we think about being used in trials. All well and good.

In contrast, familial genetic genealogy involves looking for matching single nucleotide polymorphisms (SNPs) between the biological samples. These are mutations in the DNA that are shared among family members.[101] By comparing how many shared DNA points exist within samples, investigators can make connections between them, suggesting that these two people might be cousins, brothers, or great-grandfather and great-grandson (the mutation runs through the male chromosome).[102] At best, genetic genealogy gets you close to a suspect. From there, analysts have to narrow down the connection using old-fashioned detective work. For example, in the Idaho murders investigation, police matched a DNA sample found on a leather knife sheath recovered from the scene to a male relative of the suspect, Bryan Kohberger.[103] In order to confirm the match, police needed to get DNA directly from the suspect (which they ultimately took from his family's trash can.) Note that police got the initial clue connecting the knife sheath to the Kohberger family not because the suspect's cousin was in a criminal database, but because he was curious about his family history—and that curiosity ended up providing indirect evidence of a crime.

The sheer size of these databases has been game-changing for police.[104] As the *Los Angeles Times* reported, by 2019 consumer DNA had been used to close sixty-six cases, involving fourteen suspected serial killers and rapists. But while genetic genealogy was initially used only for the most serious of cases, the cheaper and easier it becomes, the more often it will be used. The data analyzed by the *Los Angeles Times* showed that DNA was also used to identify the remains of a miscarried pregnancy, a troubling development in an anti-abortion environment where even women who experienced spontaneous miscarriages have been subject to prosecutorial scrutiny.[105]

Genetic testing companies vary in their willingness to provide data to law enforcement. Several companies allow police access as a matter of practice,[106] while others attempt to limit such access.[107] In Orlando, a police officer frustrated with a new policy limiting police access to GEDmatch went to court to obtain a search warrant allowing him to search through all the million plus DNA samples in that database.[108] To find one suspect, the officer searched millions of DNA samples from people (like your relatives) who gave no meaningful consent to such an action. But because the officer had a warrant, those people have little recourse.[109] As he casually told a reporter: "It's Big Brother, but Big Brother's been here for decades. . . . Everyone's trying to focus in on this because it's DNA, but it's no different than anything else that we do in our everyday lives. Police with a piece of paper and the judge can override almost anything."[110]

As of 2018, almost 90 percent of white people in the United States could be identified through genetic genealogy, even if they had not personally given their DNA samples to a commercial database.[111] In part because of the impossibility of truly opting out of these databases—you can't stop your cousins from mailing in the tube of spit that might eventually implicate you in a crime—governments have started to put limits on their use.[112] Maryland, for example, has limited genetic genealogy investigation to the most serious crimes, such as murder, rape, and felony sexual assault, and the state requires that DNA collected for a case to be destroyed after use.[113] Those who break the Maryland's laws concerning DNA evidence can face criminal prosecution.[114] Montana and Utah passed less-sweeping laws requiring police to get a judicial warrant before accessing commercial DNA databases.[115] At the federal level, the Department of Justice under the Biden Administration was also attempting to rein in use of the technology.[116] The idea of searching the nation's entire family tree for one bad apple was too much.[117]

Yet, even as governments and companies place limits on the use of genetic information from commercial databases, there are other ways to create a genetic surveillance net. One of the most interesting is a nonprofit that encourages people to donate DNA samples for the explicit purpose of criminal investigation. Two leaders of the genetic genealogy movement, CeCe Moore and Margaret Press, started the DNA Justice Foundation to replicate the scale of commercial DNA databases.[118] The hope is that the database can be used to identify both victims and perpetrators of crime.[119] Because participants will have actively consented to police use of their genetic information, the restrictions placed by courts or private companies won't apply.

In many ways, the DNA Justice Foundation perfectly encapsulates the troubling relationship between self-surveillance and police surveillance. A private dataset of genetic material is being created with the express purpose of identifying people who did not put their DNA into the system. While the goal of solving cold cases is noble, the cost of giving the government unfettered access to this genetic information undermines biometric anonymity and enhances police power. And as a private undertaking, the project avoids any legislative or constitutional oversight, existing outside a legal framework, subject only to whatever rules the individuals in charge deem just.

Biometric Futures

Our ability to capture and analyze more and more information about our bodies and our health has important upsides. Technological advancements like smart pacemakers and smart glucose monitors improve—and even save—lives. But the fact that such personal data is available to our doctors does not mean that it should be available to police. Perhaps the government should not be allowed to use our heartbeats against us. In the language of the Fourth Amendment, we might consider that unreasonable. Similarly, just because our faces can be scanned and sorted in public facial recognition systems does not mean that they should be (and certainly not without regulation). In a free society, such constant, persistent surveillance is arguably unreasonable.

The emergence of new technologies requires the development of new constitutional and statutory protections. The first state to enact a law protecting consumer biometric information is Illinois. The Biometric Information Privacy Act (BIPA) has been a national example of how to regulate biometric surveillance by private companies.[120] The law protects against the private collection of biometric identifiers like fingerprints, voiceprints, and scans of hands, faces, retinas, or irises[121] without formal notice of collection and written retention policies. In addition, the law forbids selling or otherwise profiting from a person's biometric identifier or biometric information.[122] The law provides for civil liability if biometric information is shared without permission, which means that it cannot be easily commercialized or commodified without risking monetary damages.[123] Lawsuits under BIPA have challenged corporate use of facial recognition, retention of images, and biometric collection without consent, resulting in significant civil penalties against tech companies both big and small.[124] The law is silent on government use of the same biometric data, however, leaving police access to it unaffected.

Some might argue that this is for the best. The stories in this chapter involve wrongdoers held to account. Facial recognition, for all the risks of misidentification, has also identified guilty suspects. DNA and other biometric data have solved otherwise unsolvable crimes, granting victims some degree of closure. If something were to happen to us, we may well be glad our cousin's DNA was in a database somewhere. Still our biometric data is perhaps the most personal data we have, and allowing police and others to have access to it carries significant costs for our privacy, security, and autonomy. Protests against the government take place in public, and facial recognition technologies will discourage dissent. Constitutionally protected activities from praying at religious institutions to practicing at shooting ranges can be virtually gated by government surveillance. We can ditch our cars or phones or Echo Dots, at least in theory. We can't ditch our DNA, or our hearts, or our faces. And that makes protecting them all the more important.

4

Our Cities

Bourbon Street in New Orleans, Louisiana, is one of the best places to have a good time. It is also one of the most surveilled. Every drunk tourist and fruity hurricane drink is being watched by a system of sophisticated cameras that record and respond to crime.[1] It makes sense. It's hard to imagine a better target for a would-be thief than an intoxicated, out-of-state partygoer with money to spend.[2] Police officers in the Real-Time Crime Center watch the streets via a live video feed, while the system archives the digital recordings. If there is a shooting or robbery or drunken brawl, police can search those recordings for evidence.[3] But rather than painstakingly scan hours of footage looking for a clue, police rely on artificial intelligence to do the work for them. If you report being assaulted by a person wearing a purple jacket, the software can pull up images of all the purple jackets seen in the area over the last twelve hours and track them from camera to camera across the system. It's like an investigative time machine.

Cape Cod, Massachusetts is famous for its picturesque beach towns and infamous for its traffic. Separated from the mainland by a canal, the Cape can only be reached by car via one of two bridges, the Bourne or the Sagamore. The bridges act as chokepoints for thousands of vehicles each day.[4] But what's frustrating for drivers can be useful for investigators. Based on a confidential informant's tip, police in Barnstable County believed Jason McCarthy was trafficking heroin onto the peninsula.[5] To bolster their case, they programmed McCarthy's license plate number into the state's Automated License Plate Reader (ALPR) system. ALPRs rely on cameras equipped with character recognition software to read license plates on passing vehicles.[6] Detectives programmed the system to take a photograph every time McCarthy's car crossed either the Bourne or Sagamore bridges, recording the time, location, and direction of travel. ALPR alerts showed that McCarthy was making dozens of trips back and forth across the bridges, sometimes multiple in one day. Once alerted to McCarthy's presence on the Cape, police were able to follow his car to the home of a suspected drug dealer, who was found to be in possession of heroin.[7] McCarthy was arrested and charged with illegal distribution of a controlled substance.[8]

Smart Cities

For most of the twentieth century, cities were built with concrete, steel, asphalt, and glass. Today, they're also built with computer chips.[9] Smart roads, streetlights, power grids, and sewers connect homes, cars, and businesses. Digital sensors collect data on everything from traffic patterns and electricity use to wastewater composition and air quality.[10] Networked video cameras record public spaces and feed the information into software programs that can track people or things through the city.[11] Each of these sources of data is revealing. Collectively, they promise to map out the patterns of civic life and transform our creaky, inefficient municipalities into smoothly running "smart cities."

The term "smart city" was coined by IBM and eagerly embraced by other technology companies, which have aggressively marketed their data collection and analytics to cities across the United States.[12] A cynic might argue that these companies are just monetizing public goods by digitizing them. After all, if one is in the business of selling data analytics, it is hard to envision a bigger goldmine than an entire municipality. At the same time, citizens are seduced by the promise of smart cities to improve their quality of life and save taxpayer dollars.[13] Both private profit motive and public demand have spurred municipalities to invest in digital infrastructure. But smart cities are also surveillance cities.[14]

City data collection is not necessarily nefarious. Take transportation. By collecting transit data and making it accessible, cities can inform residents when the next bus will arrive, or where there might be parking available downtown. The cities themselves can use the information to improve services. New York City has set up sensors in a dozen locations to track the paths of people, bikes, scooters, cars, vans, trucks, and buses.[15] The goal is to identify the busiest times of day and shape traffic patterns to minimize delays.[16] If the data reveals that a particular bus is always running late during rush hour, the city can act accordingly—by running more buses at busy times or installing a bus lane.[17] And the more granular the information, the more efficient the city can become. If your parking meter app tells you exactly which meters are in use, you can avoid fruitlessly circling the block, contributing to traffic congestion and air pollution. But, of course, once you pay your meter, the city knows exactly where you've parked, and for how long.

Municipalities also monitor environmental conditions, as well as utilities like water, electricity, and gas.[18] Pollution sensors can alert members of vulnerable groups about air quality. Smart energy grids can balance the electrical load during hot summer months to avoid blackouts. However, those same technologies can also identify which homes are using excess electricity to mine bitcoin or manufacture methamphetamine.[19] Similarly, smart wastewater systems filter waste, but they can also identify elevated levels of COVID-19—or cocaine.[20] Some business leaders such as Dan Doctoroff, once the head of Google's Sidewalk Labs, have promoted even grander plans, envisioning "build[ing] a city 'from the Internet up.'"[21] In this vision, the city could become the digital platform from which industry and consumers can program daily life. Or as Paul McFedries once imagined:

> [T]he city is a computer, the streetscape is the interface, you are the cursor, and your smartphone is the input device. This is the user-based, bottom-up version of the city-as-computer idea, but there's also a top-down version, which is systems-based. It looks at urban systems such as transit, garbage, and water and wonders whether the city could be more efficient and better organized if these systems were 'smart.'[22]

Building the infrastructure to support all this physical monitoring has become a priority for cities, with sensors becoming a core part of urban planning. In proposed plans for traffic congestion fees, or high-speed toll roads, for example, the systems only work by matching license plates and toll accounts, deducting fees for use.[23] Those systems also know which cars are in the city, and where, when, and perhaps, by inference, why. The same is true when you use a digital swipe card, linked to a payment method and your name, to take the bus or subway.[24] As public transit authorities transition away from physical cards to smartphone apps, the ability to track riders increases.[25] Each of these innovations—useful in its own right—has consequences for the ability of governments to monitor their citizens or investigate crimes. In the hands of an authoritarian government, smart cities seem pretty dumb.

Surveillance Cities

Municipalities must prioritize public safety, and for many cities, that means investing in citywide police surveillance systems. Real-Time Crime Centers like the one in New Orleans are popping up in other major cities, but also in smaller jurisdictions like Forsyth County, North Carolina, and New Haven, Connecticut.[26] These local surveillance centers serve as a central hub for video feeds and sensor data, which police use to investigate criminal incidents and disturbances.[27] The idea is to integrate multiple streams of information, including emergency services, so that police can respond to incidents more quickly and with more information already in hand.[28] Instead of calling 911 to report a mugging, you could upload your iPhone video of the suspects and watch as police turn the neighborhood cameras on to track their getaway.

Cameras

The Bureau of Labor Statistics estimates that there are 85 million surveillance cameras in the United States, and the number is growing daily.[29] Los Angeles has one of the highest numbers of surveillance cameras per person in the world (although it has nothing on Chongqing, China, which boasts more than 2.3 million—or one for every fourteen residents.)[30] In Chicago, more than 30,000 video cameras encircle the downtown area, feeding into district-level command centers where information about incidents, suspects, and other crime data can be analyzed.[31] In New York City, the NYPD's Domain Awareness System can track individuals as they walk down the street via thousands of cameras and sensors.[32] Should a person of interest enter the subway, cameras will track them there, too. As Mayor Eric Adams proclaimed—without a trace of self-awareness—"Big Brother is protecting you."[33]

In New Orleans, police have access to footage from more than 1200 cameras—550 installed by the city, plus another 700 installed by residents and businesses participating in the city's SafeCam system, which allows police to view recordings stored in the cloud from private cameras.[34] As you might expect, the police are not just interested in monitoring tourist hotspots. Many of the cameras watch over less affluent areas, such as the Seventh Ward, where a young man named Michael Celestine stepped outside one afternoon and found himself under the camera's gaze. A portion of the captured video is available on YouTube, where you can watch the mundane reality of video surveillance.[35] It's a brisk January day, and Celestine is wearing a white Tommy Hilfiger jacket. He walks down the street with his hands in his pockets. He chats with his friend. He goes inside another house. It's remarkably unremarkable. But the police officer conducting the "virtual patrol" sees what he considers a suspicious bulge. He informs local patrols that he thinks Celestine has a gun in his pocket. Two hours later, officers on a real (nonvirtual) patrol see Celestine again. He is wearing a different jacket, but the police approach him to investigate the prior suspicion. He runs. Police officers chase him, Taser him, and handcuff him. The officers claim they found a weapon, but prosecutors dismiss the case after watching the tape. The lack of a crime—or any reason to suspect one—was all caught on video. Still, Celestine spent months in jail waiting for the case to be resolved.[36]

Video Analytics

In addition to watching the live video streams, New Orleans police rely on video analytics,[37] a form of artificial intelligence that can identify, sort, match, and catalog objects, allowing police to search in the stored video data.[38] Want to find a suspect wearing a purple shirt and a Saints hat? Query the stored data, and the computer vision system will serve up every purple shirt and Saints hat it's seen recently. While New Orleans doesn't officially use facial recognition, the ability to track objects with such granularity makes it almost unnecessary.

The BriefCam system used in Hartford, Connecticut, is similarly powerful.[39] BriefCam can identify classes of objects appearing in a video—person, man, woman, child, bicycle, motorcycle, car, truck, van, bus, airplane, boat, animal—and tag them with attributes including (but not limited to) clothing color, sleeve length, hair color, sex, age, license plate number, car color, and direction of movement.[40] Video analytics companies like BriefCam also sell their wares to retailers and other businesses, who can use video cameras to identify all people wearing high heels, for example, and follow them around a store to see what they buy and how long they linger in certain aisles. Facial recognition can alert stores to known shoplifters, or let managers know that a VIP has entered the premises so that they can be recognized and treated accordingly (a feature especially popular with casinos).[41] Future AI-enhanced systems will be able to recognize small details like clothes with too many pockets or particular brand-name products.

All of these matches are time-stamped and geocoded.[42] Police can sort through days of footage to find an event, object, or person in seconds. This ability of video analytics to compress time and space is a tremendous boon for investigators. By separating dynamic images in the foreground of a video (a red pickup truck driving by, or a child with a backpack) from a static background (the city street),[43] the software can cut out minutes or hours of irrelevant footage.[44] If a suspected bank robber escapes in a blue van, video analytics can identify all the vans in the city, then narrow that search to blue vans and arrange them by time, place, and direction, allowing investigators to track them as easily as if they'd had a single video camera trained on the truck the whole time. Hours and hours of video can be collapsed into a few seconds, significantly reducing the amount of time and resources needed for investigation.[45]

Video analytics tools can also help police identify suspicious patterns of behavior, which is critical to police investigation. If you want to find the local motel that doubles as a brothel, for example, check to see how many trucks make quick pitstops there late at night. The artificial intelligence that powers video analytics tools can highlight such patterns with minimal effort. Perhaps police have received reports that a house is a front where people go to buy illegal drugs. In the past, an officer might have staked out the house, hanging out for hours in a sleeping bag with a camera and cold coffee.[46] With video analytics software, police can map the heat patterns of a neighborhood and see that several hundred people, represented as a glowing red line, visited the house over the course of a week. By aggregating data in this way, heat maps of certain homes, corners, or abandoned lots can support the inference of illegal activity. There are plenty of noncriminal reasons for people to be drawn to certain areas at certain times. (Maybe neighbors have turned the abandoned lot into a community garden.) But if instead it's turned into an open-air drug market, heat maps like these allow police to identify it with relative ease.

With enough training, the object recognition systems can identify patterns on a broad scale and alert police when something unexpected happens.[47] If a camera detects human movement in a park at midnight, at a time when the park is typically empty, the AI system can alert police that something is out of the ordinary.[48] Unexpected or anomalous activity around a building or parking lot, for example, might prompt the system to awaken dormant cameras.[49] If sensors sense a car driving the wrong way down a one-way street, the system can immediately send an alert, and in rare cases, it might automatically call the police to the area to check out the anomalous event.

These AI systems wouldn't be able to provide much useful information without a regular stream of data coming in from cameras and sensors. The quality of the output reflects the quality—and quantity—of the input. Thousands of jurisdictions now equip police officers with surveillance cameras on their chest.[50] While ostensibly deployed as an accountability measure, the cameras are also recording city streets all day, every day, generating hours on hours of footage.[51] Seeing a business opportunity in this deluge of data, Axon, one of the largest manufacturers of police cameras built Evidence.com, which allows government agencies to sort through bodycam footage. If police need a video clip for trial, or prosecutors need a transcription of a conversation, it is all stored on Axon's servers.[52]

In addition to the cameras worn by police, private surveillance cameras on the street can be linked to central police command centers for analysis and storage. In New Orleans, a private foundation run by a former police officer raised tens of thousands of dollars to install cameras in local businesses with direct linkages to the police department.[53] In San Francisco, billionaire tech executive Chris Larsen helped subsidize cameras to be installed in private businesses in several business districts, with the understanding that the San Francisco Police Department could access the footage when needed.[54] Under the Biden Administration, tens of millions of COVID-19 and infrastructure funds have been used to support the creation of local Real-Time Crime Centers and increase the number of public and private cameras that feed into their centralized data flows.[55]

One start-up, Fusus, offers a cloud-based video analytics hub that "fuses" data from both public and private surveillance cameras into one central location, accessible by police.[56] If there is a robbery at a particular address, for example, police can use video analytics to access footage from the closest private cameras at homes, businesses, or apartments.[57] Before officers respond, they can consult a live feed of the area from those same cameras. In this way, police are essentially crowdsourcing massive surveillance. In 2024, Axon announced it would buy Fusus, making the company an even bigger player in law enforcement surveillance.[58]

Drones and Aerial Surveillance

A few jurisdictions have gone further by adding cameras to drones. Police in Beverly Hills, California have initiated what they call the "Overwatch."[59] Seven days a week, several thousand times a month, drones hover over the city streets checking for suspicious behavior, responding to altercations, and reporting back to the Real-Time Watch Center. The drones can follow a person, zero in on a license plate, or watch an event unfold. As Patrick Sisson and Bloomberg's *CityLab* reported, the drone footage is combined with data collected by street-level cameras and other sensors.[60] In Chula Vista, California, drones are sent out to almost every routine 911 call.[61] The pilot project has twenty-nine drones available to deploy, which respond to a wide range of incidents—from a person sleeping on the sidewalk to murder.[62] Of course, the cameras on the drones, which are equipped with zoom lenses also capture everything else on their way to the scene. As of 2023, police in more than 1500 jurisdictions are using drones in some way,[63] with 225 jurisdictions receiving a special waiver from the US Federal Aviation Administration that allows drones to play the role of first responder.[64]

These numbers are sure to increase. In what is likely a taste of future surveillance capabilities, Amazon applied for a patent for an officer-enabled "shoulder drone" that would deploy above police officers during traffic stops, filming the police-citizen interaction from above.[65] The camera would provide a bird-eye's view of the events, all recorded and stored for future use.[66] While obviously invasive from a privacy perspective, the camera footage might provide a less officer-centric angle on events than body cameras, reducing perspective bias, and depending on who maintains access to the footage, an additional measure of accountability.

Small drones are not even the most ambitious aerial surveillance technologies being piloted. In Baltimore, Maryland, the city contracted with Persistent Surveillance Systems (PSS), an aerial surveillance company that promised to record the entire city from above.[67] The city's Aerial Investigative Research (AIR) program involved two Cessna planes filled with super-advanced cameras, which flew over the city for twelve hours at a stretch.[68] If there were a robbery at a particular bank, police could search through the overhead footage for the incident, then track the getaway car to its final destination (or backtrack to see where it came from.) The aerial cameras could also be integrated with street-level CitiWatch cameras, so even though the resolution of the aerial cameras precluded seeing faces or license plate numbers, the ground-level cameras filled in the gaps.[69] Ross McNutt, who created the system, called it "Google Earth with TiVo capabilities."[70]

Sociologist Ben Snyder wrote a book about the Baltimore AIR program which he was able to observe in action. In *Spy Plane: Inside Baltimore's Surveillance Experiment*, Snyder describes a group of analysts using AIR to solve a murder.[71] The work required hours of painstaking review. Analysts diligently tracked the getaway car frame by frame and matched those images to footage from CitiWatch cameras that had captured the suspect's face.[72] Not all the technologies worked as hoped, and because the tracking was manual (albeit enabled by digital systems), the risk of human error was ever-present. But the reality is that a murder was solved because the shooter could not escape the cameras in the air.

This kind of surveillance in a city fractured by poverty and race like Baltimore creates issues of equity and fairness. Since policing tends to center on the less powerful, so does surveillance. Professor Snyder concluded that AIR was "another in a long line of surveillance experiments that promised to alleviate crime through a technical fix, but ended up unleashing unforeseen harms primarily shouldered by residents in majority Black neighborhoods."[73] The problem wasn't that the technology did not always work, but that it came with real costs that were not always anticipated by the companies selling it to the police.

The Baltimore spy plane was challenged in federal court. Community organizations, including Leaders of a Beautiful Struggle, joined with the American Civil Liberties Union (ACLU) in a lawsuit intended to stop Baltimore from using mass surveillance planes and they won in the

U.S. Court of Appeals for the Fourth Circuit.[74] The *en banc* court (the full court) decided that this type of surveillance constituted a Fourth Amendment search. Chief Judge Gregory wrote:

> The AIR program records the movements of a city. With analysis, it can reveal where individuals come and go over an extended period. Because the AIR program enables police to deduce from the whole of individuals' movements, we hold that accessing its data is a search, and its warrantless operation violates the Fourth Amendment.[75]

The Fourth Circuit opinion is controlling law only in Maryland, Virginia, and the Carolinas, and it is an open question whether its constitutional analysis will prevent other jurisdictions from trying to build similar citywide video surveillance systems.

AI Sensors

Beyond camera systems, other police sensor technologies have begun populating urban areas. SoundThinking sells ShotSpotter, which promises to identify gunfire and alert police more quickly than a 911 call can.[76] In fact, in some urban areas where police have lost the trust of the community, audio gunshot sensors can be a more reliable (although not always accurate) way for police to learn about a shooting. Las Vegas, Washington D.C., and New York State all use ShotSpotter,[77] which relies on sensors to identify loud sounds and triangulate the location of a suspected gunshot, then sends police and emergency responders to the scene. In theory, this quick response means gunshot victims can receive faster medical attention and police can gather more clues for criminal investigations. In practice, critics have questioned the technology's effectiveness in reducing gun violence[78] and raised privacy concerns, given that the system relies on placing hidden microphones on city streets.[79] Furthermore, reports have shown that ShotSpotter primes officers to be hypervigilant, because an officer alerted to gunfire will naturally arrive at the scene concerned about possible weapons.[80] Police primed to expect an armed suspect are more suspicious of the people in the identified locations and more prone to use violence when responding to the call.[81] Because the sensors tend to be concentrated in poor communities with higher instances of gun violence, this means that already overpoliced areas are further burdened by potentially violent police responses and continued suspicion.[82]

Finally, there are automated license plate readers (ALPRs) like the ones that helped police on Cape Cod arrest Jason McCarthy. ALPRs are deployed not only on stationary locations like bridges, telephone poles, traffic lights, freeway ramps, and overpasses, but also on police cars and traffic enforcement vehicles.[83] They record cars driving and parked on the streets and traveling between cities,[84] tagging them by date, time, and location.[85] A single ALPR camera can record thousands of images an hour. Statewide sensor systems record millions of images a year.

Police view ALPRs as useful tools to alert them to stolen cars or drivers with outstanding warrants. One company that sells ALPRs marketed a service that would alert police officers to cars with unpaid fines; when the fine was collected, the private ALPR company would take a percentage as a sort of service charge.[86] This arrangement gives both the company and the police department obvious incentives to increase surveillance. Also troubling is that the cameras that power license plate readers don't just capture license plates. They also take photographs of cars, people standing by their cars, people in their cars, bumper stickers on cars, and details of the surrounding location, all of which can reveal insights into a person's identity, religion, and protected speech. Did you travel from one state to another to seek medical services? Did you park in front of a mosque or a mental health clinic? Does your bumper sticker profess an unpopular political stance? Anyone searching the ALPR image databases can find out.[87]

ALPRs from different states share license plate information across state borders, even when there are different laws (around abortion, for example) that create criminal liability in one state but not the other.[88] In 2023, seventy-one California police departments were caught sharing ALPR data with out-of-state law enforcement agencies—despite a state law forbidding the practice.[89] And while ALPRs are largely accurate, they do make mistakes. In one awkward case, Brian Hofer, the chair of the Oakland Privacy Advisory Commission—the community body that approves police surveillance technology in Oakland, California—was detained after an ALPR mistakenly flagged his car as stolen.[90] If the man in charge of overseeing surveillance in a city can be wrongfully targeted, no one should feel safe.

As we've seen, these various forms of surveillance are especially powerful in combination. State and local governments are working to create centralized operations centers where information from 911 and other emergency alerts can combine with real-time video footage and other digital data streams to allow for a quick and accurate assessment of an emergency situation.[91] Modeled on federal fusion centers, which share information between law enforcement and intelligence agencies at various levels of government, these centers are capable of expanding their capacity to incorporate any data stream that can be digitized.[92] Such integration allows local surveillance schemes to become national, giving artificial intelligence more data to comb through so it can find—and flag—more patterns and alert police to them.

In 2022, a suspicious pattern, detected by AI, prompted New York police to pull over a car driven by David Zayas.[93] Like many states, New York has hundreds of ALPR readers spread across various jurisdictions. Over a two-year period, those cameras identified 1.6 billion license plates and shared the information with forty different jurisdictions. According to court papers filed in his criminal case, Zayas's car was flagged because the computer thought his driving patterns—nine short trips from Massachusetts to different parts of New York—were typical of someone trafficking drugs. The algorithm was right. When Westchester County police searched Zayas' car, they found 112 grams of crack cocaine, $34,000 in cash, and a gun. We don't know how often AI systems like these get it wrong, or how many innocent drivers are pulled over for every one David Zayas, but even if they were 100 percent accurate, the implications for personal privacy are chilling. If a machine learning algorithm can identify someone as a drug dealer based on their driving patterns, surely it could also identify a parent driving their trans child across state lines for medical appointments, or labor organizers rallying workers around a factory, or anti-government activists entering a city.[94] Public movements now can be tracked in ways deeply harmful to autonomy, anonymity, and liberty.

Are Smart Cities Unconstitutional?

The rise of smart sensors and structural surveillance systems raises many of the same constitutional questions as other forms of location tracking. On the one hand, the general rule is that we can expect little privacy in public, so police can capture our activities in public without a Fourth Amendment concern. At the same time, the Supreme Court in *Carpenter* and *Jones* recognized that long-term aggregated tracking via location data is a Fourth Amendment search requiring a warrant.[95] So what does one make of a smart city like Chicago, with its 30,000 networked cameras? In a place like Chicago, covered in cameras and sensors equipped with artificial intelligence, you or your car can be tracked anywhere over the last week or month. Should prosecutors be able to use that information against you in court? The law points both ways, and the courts have not resolved the matter.

In Part III, I consider how courts *should* view this type of persistent digital surveillance. At present though, there is no clear constitutional or statutory law that would prohibit police from creating a large-scale, city-wide surveillance system and using that system to track people. Unlike some other technologies discussed in this book, smart city and smart surveillance technologies avoid the problem of third-party access. The government controls the cameras. The government controls the sensors. And the government controls the databases that process and store the information those cameras and sensors collect. Police therefore have easy access to the data for criminal prosecution. Any limits would have to come from courts, legislative rulemaking, or internal policies—and so far, limits have been few. While Baltimore's Persistent Surveillance Systems plane was judged unconstitutional, federal courts have allowed prosecutors to introduce evidence collected from Real-Time Crime Centers, ShotSpotter sensors, ALPRs, body cameras, and networked private camera systems. These decisions have been based on old-fashioned, analog thinking, but that remains the current thinking. In the absence of legal restrictions on their use, police departments and cities are investing in smart surveillance technologies at a rapid pace.

Why Are We Buying Smart Cities?

Good governance means addressing community needs, and for all the privacy concerns it raises, smart infrastructure can help cities understand and meet those needs. An app that allows you to report a pothole on your street using GPS is a pretty amazing innovation (assuming the city gets around to fixing the pothole.)[96] Smart technology involves an up-front cost, but over time, it can deliver significant cost savings. You don't need to pay a human to answer 311 calls if artificial intelligence can automatically route complaints to the right agencies.

Public surveillance, too, is paid for with public funds on behalf of taxpayers.[97] When cities invest in these systems, they are responding to a perceived desire for public safety.[98] Critics contest the premise that surveillance equals safety. These critics are not wrong. Few studies, if any, link increased expenditures on high-tech policing tools with sustained decreases in the crime rate. Investing in these tools also carries significant opportunity costs: Taxpayer money spent monitoring crime and social disorder is money that is not being used to address the underlying economic and public health problems that feed those societal issues in the first place.

Still, the lure of technology-driven policing remains hard for many to resist. In a previous book, *The Rise of Big Data Policing*, I argued that much of the allure of smart surveillance is that it gives police chiefs a way to answer an otherwise unanswerable question: "What are you going to do about crime?"[99] A truthful answer would require them to confront the fact that police can respond to crime but cannot fix its root causes—like structural inequality, housing and education discrimination, and a lack of economic or social opportunity—without dramatically transforming their mandate. It is much easier to tout a shiny new technological fix than fund social services programs that address poverty and inequality directly.[100] When the police abolition movement calls to "Defund the Police," this is what they mean. It's about decentering police power while building community power. It's about building childcare centers instead of detention centers. But in the heated rhetoric of political campaigns, this argument has not always won out.

The truth is that many of the pro-carceral forces in society would rather prevent short-term property losses than invest (via taxes or charitable contributions) in long-term structural solutions to poverty and thus crime.[101] Whether police are guarding the boundaries of affluent communities to keep out "the Other," patrolling poorer communities to maintain social control, or responding to the consequences of unaddressed poverty (like shoplifting, drug dealing, addiction, and mental health crises), modern law enforcement is largely in the business of protecting privilege and policing poverty. And deep down, that's exactly what many private property owners and business interests want.[102] Accepting this reality allows us to see the growth of citywide sensor technologies as a form of democratic self-surveillance. "Democratic," of course, is qualified, limited to those with the power to speak in a democracy marked by inequalities in access, resources, votes, and power. Within that unequal democracy, we are the ones choosing to buy technology to spy on our fellow citizens, making a multibillion dollar investment in police surveillance power rather than funding other services that could also improve public safety.[103]

Adding another level of complexity, local budgets are heavily influenced by "free" federal dollars. Many policing technologies are funded by federal grants that can only be used to enhance law enforcement capabilities.[104] The amount of money involved is staggering. The Department of Justice has provided hundreds of millions of dollars for research to improve policing, while the Department of Homeland Security's Urban Areas Security Initiative (UASI) provides over half a billion dollars every year to cities looking to improve their capacity for public surveillance.[105] Almost every technology mentioned in this book is, in one way or another, subsidized by federal grants to create, test, and pilot technologies—which means they're subsidized by your federal tax dollars. Although it might seem that smart surveillance is driven by local pressures, the truth is that the federal government is complicit in fueling those advances with significant and largely opaque financial support.

Finally, we are buying smart city surveillance technologies because companies are good at selling them.[106] If today isn't perfect, tomorrow can be, provided we have the right technology—or so the sales pitch goes. The resulting public-private partnership is mutually beneficial. Private companies involved in surveillance and other smart city infrastructure donate to candidates who share their vision, and those candidates get to campaign on the promise of a safer future. Once in office, they have a vested interest in following through.

The Cost of Surveillance

What do we lose when our cities become too smart? As with other smart technologies, we give up some of our privacy and some of our power.

But "surveillance cities" also shred the fabric of urban life. Video analytics turns citizens into literal objects of police surveillance.[107] A woman walking down the street becomes identified as an object (woman) and tracked as an object because that is what the technology has been trained to do—track objects.[108] Turning citizens into objects is dehumanizing, and when the purpose is to maintain social order, the whole process feels vaguely Orwellian. Ordering, cataloging, and sorting the lived experience of a city seems un-American.

This latter point is important to remember. The intrusion of video analytics and sensorveillance into ordinary life reverses the normal (or traditional) relationship between citizens and police. In the United States, "the people" are supposed to be able to go about their business without government monitoring unless and until police have some reason to suspect them of a crime. While communities of color long burdened with surveillance cameras and oversaturated with police patrols are right to contest this characterization (as it is not applied evenly across society), the legal rules still require probable cause or reasonable suspicion before police search or seize someone. The default condition of American life is supposed to be freedom from surveillance. Digital surveillance—especially integrated systems like citywide Real-Time Crime Center cameras and ALPR sensors—reverses that default, surveilling everyone all the time. In the hands of an authoritarian-minded government such surveillance power will be used to target disfavored groups, chill protest, and otherwise suppress free movement and travel.

In the same way that police turn people into objects, companies turn public space into data. Citizens in public spaces become commodified and commercialized, experimented upon so that the results can be sold for a profit. One of the most audacious experiments in this space was the Google project, Sidewalk Labs. For a few years, Sidewalk Labs was proposing to redevelop a portion of Toronto, Canada, as a prototype—a digital downtown filled with smart sensors from the streets to the stores, from the apartments to the parks, which would feed information back to Google and, in theory, help make the city run better.[109] Everything from residents' door locks to their ebike to their morning coffee would be digitized via electronic payment and security systems. Privacy advocates and community members expressed alarm about the proposals, and after several years of public debate the project was cancelled.[110] While the grand plan of building a single area under the eye of Google's data-obsessed engineers did not pan out, many of the company's innovations in transit, parking, access, and lighting will make it into smart cities soon. And all that sensor technology will also be available as surveillance technology unless privacy-protective steps are taken at the front end.

One reason Toronto rejected Sidewalk Labs was that the company failed to give citizens a full say in what would happen to their data. The decisions about what data would be collected, and from whom, were opaque, and had been made with little democratic oversight. The same is true when it comes to who gets targeted for police surveillance in the United States today. In the digital city, the objects of surveillance are usually people living their lives—walking down the street, driving a car, using electricity. Sometimes those people are involved in criminal activities and rightly targeted for police investigation, and sometimes not.

The Benefits of Surveillance

The costs of surveillance are real, but they also have hidden benefits. For example, the same surveillance cameras that zoomed in on Michael Celestine as he walked around his neighborhood in a jacket also capture instances of police abuse, substandard housing, and the results of failed social programs (people with serious, untreated mental illness, for example, or people living on the streets.) If society wanted to turn the cameras and sensors to expose those systemic problems, we could. Urban surveillance is double-edged, watching the watchers almost as much as they watch the people. Police officers patrol in public. Their cars and uniforms can be turned into trackable objects. In fact, because police cars and uniforms are so identifiable, it is easier to track police patrols than most other objects.

For decades, police departments have faced Department of Justice investigations for what are called "pattern and practice" violations—patterns of constitutional violations and civil rights abuses.[111] In Chicago, Baltimore, Oakland, Los Angeles, and Ferguson, Missouri, as well as dozens of other cities, DOJ lawyers from the Civil Rights Division interviewed community members and police officials and developed a record of illegal stop and frisks, excessive force, and other misconduct.[112] It is exhausting, labor-intensive work. Now imagine that these investigators could sort through BriefCam for every traffic stop, every moment when a police officer pulled a gun, every police chase. With a few search queries, they could isolate and superimpose all the events in time. They could track particular officers or cars. They could find patterns of police abuse.[113] Now imagine that the data from the drones in Beverly Hills were used for police oversight, or the Evidence.com data vault was handed over to DOJ to search with AI pattern recognition systems to find police misconduct. Companies already offer services utilizing AI to scan police worn body camera data to identify a lack of professionalism, now they could do it at scale across a city.

The surveillance has been done. The question is who gets to access it, and what they use it to do. With the political will, we could transform all the data flowing through the Real-Time Crime Center into what I've called "Blue Data," surveillance data used to police the police.[114] The Department of Justice or private litigators could use it to investigate civil rights violations. Police administrators and community groups could use it for training and accountability.[115] We could build its collection into the architecture of our digital cities. This would be true democratic self-surveillance but turned against the government. All it takes is citizens wanting access to the data.

5

Our Papers

Sometime during the early hours of New Year's Day in 2023, Ana Walshe disappeared. Walshe's husband, Brian, told police that his wife had left early for a work trip and he hadn't heard from her since. When elements of Brian's story didn't check out, he became the prime suspect in what police were now treating as a likely homicide investigation. But Walshe's body hadn't been found, which made it hard to prove she had been murdered. Hard, that is, until police obtained her husband's Google search history.[1]

Jan. 1

- 4:55 a.m.: "How long before a body starts to smell"
- 4:58 a.m.: "How to stop a body from decomposing"
- 5:20 a.m.: "How to embalm a body"
- 5:47 a.m.: "10 ways to dispose of a dead body if you really need to"
- 6:25 a.m.: "How long for someone to be missing to inherit"
- 6:34 a.m.: "Can you throw away body parts"
- 9:29 a.m.: "What does formaldehyde do"
- 9:34 a.m.: "How long does DNA last"
- 9:59 a.m.: "Can identification be made on partial remains"
- 11:34 a.m.: "Dismemberment and the best ways to dispose of a body"
- 11:44 a.m.: "How to clean blood from wooden floor"
- 11:56 a.m.: "Luminol to detect blood"
- 1:08 p.m.: "What happens when you put body parts in ammonia"
- 1:21 p.m.: "Is it better to throw crime scene clothes away or wash them"

Jan. 2

- 12:45 p.m.: "Hacksaw best tool to dismember"
- 1:10 p.m.: "Can you be charged with murder without a body"
- 1:14 p.m.: "Can you identify a body with broken teeth"

Jan. 3

- 1:02 p.m.: "What happens to hair on a dead body"

- 1:14 p.m.: "What is the rate of decomposition of a body found in a plastic bag compared to on a surface in the woods"
- 1:20 p.m.: "Can baking soda make a body smell good"[2]

The keyword searches suggested a guilty mind filled with increasingly incriminating questions. Prosecutors used them as evidence to charge Walshe with murder.[3]

Everyone has gotten busted texting when they hoped people weren't watching. In a meeting, in a classroom, during a bad first date—you thought you were being subtle, but you weren't, and now your date is calling you out. The only thing worse might be getting caught texting during a drug bust. That was the position Brandon Sykes found himself in on the Eastern Shore of Maryland.[4] Sykes was riding in his girlfriend's car when it was pulled over for a broken taillight. When the police approached, Sykes's girlfriend seemed nervous. Suspicious that the couple was hiding something, police used a drug detection dog to sniff around the car. The dog alerted to the presence of narcotics, and a search of the car uncovered eighty-four bags of heroin. Both Sykes and his girlfriend were arrested. Both denied knowing about the heroin in the car. Sykes, however, was observed using his cell phone during the arrest process. Police obtained a warrant for Sykes's texts and discovered incoming messages like, "I need 5 more," "Can u thro 1 in so I can make something please that's 230 already," and "I need like 2. . . . 50,"[5] and outgoing messages like "bring me another 8th."[6] Texts from the ten days leading up to the arrest established a consistent pattern of communications that suggested drug dealing using that phone. Sykes denied that the texts (and the phone) belonged to him—which might have been more convincing if police officers hadn't witnessed him using it. The texts provided the strongest evidence that the drugs hidden in the girlfriend's car belonged to Sykes, who was ultimately convicted of drug distribution and sentenced to eighteen years in prison.[7]

Digital Papers

Search queries and text messages are digital examples of what the Fourth Amendment refers to as "papers." In using this term, the Founders of course had in mind physical documents, not gifs. But while today's "papers" may be made of pixels, James Madison would have recognized them as similar to the ones he sought to protect with the Bill of Rights. In the eighteenth-century, as today, people had two types of papers to keep private. The first type was personal in nature—diaries and journals, as well as letters to friends, family, and romantic partners.[8] The second type involved commercial affairs, including business records.[9] Both types of papers were of interest to the British government during the revolutionary period because they could reveal whether Americans were fomenting sedition or evading taxes (many were).[10] By securing physical papers from unreasonable search and seizure, the Founders aimed to protect the ideas, information, and communications they contained.

Today, ideas, information, and communications are collected in digital form. This book was written on a laptop, not a parchment scroll, but the intellectual work of notetaking, writing, and editing otherwise hasn't changed much in 200 years. When I communicate with friends and family, I email or text rather than handwriting a formal letter, but the information I share about myself and my family could be conveyed in either form. My online bank account allows me to monitor my checking and savings accounts through a computer connected to my bank's cloud server, but it offers me the exact same insights as the paper bank records my parents received in the mail and kept in a shoebox in the attic for fifty years.

What's changed isn't really the content of the papers, but how easily that content can be obtained—and used against us. There was a time when phone numbers were handwritten in little paper address books and shopping lists were jotted on the back of an envelope. There was a time when photographs were viewable only after being developed in a lab, and love letters had to be physically mailed. Now that these records are digital, it's much less difficult for police to get their hands on them. It's not that detectives in the past couldn't confiscate the box of photos stuffed in the back of your closet if they wanted to. They could. But now, those photos are on your phone, in chronological order, stamped with the time, date, and location, and duplicated on a cloud server. The digital paper trails we create today—our texts, notes, photos, contacts, calendars, purchases, and queries—contain a significant amount of information about who we are, what we think, and what we do. And unlike analog records, they're almost impossible to destroy.

Part of what makes our digital papers so revealing is that we produce—and keep—so many of them. In the pre-Internet age, someone who never threw away a single grocery list, work memo, wall calendar, or dry-cleaning receipt would likely be branded a hoarder. Today, that degree of retention is the default. In their investigation into the NXIVM "sex cult," police obtained over twelve terabytes of data from computers.[11] A single terabyte can hold as much information as a twelve-story library.[12] Twelve of them contained more than enough evidence to prove that NXIVM's leader, Keith Rainiere, and his associates had engaged in racketeering conspiracy to commit sex trafficking, forced labor, wire fraud, identity theft, money laundering, and obstruction of justice.[13] Some of the material was salacious: New members were recruited by existing members (some of whom were minor celebrities) and forced to provide incriminating "collateral" to join,[14] such as "sexually explicit photographs and videos of themselves, rights to financial assets, and letters containing damaging accusations—whether true or untrue—about family members and friends."[15] But most of the records that sunk NXIVM were mundane papers, the kind of information associated with any commercial enterprise—such as emails, Excel spreadsheets, and bank accounts hosted in the cloud.

In the past, someone in Raniere's position might have opened up his filing cabinets and started shredding. If he was fast enough, he might have managed to destroy some of the evidence. But even if Raniere had lit all his computers on fire the minute he found out he was under investigation, investigators would likely have had little trouble finding the incriminating evidence elsewhere. Much like the data produced by our smart home devices, cars, and cell phones, our papers aren't ours alone. You cannot edit a shared document without accessing a cloud-based, third-party service like Google Docs or Dropbox. You cannot email someone across the world without a third-party email service provider like Gmail or Microsoft Outlook. In short, you cannot connect with other people or services without a technology company doing the work at the backend. The result is that these technology companies mediate access to most of our digital papers.[16]

Digital Currency

Consider money, for example. Money in the form of cash is largely untraceable. The ten-dollar bill in your wallet has been used before, but you do not know where or why or by whom. If you use it to buy an ice cream (or cocaine), there won't be an easy way to trace it back to you. Now think about the digital transactions you make using Apple Pay, Google Pay, or any of the other apps that function as cash equivalents. These mobile wallets are creating digital paper trails, recording not only what you buy, but also where and when.[17]

At first glance, this may not seem all that different from the records generated when you purchase something with a credit card, which police have been able to track for years. But fintech can provide a more comprehensive picture of your activities that incorporates not only the purchases themselves, but also the geolocation data and other context surrounding those purchases.[18] If you use a payment app when you stop at a drugstore for cold medicine, an auto repair shop for brake cleaner, and a hardware store for paint thinner, acid, or batteries, and then use it again to book a short-term rental, anyone with access to that app's data will be able to see that you've "invested" in a pop-up methamphetamine lab.[19] Once the payment pattern has triggered suspicion, the GPS data can be used to pinpoint the location of the lab.

Apps like Venmo can also reveal your associations. If you grab lunch with a friend and hand them a twenty-dollar bill to cover your share, your friend's credit card statement won't reveal the fact that the two of you were dining together. But if you Venmo them that twenty dollars, it's a different story, as a disturbing case from Salt Lake City, Utah, illustrates. After the murder of George Floyd in the summer of 2020, Madalena McNeil took to the streets alongside many of her neighbors to protest police brutality.[20] To symbolize blood spilled by police, she and a few friends threw red paint on the street. After that protest, McNeil solicited money to help pay for future protests. Among those who donated was a local politician, State Senator Derek Kitchen, who sent her ten dollars via Venmo.[21]

Then things got strange. After the local district attorney refused to prosecute a police shooting, protesters returned to the streets, again throwing red paint—this time outside the district attorney's office. Police began investigating McNeil because she had purchased twelve buckets of red paint at Home Depot.[22] Prosecutors charged her with a first-degree felony and gang enhancement, exposing her to life in prison. They also began investigating everyone who had donated to the protest as possible participants in a conspiracy to destroy public property. This included State Senator Kitchen, whose entire Venmo history was searched because of his ten dollar donation. What began as a protest against police brutality turned into a serious felony case based on digital papers with chilling impacts on all who had donated to the cause.

Digital Demands

Transparency reports from technology companies reveal that police regularly ask them to hand over digital papers and that they generally comply, at least when there is a warrant. For example, in the six months from January to June 2022, Google received 30,030 demands via warrant for information on 42,518 accounts and provided some information about 86 percent of them.[23] Google also received 21,162 requests via subpoena on 49,097 accounts and provided some information on 83 percent of them.[24] Facebook received 65,420 legal process requests (not broken down by warrant or subpoena) on about 146,122 users/accounts, and granted some information 87 percent of them.[25] Microsoft responded to 5,560 requests from law enforcement for information on 17,337 accounts and provided some information on 9 percent of the requests.[26] The number of requests have increased year after year and they also involve smaller tech companies with other types of digital information.

The numbers tell only part of the story. While cheap computer memory allows us to store more information, the interconnected nature of the services that host our digital papers has made that information more valuable. If police searched your wallet and found a scrap of paper with a phone number, they'd have a scrap of paper with a phone number. If, instead, they found the same number on your smartphone listed as a contact, they would be able to see all the times you texted that number late at night and all the Venmo payments you made soon thereafter, helpfully revealing the approximate quantity of cocaine you purchased. The aggregation of details is more telling than any single clue.

For police, a suspect's phone can be a gold mine of digital papers. It might contain direct evidence, like a photo of the murder weapon. Or maybe they'll find indirect evidence—say, a suspicious sounding text.

Caroline Torie, the codirector of the St. Joseph County Prosecutor's Office Cyber Crimes Unit in Indiana told *Police Magazine* that the average iPhone has about 800,000 stored digital artifacts, with some smartphones having more than a million digital clues.[27] And because this information is helpfully located all in one place, it's easy for police to access. With extraction tools for mobile devices, police can copy a phone's data for later study.[28] In a few jurisdictions, police were using these tools during routine traffic stops.[29] You get pulled over, get a ticket, and have your phone's data downloaded by the police.

The sheer amount of information we store digitally gives the government access to our private acts, thoughts, and opinions in ways that are far more invasive than ever. Even if the British authorities had confiscated every single one of John Adams's papers, the documents would have limited value compared to the emails, texts, photos, contacts, calendars, banking information, and other personal notes in a modern smartphone, tablet, or computer. As Chief Justice Roberts wrote in *Riley v. California* about smartphones:

> Cell phones differ in both a quantitative and a qualitative sense from other objects that might be kept on an arrestee's person. The term "cell phone" is itself misleading shorthand; many of these devices are in fact minicomputers that also happen to have the capacity to be used as telephones. They could just as easily be called cameras, video players, rolodexes, calendars, tape recorders, libraries, diaries, albums, televisions, maps, or newspapers.
>
> One of the most notable distinguishing features of modern cell phones is their immense storage capacity. Before cell phones, a search of a person was limited by physical realities and tended as a general matter to constitute only a narrow intrusion on privacy. . . . Most people cannot lug around every piece of mail they have received for the past several months, every picture they have taken, or every book or article they have read—nor would they have any reason to attempt to do so.[30]

As Roberts suggests, someone who had access to all the content on your phone—photos, email, texts, calendars, budget apps, mobile wallets, health trackers, news sources, Google searches—would have a pretty good window into who you are and what you care about. Think about it:

Which is more personally revealing, a search of your bedroom or a search of your smartphone? Which would you rather expose to the world?[31]

The case that inspired Roberts to make these remarks involved a young San Diego man named David Riley. Police initially stopped Riley for driving a car with expired registration tags.[32] During the traffic stop, police learned that Riley's license had been suspended, so they impounded the car. In the process of inventorying the car, officers discovered two illegal guns taped under the hood and placed Riley under arrest. Suspicious that Riley was involved in gang activity, police scrolled through his smartphone, looking through his contacts, photos, and videos. Intriguingly, one of the photos showed Riley in front of a car that police believed had been involved in an earlier gang shooting that was still under investigation. That photograph—which had been found somewhat fortuitously by the officers—became a key piece of evidence against Riley, who was charged with attempted murder for his role in the shooting. Riley was convicted and appealed the warrantless search of his smartphone.[33] The legal issue in *Riley* was whether police could rummage through any phone recovered incident to arrest to find evidence of other crimes unrelated to the reason for the arrest.[34]

The Supreme Court, in what is widely understood to be the first case recognizing that "digital is different" for Fourth Amendment purposes, held that even though Riley had been lawfully arrested, police still needed to obtain a judicial warrant before searching through his smartphone.[35] Police could search his physical things incident to arrest, including the physical cover of the phone, but the data in his phone was too personal and revealing. Because there was no warrant in Riley's case, the discovery of the photograph violated the Fourth Amendment and had to be suppressed.[36]

The *Riley* case was considered a watershed moment in Fourth Amendment law. But as you might now recognize, it left a significant loophole. *With a warrant*, all of Riley's digital papers would have been open for inspection. In a case where a young man, alleged to be a gang member, was found with two guns taped to the hood of his car, it is not hard to imagine a judge signing a warrant allowing police to search for gang-related evidence on the suspect's phone. Which means all of Riley's smartphone data—and all of everyone's—is only a warrant away from exposure.

Searching Your Searches

The websites we visit, the videos we watch, the texts we send, and the photos we save can be very revealing, but to really get inside our heads, all anyone would have to do is look at our search history. The average Google user searches for something three times a day, every day.[37] Queries about politicians, celebrities, cheesecake recipes, football trivia, mental health symptoms, sexual fantasies, weird rashes—all live in your search history, like a direct link to your subconscious. People reveal to Google fears and desires they would never reveal to their spouse, their best friend, or even their therapist. And yet all these queries are captured and can be made available to law enforcement.

A surprising number of people ask Google for help with committing their crimes—like the would-be burglar who Googled "how to open a locked window."[38] Others seem to be attempting to assuage their anxiety in the aftermath of a crime, like the January 6th Capitol rioter whose somewhat belated search "Is it illegal to go into Capitol?" helped prosecutors charge him with having done just that.[39] Other searches might not be as directly incriminating, but they can still become evidence against you under the right circumstances. A search for an address might not directly reveal a crime, but it might point to one if that address is a known brothel.

All of this assumes police have a suspect in mind. If they don't, they can still take advantage of the revealing nature of search engine data by performing what's known a reverse keyword search[40]—a request for a third-party search engine like Google or Bing to reveal the identity of users who searched for a particular word or phrase.[41] While these searches are directed against the entire dataset of search queries, the requests can be narrowed by date and location.[42] For example, after the bombing of a church, police might request the identifying information of anyone who had recently Googled the church's address or inquired how to build a bomb. Of course, there are plenty of innocent reasons to Google the address of a church, like wanting to attend services. But close to the time of the bombing, that query might also be a clue.

In Denver, Colorado, police used a reverse keyword search to find suspects in a felony-murder arson case.[43] The facts offer layers of warnings about our digital future. According to police reports, three teenagers sought revenge for an iPhone robbery that had occurred a week earlier.[44] Using Apple's Find My iPhone service, the teens tracked the stolen phone to a home in a residential neighborhood. Then, they set the home on fire. But, tragically, Find My iPhone had provided an incorrect location. The fire killed a family of five, including two young children.

Police had no leads, so they began issuing a series of warrants intended to identify phones (and by extension, people) that had been near the home at the time of the fire, including two geofence warrants sent to Google and requests for CSLI from four separate cell phone services. None of the digital searches provided a useable clue until police requested a keyword search for the address.[45] Investigators asked Google to identify anyone who had queried "5312 Truckee Street" or a variation in the fifteen days prior to the arson.[46] After much back and forth with Google's lawyers to narrow the request to particular IP addresses, Google finally provided information identifying sixteen-year-old Gavin Seymour. Seymour's device was one of three that had queried the address multiple times. Police then sought additional warrants for Seymour's Snapchat, Instagram, and Facebook accounts, and for his Apple iCloud data, along with his text messages and historical cell-site locational data. The combination of digital clues led to his conviction for the murder of the family.

To identify Gavin Seymour, Google had to sort through billions of search queries. As Seymour's lawyers argued before the courts, that makes it one of most extensive general searches in world history[47]—billions of bits of personal information to find one IP address. The police in the Seymour case had obtained a warrant for their search, presumably in large part because Google had demanded one. But as a constitutional matter, it's not necessarily obvious that such a search would require a warrant, despite its breadth. Typing a query into a private company's algorithmic search bar is not clearly a private act that the company must keep secret. In fact, we know that companies do not keep these searches secret—instead, they monetize them by selling the sponsored ads that appear in your search results. Google searches may feel intimate, but from a legal perspective, it's hard to articulate why a person would have a reasonable expectation of privacy in regard to a question asked of a computer algorithm. And yet, asking questions about abortion, sexual identity, health, freedom of speech, and subversive and unconventional thinking feels private and something that we do not want to share with the government. The idea that the FBI could start investigating us because of our curiosities or interests revealed by our Google searches is a frightening but all too real possibility. Anyone searching for "nearby protests" or arguments as to why the current government is doing a bad job could be targeted for investigation. Even something innocuous as querying "immigration laws" or "gender identity" in a search field could lead to unwanted scrutiny.

The Law of Dearest Papers

While Congress has yet to consider many of the privacy questions arising from digital technology discussed in previous chapters, the question of our papers is an exception. The Electronic Communications Privacy Act (ECPA) protects electronic communications, such as email, in three ways.[48] First, it extends the protections of the Wiretap Act to email, preventing police from intercepting messages in transit.[49] Second, ECPA protects stored emails, requiring a warrant to obtain the content of emails sent or received within the past 180 days.[50] Third, ECPA establishes some lesser protections for email that has been stored for more than 180 days.[51] The 180-day cutoff may seem strange or arbitrary today, but it reflects the state of technology in the year ECPA was passed 1986, four years before the introduction of the first web browser.[52] In the early days of the Internet, email was largely kept on personal computers (not large cloud providers) and typically not stored for very long, because storage was limited.[53] If all you were concerned about was the government intercepting your emails or obtaining them from your computer (before you deleted them to save storage), ECPA was a fine protection.[54]

Today that logic has almost reversed itself. Few people download emails, preferring to keep them forever in the cloud. (I still have emails I received in 2007.) The privacy danger arises primarily from those cloud-stored emails, which remains outside ECPA protection. In addition, other forms of digital papers that are not considered communications (like the contents of your notes app, or your calendar entries) fall outside of statutory protection under ECPA. While ECPA has been amended, it has not been fully updated to address the realities of the modern digital world. As a result, the full scope and scale of modern digital papers remains largely unprotected under federal law. Congress after Congress has acknowledged the need to update ECPA—and then inevitably moved on to other pressing problems (like naming a new post office)[55] without doing anything about it.

If federal statutory law is incapable of protecting our digital papers, the U.S. Constitution may hold more promise. At the time of the Founding, papers were highly protected. In fact, for the first hundred years of the Fourth Amendment's existence, the protection of papers was almost absolute.[56] Historians largely agree that the Fourth Amendment arose in response to two forms of British oppression, the writs of assistance and general warrants.[57] As legal scholar Donald Dripps has recognized, the writs of assistance granted English authorities almost unlimited government search powers, but did not authorize the seizure of papers.[58] The general warrants, in contrast, specifically allowed the collection of personal papers.[59] Together, the two laws represented a significant threat to privacy, autonomy, and political freedom.

To fully understand why the Founding generation cared so much about papers, all one needs to do is look at the seminal English cases influential at the time. Two cases—*Wilkes v. Wood*[60] and *Entick v. Carrington*[61] are famous examples of government overreach with respect to private papers, and both contain lessons for today's digital world.[62] John Wilkes was a member of Parliament who anonymously published *The North Briton*, a publication that criticized King George III.[63] At the time, criticism of the king was a crime, and authorities were dispatched to Wilkes's home to look for these seditious and treasonous papers.[64] The agents ransacked Wilkes's home, took his papers, and generally behaved in an insulting and demeaning manner. Wilkes sued the king's agents, claiming that the warrant for his papers was unlawful and unreasonable.[65] In a case that was read widely in the Americas, the British court agreed with Wilkes about the harms involved and awarded damages for the seizure of all the papers and manuscripts from his private office.[66]

John Entick came from the other side of the English class divide, publishing his pamphlet called *The Monitor* from London's Grub Street, a haven for marginal "hack writers."[67] Entick was paid to criticize the king and did so with gusto, especially when it came to how the king was conducting the war against the Spanish. Peeved by the criticism, agents of the king searched Entick's home looking for private papers to confirm the authorship of the suspected seditious libel.[68] The agents walked off with one hundred pamphlets and hundreds of other documents. Like Wilkes, Entick sued the offending agents, claiming that his papers and books had been seized based on an unreasonable warrant.[69] In an opinion that not only influenced the Founding generation but also is still cited by the modern U.S. Supreme Court, Lord Camden wrote about the privacy and exposure harms of these invasive searches of personal papers:[70]

> Papers are the owner's goods and chattels; they are his dearest property; and are so far from enduring a seizure, that they will hardly bear an inspection; and though the eye cannot by the laws of England be guilty of a trespass, yet where private papers are removed and carried away the secret nature of those goods will be an aggravation of the trespass, and demand more considerable damages in that respect. Where is the written law that gives any magistrate such a power? I can safely answer, there is none; and, therefore, it is too much for us, without such authority, to pronounce a practice legal which would be subversive of all the comforts of society.[71]

"Where is the written law that gives any magistrate such a power? . . . There is none" is a bold statement limiting executive power to seize papers. It was a case and a principle that echoed across British courts and filtered to the Americas.

Despite these cases, British agents in the American colonies continued to conduct invasive searches, and opposition to those searches became a rallying cry for revolutionaries.[72] After independence, Anti-Federalists reminded Americans of these abuses as they promoted a Bill of Rights, with the Fourth Amendment as a check on government search power.[73] The proponents of the Bill of Rights feared that without special protection, all of our written materials could be seized with a warrant provided by a newly empowered federal agent. After all, the searches that had been so objectionable to the colonists had been authorized by a magistrate's warrant.[74]

The best example of the U.S. Supreme Court's once-strong support for private papers arises from the Court's first major Fourth Amendment decision, *Boyd v. United States* in 1886.[75] The case involved the subpoena of business records (receipts from a glass company), which helped the government convict Boyd of tax evasion. Boyd challenged the seizure of his papers, and the Supreme Court agreed that the Fourth Amendment had been violated, citing to none other than Lord Camden and *Entick*, and holding that such a request for private papers was unreasonable. Even one hundred years after the Founding, papers (both commercial and personal) were protected from government seizure.

Over time, however, this understanding fell apart.[76] Whatever protection was once granted to papers has been undercut by Supreme Court decisions that allow their use as evidence in a variety of cases. Police routinely seize documents that prove crimes (photos, emails, texts, threats) as well as documents that are crimes themselves (child sexual abuse material), and all of it is admissible in court. The information may not be on parchment or even on paper, but if it is evidence of a crime, the Fourth Amendment now offers little protection.

Today, the general rule is that the search and seizure of digital papers located on personal computers or tablets requires a warrant.[77] Courts have analogized computers to closed containers (like suitcases) that require legal justification to open. Of course, unlike the items in our suitcase, many of our digital papers live both on our computers and on a cloud server, which makes the analogy less helpful. Still, police do generally get a warrant for digital papers unless a legal exception applies. As it turns out, however, there are many such exceptions. For example, if a private party (like your nosy roommate) searches your computer and finds contraband (photos of illegal acts) and then turns the computer over to police, the "private-search doctrine" allows police to see everything the private party saw.[78] If the device's owner (or their spouse) consents to the search, any Fourth Amendment claim is rendered moot.[79] If there is an emergency and "exigent circumstances" make searching the device imperative (for example, if the device may reveal the location of an abducted child, or a bomb that is about to detonate), police can do so right away, without waiting for a warrant.[80] The exceptions go on, and as a result, police have been able to gain access to many electronic devices without a warrant. And, as with much of our other personal data, if investigators do get a warrant, they can access almost anything.

The Problem with Warrants

One of the reasons the Founders considered searches of papers so invasive, even when authorized by a warrant, is that they can be unavoidably overbroad, capturing innocent materials that must be read to find the incriminating facts. This is arguably even more true when it comes to digital papers. Assume for the sake of argument that photographs, texts, digital health records, and other stored notes are "papers" for the purpose of the Fourth Amendment. After all, in an earlier time, all these documents would have been memorialized in paper form. Now recall the case involving a series of nighttime burglaries, during which witnesses saw the burglar using an iPhone flashlight app while creeping around their bedrooms. The geolocation data captured by that free flashlight app provided strong evidence that a particular suspect was behind the robberies. The police, however, wanted more. In their warrant to search the suspect's smartphone, police asked for access to any potential clues that could help them win a conviction, including:

> The memory/data storage of a black iPhone 6 cellular handset belonging to [suspect] for data/information, and any "cloud" storage applications connected to the cellular handset, concerning any of the following on October 13, 2019, October 31, 2019, and November 2, 2019: use of the flashlight; Apple Health data; use of the camera application to take photographs or record video; use of any applications requiring the use of the phone's keyboard, including text, photo, or video message applications, Internet browsers, and applications for voice or video calls; locational data, as compiled by the phone's internal GPS device or other components or applications of the phone capable of identifying and memorializing the geographic location of the cellular handset. The search is to be conducted for evidence, direct and corroborative, of the criminal offenses identified in the Affidavit of Probable Cause to this warrant application, incorporated herein by reference in its entirety.[81]

The logic behind the detective's request makes some sense. Maybe the burglar took photographs of the homes' sleeping residents (frighteningly enough, he did).[82] Maybe his health records reveal an elevated heartbeat (they did not). Maybe the burglar texted someone about his plan to commit a crime (he did not). The requests were speculative, but not irrational.

The harder question is whether police should get access to all of our digital papers just because some of that data could contain incriminating clues. Sure, it's possible that the burglar kept an Outlook calendar where he scheduled his crimes, but to find those entries, police would need to look through his entire calendar, going back months to see every other event in his life. Is that reasonable? Somewhat strangely, in the physical world, police do receive broad access to search and seize evidence. It is common, for example, for police investigators who have identified a burglary suspect to ask a judge for a warrant to search that person's entire home. The thinking is that investigators might find stolen items or recover clothing that the suspect had been wearing. Even if the logic is a bit speculative, judges typically sign such warrants. And if police officers find evidence of another crime during their search, stumbling across a pile of cocaine or a dead body while looking for the burglar's clothes, police can seize that evidence because it is in plain view (in accordance with a rule known as the plain view doctrine).[83]

Should this logic hold in the digital realm? Does the fact that the burglar had a smartphone give the police the right to rummage through the phone's stored data looking for incriminating clues? Can that search go back in time indefinitely? What if, while looking for pictures taken at the crime scenes, investigators stumble across photos of piles of cocaine, or texts about moving a dead body? What happens with incriminating information uncovered incidental to the original reason for searching?

There is no easy answer. In the Pennsylvania case involving the iPhone flashlight burglar, the appellate court took the middle ground. The court allowed the warrant for the suspect's geolocation data and the data from his flashlight app but denied access to his other personal data, including photographs, health data, and texts.[84] The court offered two clarifying justifications for denying the warrant request. First, the court found that the request for other data was not particularized enough.[85] The requirement of particularity comes directly from the text of the Fourth Amendment, which states that "no Warrants shall issue, but upon probable cause, supported by Oath or affirmation, and *particularly* describing the place to be searched and the persons or things to be seized."[86] The terms of the warrant are supposed to limit what can be searched and seized, removing the police officer's discretion to pick and choose as they rummage through someone's things.

Second, the court found the warrant overbroad.[87] Under the Fourth Amendment, there must be a clear connection (a "nexus") between the crime and the search location. The goal of a warrant is to prevent generalized rummaging outside the bounds of probable cause.[88] While police had reason to believe that the location data (keyed to the time and place of the suspected crime) and the flashlight app (observed by a witness) would provide information about the burglaries, they could only speculate about the evidence that the other digital papers stored on the phone might reveal. It was a fishing expedition, and the court limited the warrant accordingly. But this is not settled law nationally. Many courts might come to a different decision. Judges sign warrants every day granting investigators access to entire computer hard drives and smartphones without a careful analysis of the nexus requirement. Until the Supreme Court makes a definitive ruling on the matter, the safety of the data on our devices will remain in question.

Can We Escape Our Digital Papers?

The conversion of our physical papers into digital data creates a difficult problem for those who would avoid surveillance. There is almost no escape from digital creation, which means almost no escape from police or government monitoring. Our communications, purchases, and work take place largely in the digital realm and exist somewhere in digital form. Even the papers that filled James Madison's desk drawers are now on a cloud server or cached on the Internet somewhere and available for download. Only the most sophisticated technologists could create their own email system or storage system protected from third parties. And unless their interlocutors are equally savvy, even that isn't likely to protect them. Securing only one side of an email or text exchange means not securing it at all.

It is hard to imagine a world without digital papers. Yet it should be possible to imagine a world where the government does not get access to the content they contain. The government's interest in accessing this information must be weighed against our claims to secrecy and privacy, and the balance should not always tilt toward the government. It is no accident that the Fourth Amendment arose as a response to political repression and attempts to stifle dissent. Those who challenge government power can always be exposed by their digital papers that reveal their critiques or just different ways of existing.

Our expectation of privacy in our papers has eroded significantly since the early days of the republic. But further erosion isn't inevitable. Papers are the only digital medium that has had legislation written to protect it, and while that legislation is now dated, the fact that it exists at all helps smooth the way for future regulation, updated for the realities of today's technology. In addition, papers can be encrypted. During the American Revolution, John Adams, James Madison, Thomas Jefferson, and others kept sensitive messages secret by writing them in code.[89] Today, communication services like Signal use end-to-end encryption for similar purposes.[90] Texts sent via Signal cannot be obtained by the police because they are encrypted and not stored on third-party platforms.[91] There is no place for police to obtain Signal data because the app doesn't keep any of it. Other communications providers like WhatsApp (owned by Meta) and Telegram also offer a limited form of end-to-end encryption.[92] VPNs (virtual private networks) can offer some privacy from geolocational clues by masking the user's IP address and thus shielding them from identification by their Internet service provider.[93] As I'll discuss in Part III, these technological methods of protecting our digital papers can serve as models for safeguarding other parts of our digital lives. In the meantime, they represent one way to resist the encroachment of government oversight of our "dearest" information.

6

Our Likes

If you're lucky, you grew up with a tight-knit circle of childhood friends—a group of people who protected you and defined you, who shaped the person you became. If you grew up as a digital native, always interacting through social media, these friend groups are memorialized in photographs, videos, and social media posts.[1] The dance video you filmed together and posted to YouTube, the birthday party photo you added to Instagram, the memes you sent each other on Snapchat—all these are posted and shared. For Jelani Henry, a teenager from Harlem, New York, the documentation of this natural bonding process became circumstantial evidence when he was arrested for attempted murder.[2] Prosecutors found that Jelani had liked videos on social media featuring a crew of his childhood friends who called themselves "the Goodfellas."[3] Some of those friends were later arrested as part of a large-scale criminal conspiracy case for allegedly assaulting members of other, rival crews. It was pretty simple for prosecutors to link Jelani to the Goodfellas crew through his social media likes, photos, and friends.[4] But Jelani was innocent. Even though police had no evidence that Jelani had committed a crime, he spent nineteen months in jail at Rikers Island before he was released and the case dismissed.

In Memphis, Tennessee, a white police detective went undercover to monitor a local Black Lives Matter (BLM) group, whose members were active on Facebook.[5] Hiding behind an avatar of a Guy Fawkes mask, "Bob Smith" liked various Facebook posts about social justice, friended hundreds of BLM activists, and became privy to the group's plans.[6] Because the local BLM movement used social media to coordinate activities and shape strategy, "Bob" knew about protests before they happened. He became a virtual informant, lurking in meetings and tipping off police to planned events.[7] As in the 1960s when the FBI infiltrated the civil rights movement, a law enforcement spy had infiltrated a racial justice organization to surveil its members and undercut its political work.[8] Once again, lawful political organizing and speech has become the subject of police suspicion and surveillance.[9] And since that organizing was happening on social media, the infiltrator didn't even have to leave his desk.

Digital Communities

For centuries, our communities were defined by physical proximity—we spent time with our families, our neighbors, and the people with whom we worked, worshipped, or attended school. Over time, technology allowed us to expand our world, connecting us by mail, telephone, trains, and planes, but those connecting points went largely untracked. Sure, in theory a detective could count the number of letters sent by your Aunt Alice or surveil your family barbecue to see whether Cousin Louie showed up, but unless Alice and Louie were in the Mafia, it's unlikely anyone would have bothered. And even if someone did go to the effort of spying on your backyard barbecue, they wouldn't be able to glean much about the interactions that took place there, or learn much information about you as a result.

In the digital era, our web of social connections has expanded exponentially. On social media, friends from high school and college are linked with family, friends, and random influencers. The daily conversations and semi coherent musings you might once have shared with a roommate are now posted in a public-facing forum. Entire communities have been created through social media, allowing millions of people who share interests, passions, or politics to connect daily across the globe.[10] The family picnic is now a global platform, and everyone's invited to the party. In many ways, this is a positive development. Digital communities can give us access to perspectives we wouldn't otherwise encounter, and they can serve as lifelines for members of marginalized groups who might otherwise feel isolated. The downside is that every comment, contact, and connection we make in these digital communities is tracked, recorded, and analyzed. The screaming argument at the family picnic was never recorded, but the argument you had on Facebook is available for all to see. Social media reveals your ideas and opinions, your likes and dislikes, your relationships and associations. And when data like that exists, it can be exploited—including by law enforcement.

Social Media Detectives

When it comes to politics and activism, social media platforms have supplanted the town squares and taverns of the colonial era. Public debates take place on X (formerly Twitter) and Bluesky; organizers spread the word about actions via Instagram. And lurking at the edge of those virtual crowds is often a police officer or two, monitoring the goings-on, collecting evidence about past crimes, or simply sending a message by their presence: We're watching you.

Shanai Matteson is an artist and climate activist living in rural Palisade, Minnesota, where she became involved in protesting a proposed oil pipeline.[11] Matteson and other activists believed that the pipeline, which would run through Ojibwe land, threatened the environment and Indigenous sovereignty. They initiated a pressure campaign to stop the planned construction, and, like many activists, relied heavily on Facebook and Instagram in their organizing efforts.[12] Police monitored their social media feeds to learn when and where the events were happening, so they could send officers to those locations in advance.

During one protest, the crowd moved to a pipeline construction site, where a few attendees were arrested for trespassing. At the protest rally beforehand, Matteson had spoken about risking arrest. Though she herself had not been arrested, prosecutors used the video of her speech, which had been broadcast on Facebook Live, to charge her with a misdemeanor for "conspiring, aiding, and abetting" trespass onto "critical" pipeline infrastructure.[13] At the trial, it was revealed that the police department had been monitoring Matteson's social media posts for months. These revelations obviously unnerved her. Although she was eventually acquitted of the criminal charges, she and her fellow activists got the message: Social media is a location of police surveillance and social control.

Social media monitoring has become a routine tool for many law enforcement agencies.[14] In one International Association of Chiefs of Police (IACP) survey, police respondents stated they used social media for "soliciting crime tips (76%), monitoring public sentiment (72%), [and] intelligence gathering for investigations (70%)."[15] Some police departments have created specialized social media investigative units.[16] In Chicago, police leaders created a twenty-person unit to track potential looters by monitoring social media posts organizing such efforts.[17]

Chicago has also experimented with social media surveillance of young suspected gang members to identify areas where the gangs were active and learn about incidents of violence.[18] The idea was that "virtual" gang activity on social media (threats, planning for fights) might yield information police could use to stop real gang activity in the streets.

These social media surveillance practices are growing in scale—in large part because they make it easy to investigate crime.[19] Terrance Everett was arrested because he posted to Facebook a photo of a gun on his bedside table.[20] Everett had a felony conviction and was not allowed to own a gun. Unfortunately for him, a local detective had been keeping tabs on him, checking Everett's Facebook account up to three times a week for two years. The day after the photo was posted, police arrested Everett for gun possession[21] and he ended up being sentenced to fifteen years in prison. Such investigations can also occur at scale. In his book *Sedition Hunters*, journalist Ryan Reilly details the ease with which the FBI was able to track down thousands of the rioters who entered the U.S. Capitol on January 6, 2021.[22] Investigators were able to just sit at their desks and scroll through publicly available images or those sent to them by online tipsters.

Next-generation object recognition technology will let police automatically find clues from our photographs and videos. Law enforcement investigators can already search social media for gang symbols or graffiti tags, for example, or track down a suspect who was spotted wearing a red hat with a specific logo.[23] And while most humans focus on the foreground of a photograph, there are also clues in the background that can be identified via AI and machine learning. Computer vision technology can now separate out background objects, identifying them, coding them, geolocating them, and searching for them across all the stored images in a dataset—(such as all the photographs on Facebook).[24] Object recognition systems can detect guns, drugs, or other evidence of criminal activity in the background.[25] In child sexual abuse material (CSAM) investigations, pattern recognition technology can analyze features of a hotel room (beds, drapes, lighting, layout) to identify the specific location where the abuse occurred.[26] Similar technology may be used to analyze photographs or videos for background content that matches known trafficking images, helping investigators connect otherwise disparate pieces of evidence.[27] Few people would argue against the benefits of a technology that can rescue victims of human trafficking, but there's nothing stopping police and school administrators from targeting other images (say, peace symbols, or Palestinian flags.)

If, while searching social media, police stumble across a clue or evidence of a crime, they can save the image and deliver it to prosecutors. In fact, under certain circumstances, police can get a "communications data warrant" to watch a social media user into the future.[28] Facebook, for example, was under a court order to provide content about an alleged drug dealer's social media use every fifteen minutes for an entire month, including his interactions with public posts, reactions, comments, and private messages.[29] With this form of proactive surveillance, police can watch what suspects are doing in almost real time, just waiting for them to incriminate themselves.

As mentioned with "Bob Smith," sometimes police take a more direct approach to social media sleuthing—they go undercover.[30] In New York State, for example, the intelligence apparatus set up after 9/11 has been designed to allow for direct monitoring of social media accounts.[31] New York's social media investigation program gives police authority to create "alias online identities" with fake names and photos in order to infiltrate online groups and connect with individuals suspected of committing a crime.[32] These efforts to spy on social media via dummy accounts are not even hidden. In 2022, Governor Kathy Hochul proudly proclaimed, "We're watching you now," as she unveiled a rule giving police enhanced abilities to target potential violent actors via social media.[33] In Minneapolis, Minnesota, the same report that called out the racist policing practices that led to the murder of George Floyd also exposed illegal social media surveillance targeting racial justice activists,[34] revealing how social media monitoring can be weaponized not just against innocent individuals, but against entire communities.[35] Just think how easy it would be to wipe out dissenting voices or to suppress disfavored political speech using social media, especially if the platforms cooperated with the government.

Selling Social Media Surveillance

The explosion of police interest in social media monitoring has created opportunities for tech companies, which are racing to create analytical tools that can sort through billions of posts, comments, shares, and likes to identify active threats.[36] One form of monitoring, called "sentiment analysis," allows police to track how people online feel about a particular subject or event—say, a police shooting—by analyzing the language (and even the emojis) used in social media posts, blogs, and message board postings.[37] One such service, Babel X, which uses keyword searches to gain "situational awareness" about breaking events and emergencies, has been tested by police departments in Los Angeles and Seattle,[38] as well as the Department of Homeland Security and the FBI [39] which in 2022 purchased 5,000 licenses for the software.[40]

Other companies like Dataminer, Skopenow, and Cobwebs scrape social media on behalf of various police departments.[41] During 2020's racial justice protests, Dataminer was given access to Twitter's data "firehose" in order to conduct real-time threat assessments.[42] The LAPD, meanwhile, piloted the social media analytics tool ABTShield, created by EDGE NPD,[43] which also watched Twitter for anti-police comments and mentions of protests. MediaSonar sold social media monitoring technology to the Fresno, California police department that could track hashtags like #BlackLivesMatter and #PoliceBrutality.[44] The goal of these services is to identify social media "threats" as they happen so that police can respond quickly, which requires constant monitoring of all public social media threads.

Schools and universities also engage in threat monitoring, and for understandable reasons.[45] Over the past few decades, hundreds of children have been killed in school shootings and other acts of violence perpetrated by outsiders or by their peers. School administrators and parents desperately want students to be safe, and many have turned to social media surveillance in hope of preventing more tragedies.[46] More than one hundred schools have bought into predictive surveillance programs that promise to identify the "red flags" of violence before it is too late.[47] Of course, the idea that these programs can offer complete protection is a fantasy,[48] yet after every shooting, the calls to "do something" about the violence inspire schools to buy technology that sells the promise of security.[49]

Take, for example, the company Navigate360 (formerly known as Social Sentinel), that sells social media threat surveillance services to schools.[50] It scans social media via keyword searches and other tools in the hopes of identifying possible threats. These threats might be directed at a school or specific students, or they may be threats of self-harm or evidence of bullying, but in every case, the goal is to predict and prevent violence. Of course, to identify such threats, the software must monitor everyone, which means that every student at a university or high school becomes a target. In addition to being overinclusive (and a bit creepy), these programs often get things wrong.[51] In one case, the keyword "shoot" also alerted to a basketball team's shooting clinic, promotional events around the Mark Wahlberg movie *Shooter*, and someone pleased that their credit score was shooting up.[52]

Perhaps more problematic is that monitoring affects freedom of expression. University police have used surveillance services to monitor protests against university administrators and policies.[53] At the University of North Carolina-Chapel Hill, for example, administrators used predictive surveillance to track the movements of students who sought the removal of a Confederate monument on campus.[54] Stifling protected First Amendment activity though digital surveillance seems like an odd lesson to teach, but it has been embraced by some college administrators.

The Law of Likes

Consumers of social media have few legal protections when it comes to their use of platforms. Under current rules, any public posting on a social media site can be observed by law enforcement without any legal justification.[55] By design, public-facing posts can be seen by anyone, including the police. Depending on the service or platform, privacy-restricted communications might require a warrant or other legal process to obtain. But much of social media remains unprotected, and many of the protections that do exist are the result of corporate policy, not law.

The legal conundrum for privacy in a social media saturated world is that consumers are knowingly sharing revealing private information in quasi-public settings, and yet they do not necessarily expect that information to go directly into the hands of government monitors (especially ones looking to use that information for political advantage). Existing constitutional law does not offer an obvious basis for protecting this speech. The Fourth Amendment tends to focus on private possessions, private information, and private communications, not public communications on commercial, third-party platforms. The First Amendment tends to focus on the ability to speak freely; it remains silent about government monitoring that free speech. Taken together, these constitutional rights suggest a foundational concern with protecting speech from government intrusion and suppression, but it's unclear how they should apply in the social media age.

Consider a few different ways a person recently diagnosed with cancer might share that personal information online: (1) emailing the news to several close friends; (2) posting the news on a private social media platform, such as a closed Facebook group; and (3) posting the news publicly on social media (X /Twitter, Instagram).

Under statutory law (the Stored Communications Act and the ECPA) and the Fourth Amendment, only the first of these communication would be clearly protected.[56] Although there are no Supreme Court cases on the subject, most courts agree that the police shouldn't have unfettered access to the content of our emails.[57] This is the case even though email runs through a third-party provider (such as Google or Microsoft) that has the technical ability to scan all emails, and does so in order to detect things like child sexual abuse material.

In theory, the same logic would apply to information posted to closed social media groups. In practice, however, while social media companies have tried to require warrants or other legal processes restricting access to closed groups, it is not clear what the law actually requires. Expectations of privacy have not been firmly set in the world of shared digital communications. Finally, there are no limits on police use of information gleaned from public-facing social media posts. If, instead of "I have cancer," a post read "I have cocaine," the inculpatory information could be used against the person who posted it. This makes some sense; if you stood on the street corner offering cocaine to passersby, that, too, could be used against you.

Three caveats are in order. First, whether an email remains private depends on both the sender and the recipients. If you email something to a friend who then turns it over to police or forwards it to others, you would not be able to claim that they had violated your legal right to privacy (even if their actions clearly did betray your trust). The same rules apply to information shared orally, in conversation. The Supreme Court has termed this the "false friend" problem. Your privacy is reliant on the secrecy of those you speak to, and if a false friend happens to betray you, the Court has considered you out of luck (or, more precisely, out of Fourth Amendment protection).[58]

Sometimes, false friends are undercover cops.[59] Averyk Carrasquillo used Snapchat to connect with a small circle of friends. One day, a police officer named Joseph Connolly sent a friend request to Carrasquillo under a false name, and Carrasquillo accepted it. Although Carrasquillo's profile was set to "private," once Connolly became his friend, he could see all his postings—including photos of Carrasquillo posing with an illegal handgun at a local gym. Police went to the gym, arrested Carrasquillo, recovered the gun, and used his Snap postings as evidence against him.[60] When Carrasquillo challenged the use of the Snap, a Massachusetts court rejected the argument, asserting that he had no expectation of privacy from his "friends." Worse, just as you can't control what your friends do with the posts you share with them, you also can't control what they post themselves. In other words, your privacy is dependent on the judgment of your least responsible friend. If that friend posts an embarrassing photo of you at a party, your face, location, and activities are now available for law enforcement to see. If police want to prosecute you, they can rely on other people's images to help them.

The second caveat is that any protection that does exist applies only to the "content" of a message. The fact that you posted on social media, the time and date the post was made, and the people to whom it was sent—is all non-content "metadata" that is fair game without a warrant.[61] This distinction between content and metadata (that is, content about content) is rooted in the ECPA but also finds support in Fourth Amendment cases. Essentially, the substance of our communications is protected at a higher level than the fact that we communicated at all. And that metadata can be quite revealing. If you learn that someone called a suicide hotline at 2:00 a.m. and stayed on the line for an hour, you don't need to know exactly what they said to deduce that they're probably struggling with their mental health.

The final caveat is that, as we've seen, all our digital papers—including emails and private social media content—are available with a judicial warrant. This is true for much of the data I've considered in this book, but it's especially critical to understand in the context of social media. In the past, the everyday stuff of our lives—that inside joke with your friends, the haircut you had during your emo phase—was shared in person. Any evidence—a note passed in class, or an awkward photo—would be ephemeral and hard to locate. Most of our experiences weren't recorded or recoverable. Today, all that information is digitally stored and available to police. With a warrant, your entire social media footprint—every like, connection, click, link, and post—is open for inspection. Imagine how much of your life could be pasted together from the mosaic of your social media feeds, how many of your thoughts, moods, frustrations, challenges, and joys that information would reveal. While this picture would likely be distorted (life is not always Instagrammable), it would still offer remarkable insight into who you are, what you've done, and what you care about.

And once you've shared something, it can be hard to take it back. Currently, Google keeps data two months after a user deletes it and up to six months if the user stored it in a backup. Facebook keeps data six months after it is deleted. If you close your account, the data will be deleted after ninety days.[62] Some social media companies are less clear about their data-retention policies. TikTok, for example, retains your data for an undetermined amount of time, even after you delete it.[63] Data created is data that can be collected—and it will be, if law enforcement has an interest in it.

Swiping Likes

Social media platforms are fueled by "likes."[64] When you upvote or downvote a comment on Reddit, share someone else's story on Instagram, or express your appreciation for a photo with a thumbs-up or a heart, you're sending signals about what you like and dislike. Just look at the interface of your favorite social media site. You reveal what you care about, and the company uses that information to serve you targeted advertisements that can pinpoint your specific interests and activities with a striking degree of precision. You posted pictures of your outdoor adventures on Instagram, and now an advertiser has the perfect waterproof, vegan hiking boot to sell you, right at your price point.[65]

Even when we don't choose to share our likes, technology tends to expose them anyway. Almost everything on the Internet and in the larger mobile digital world is tracked. Embedded electronic "cookies" trail you from website to website and from click to click.[66] Search for "trip to Las Vegas" and advertisers know you are interested in a vacation escape. Search for "help with online poker addiction" and advertisers know you might have a gambling problem. The data is sold and then resold and repackaged through commercial data brokers who find ways to monetize it.

Data brokers, as the name suggests, buy and sell pieces of your data. You could consider them digital trash collectors, except they are making billions off the scraps you leave behind online.[67] Big data brokers like Acxiom, Experian, Epsilon, LexisNexis, CoreLogic, and LiveRamp are in a race to accumulate a digital profile of you and then sell that profile to marketers who want to know you a bit better.[68] As researcher Justin Sherman has revealed, these companies can confidently brag that they have billions of data points on millions of people. For years, data brokers have scraped public records from courts and other sources, bought data directly from digital services, and made inferences based on zip code, age, race, and gender.[69] For example, if you used GoodRx, which helps users find discounts on prescription drugs, to search for antidepressants or other psychiatric medications, your data was repackaged by a broker and sold to third parties like Facebook and Google.[70] The idea was that this private information could be useful to advertisers trying to sell mental health aids, treatments, or services.

The Federal Trade Commission stepped in and barred GoodRx from selling personal health data[71] and the company had to pay a $1.5 million civil penalty for the violation.[72] But the problem is not just GoodRx. As researcher Joanne Kim has revealed, as people pivoted to online mental health services during the COVID-19 pandemic, many of those services sold information about their users to third-party data brokers.[73] The information these brokers provided included demographic information, zip code data, and in some cases even the names of individuals seeking mental health care. One might imagine positive uses for this data. If a certain zip code is home to an unusually large number of people with depression, for example, public health agencies might work on improving access to care in those neighborhoods. Or someone with anxiety might be genuinely happy to receive a targeted ad for a meditation app. But in the wrong hands, this data could be used to harm vulnerable people. An insurance company might want to charge higher rates to customers in the zip code associated with depression. And police, of course, may want to subject certain populations to surveillance. One could imagine a system that automatically flags anyone who has shown interest in both depression medication and gun purchases, for example.

While users of mental health apps might expect some degree of privacy, users of dating apps know that they're putting personal information out in public—that's how the apps work.[74] Someone seeking a partner uploads personal details that reveal them to be a likable person or a potential life partner, and then waits for others to do the same so that an algorithm can match them.[75] As might be obvious, the more granular the personal data you provide, the more accurate a match you will find. Depending on the app, you might upload your name, gender identity, sexual orientation, age, height, weight, employer, financial information, religious identity, political beliefs, and alcohol and drug habits, in addition to your hobbies and tastes (sexual and otherwise).[76] Because the apps match people in close physical proximity, many also use geolocation.[77] Some apps are designed for particular groups; there are dating apps for Catholics, Republicans, goths, and the gluten-free. There are also numerous dating apps for members of the LGBTQ+ community or some subset of that group. The danger is that should police want to target members of a particular group, all they need to do is look on the apps. (Indeed, in Egypt, where homosexuality is highly stigmatized, police are already using gay dating apps for this purpose.)[78] Worse, many of these dating sites sell information to third-party data brokers who repackage and sell the data to anyone (including law enforcement.).[79] Grindr, popular among gay men, has been accused of selling data that disclosed users' HIV status, for example.[80]

In 2023, online journalism organization *The Markup* analyzed how one data-driven ad platform, Xandr, tracked people online in order to sort them by their likes, interests, and habits, creating profiles that could be sold to advertisers who wished to target users with certain characteristics.[81] *The Markup* found that the company had 650,000 different audience segments in its dataset. It could identify people prone to depression, those who "get a raw deal out of life," and those who are heavy purchasers of pregnancy tests. Some of the segments had humorous (and occasionally offensive) titles. If you were an advertiser, you could choose your segment. Maybe you wanted to sell to wealthy people in the "Birkenstocks and Beemers" or "Silver Sophisticates" segments. Or if your product targeted consumers on a budget, you might choose from groups entitled "Small Town Shallow Pockets" or seniors "Retiring on Empty." Some segments were strikingly particular ("Dunkin' Donuts Visitors") and others puzzlingly vague ("Receptive to emotional messaging").

The categories might be odd, but they come from our own likes and purchases. You are in the data broker dossier because you went to Dunkin' Donuts, and now someone is trying to sell you Dunkin'-branded Keurig cups. Your coffee habit might not be as revealing as your neighbor's pregnancy test purchases, but both profiles are granular and accurate.[82] One could imagine that if the data brokers' focus was not on selling products but on surveilling groups, the same type of segmentation could identify suspected domestic extremists, people struggling with substance abuse, or those prone to reckless acts. It could also identify families with trans or queer children, or people who have had abortions.[83] This data reveals who we are, and in a world that wants to expose some of us for our acts or identities, that can be a big problem.

Other companies have gone even further, attempting to synthetize all the information available about us online, including our social media activity and browsing history, in one large-scale surveillance system sold to police. In 2021, *The Intercept* revealed that Michigan State Police had secretly contracted with the security company Kaseware to deploy a tool called ShadowDragon, which purports to search through hundreds of online platforms to develop profiles on suspects police are investigating.[84] ShadowDragon's founder, Daniel Clemens, described the product's aims: "I want to know everything about the suspect: Where do they get their coffee, where do they get their gas, where's their electric bill, who's their mom, who's their dad?" Helpfully, all the information ShadowDragon gleans from across the web can be organized geographically to find significant places, or into a timeline to find patterns of behavior, or in a network to find connections. The software has also been purchased by the Massachusetts State Police and the U.S. Immigration and Customs Enforcement Agency.[85]

Finally, in an odd combination of corporate undercover surveillance and police purchasing power, some companies like Voyager Labs have created fake social media accounts to scrape platforms like Facebook and then sell that data to police. In fact, Meta, the corporate owner of Facebook, is suing Voyager for creating tens of thousands of fake profiles for that purpose. Meta's complaint states that Voyager "created and used over 38,000 fake Facebook user accounts and its Surveillance Software to scrape more than 600,000 Facebook users' viewable profile information, including posts, likes, friends lists, photos, and comments, and information from Facebook Groups and Pages."[86] Both fake accounts and data scraping are against Facebook's terms of service. As the Brennan Center reported, the users whose data was captured by Voyager "included employees of nonprofits, news organizations, and government agencies, along with parents, retirees, and union members."[87]

Notably, Voyager markets itself to law enforcement as providing "traceless" data collection.[88] In other words, the company does the dirty work of collecting and sorting social media data, and all the police have to do is pay for it. More traditional commercial data brokers also sell directly to police, allowing investigators to circumvent warrant requirements. Once your data is commodified, anyone can buy it.

Sometimes law enforcement even bypasses a company's own process for data disclosure and just pays a confidential source inside the company for information.[89] An Inspector General's Report showed that the Drug Enforcement Administration (DEA) paid over a half a million dollars to an airline employee and a parcel employee for tips about travel and delivery patterns.[90] Amtrak employees, bus employees, and Transportation Security Administration (TSA) employees also became DEA informants, tipping off the government about passengers' travel plans—departure times, seat assignments, and other details—outside the warrant context.[91] Some members of Congress have tried to expose and ban these practices. The Fourth Amendment is Not for Sale Act would prohibit police from exchanging anything of value (like money) to obtain user data and place limits on the use of information illegitimately obtained by third parties, but as of 2025, the bill has stalled in the Senate.[92]

Tools like ShadowDragon are powerful in large part due to their ability to connect the moves you make online with the moves you make in real life. Remember how much Google knows about your location? They're far from the only company tracking you.[93] Let's say you download an app for your favorite coffee shop. The app knows that you usually order a skim milk latte, but it also tracks your location so it can time your morning pickup and keep the coffee hot. All that information is associated with your phone's advertiser identification number (AIN), which is unique to your device. The problem is that information associated with your advertiser number is sold to data brokers, who sell it to third parties, including law enforcement.

Next-generation data brokers have gone so far as to repackage and sell advertising data—including geolocation—directly to police.[94] The Fog Data Science Reveal portal (Fog Reveal) allows police to search records from 250 million mobile devices, likely by using the same sort of advertising IDs that can track individual phones through commercial transactions and sites with weaker data protection policies.[95] The idea is simple: Patterns of individual consumer behavior are revealing.[96] While advertising IDs are not connected to a person's name (unlike location data from Google or a cell phone company), they can be used to track a device for months at a time.[97] With enough location data, police can infer the identity of the person carrying that device.[98]

Fog Reveal allows police officers direct access to a portal where they can search the time and coordinates of a crime to find devices in the area, then track those devices backward and forward in time—for months.[99] If they believe a suspect is connected to multiple crimes, they can search those locations to identify any devices that popped up at more than one. Detectives in Chino, California, used this tool to capture thieves who robbed a bicycle store. Surveillance camera footage captured two men walking into Incycle Bicycles and walking out with a $10,000 bike.[100] On their way out, the thieves tried to run over an employee who was attempting to stop them.[101] In spite of the camera footage, police had no leads, but they did know that three other local sporting goods stores had been robbed in recent weeks. Detectives ran a query through Fog Reveal to see if any mobile devices happened to be at the location of all four thefts. Three different AINs showed up at each of the four locations. Tracing those AINs back in time led police to three people, who were eventually convicted of the crimes (and who also happened to be roommates). The AINs revealed their presence at the crime scenes and followed them back to where they lived.[102]

To be clear, officers could have gotten this same information—plus the names of the suspects—from Google by making a geofence request and following the company's three-step warrant process. But Fog Reveal doesn't require a warrant. In fact, one detective admitted that Fog Reveal shortens their investigative time from six weeks to two days, because police can just search the data and connect it to a suspect themselves, rather than waiting for Google to do it. And while in Google's business model, location data is a byproduct of advertising, selling unstructured geospatial data gathered from your purchases and preferences to law enforcement is what Fog Reveal was designed to do. Of course, that means that everyone is now at risk to be tracked for really any reason because some tech genius invented a system to do so.

The Lawlessness of Data Brokers

Federal law prevents data brokers from selling to the Chinese government and other entities deemed hostile to U.S. interests, but within the United States, there are few legal restrictions on what brokers can do with the data they collect.

This is not to say that regulators have ignored the issue. In 2014, the Federal Trade Commission released a scathing white paper highlighting the abuses in the commercial data collection industry, which, the agency pointed out, involved millions of data points on every single American.[103] In addition to bringing suit against femtech companies that sold data on users' reproductive health,[104] the FTC has begun enforcing existing rules on deceptive advertising against data brokers that, it argues, failed to get users' consent before reselling their data. The data aggregator InMarket Media, for example, was prohibited from selling location data about its audience segments, which like other data brokers had colorful and illustrative names like "Wealthy and not healthy."[105] The FTC also brought a case against X-Mode Social for allegedly selling location data that tracked people to reproductive health clinics, domestic abuse shelters, and places of worship, among other sensitive locations.[106]

The FTC's regulatory response shows a growing concern with the privacy issues inherent in data broker sales. A few states have also moved to fill in the regulatory gap, creating registries for data brokers that operate in those states. Montana, Vermont, and California have taken the lead, passing laws that put some limited restrictions on how brokers can operate.[107] Other states like Colorado have moved to protect personal data that can identify people via geolocation.[108] The state's rules require brokers to operate more transparently, which is a good thing, but the laws do not change the reality that your likes are still a commodity to be bought, sold, and repurposed.

Many brilliant advocates and scholars have detailed the harms of commodifying our digital likes. Julia Angwin's seminal *Dragnet Nation* and Shoshana Zuboff's comprehensive *The Age of Surveillance Capitalism* brought the surveillance economy into public view and exposed its frightening scale.[109] But while nearly everyone in the United States is swept up in the surveillance economy, its effects are experienced differently depending on who you are. Bias in the digital systems unfairly penalizes those without economic or political capital, reflecting many of the same inequalities that exist in the nondigital world. As scholars like Ruha Benjamin, Meredith Broussard, Safiya Umoja Noble, Virginia Eubanks, and Frank Pasquale have shown, racial and gender biases are baked into the systems.[110] After all, data broker and digital advertising firms actually built their business model on discriminating between different groups based on money, gender, age, race, and interests. It should not be surprising that these systems also discriminate in the more ordinary meaning of the word.

This discriminating (and discriminatory) data feeds into a system of policing that both reflects and perpetuates existing structural inequalities of race and class. In 2018, Richard Dilworth sued the Boston Police Department for targeting Black people on Snapchat. Dilworth had been arrested on gun charges after posting pictures of his guns on the app—which, yes, was both dumb and criminal. But he quickly realized he was not alone in having his social media on the police's radar. According to the pleadings, the people Boston police followed through the app were disproportionately young Black men.[111] Essentially, Boston police figured they could find suspects more efficiently by watching only a subset of the population. It was like real-world racial profiling, only easier.

Population segmentation data allows this kind of profiling to happen on a large scale. In 2020, reporting by *Vice* revealed that the U.S. military had purchased location data from users of popular Muslim prayer and dating apps. The apps gathered location data for seemingly legitimate reasons—to help users find the direction of Mecca, or to meet single Muslims in their area—but they also sold it to the data broker X-Mode, whose customers found a different use for that information.[112] These customers included contractors associated with the U.S. military.[113] The subjects of military surveillance in this case were mostly not in the United States (and therefore not protected by the Constitution), but there's nothing to prevent domestic police from purchasing similar data. If, hypothetically, domestic police sought to surveil Muslim communities in the United States, as they did after the terrorist attacks of 9/11, brokers like X-Mode would provide ready-made surveillance targets. The "discrimination" is built into the service being sold.

Even people who are not members of marginalized groups have reason to be wary of targeted surveillance. For years, Second Amendment advocates have fought against establishing a nationwide gun registry, fearing that such a list would enable "the government" to come and take their guns someday. But the truth is putting together a list of gun owners doesn't require any action by the federal government. There is geolocational data from gun ranges and gun shows and consumer data from ammunition and gear purchases. If you bought a gun lock box on Amazon, odds are there is a gun in your home. Even identity clues like hunting catalogs, t-shirts with pro-gun slogans, and of course membership in the National Rifle Association might place you in the "gun owner" data segment. If police wanted to target gun owners for surveillance or harassment, it would be easy for them to do. The data exists, and it's for sale.[114]

Liking Self-Surveillance

Social media offers a distorted vision of ordinary life. The personas we create there are exaggerated or partial. Professionals might curate a version of themselves by only listing successes and celebrating their achievements while hiding their failures. Influencers might hawk a product they'd never buy themselves. Young men might rap about the drug trade for attention and virtual fame without having ever sold drugs themselves. But for police and prosecutors watching the posturing, it can be hard to tell the difference. Targeting individuals for suspicion based on their social media posts risks misunderstanding the context of that activity.

And yet many times we do reveal our true selves on social media. It is much easier to threaten a rival crew online than in person. Both might result in real physical violence, but one involves less immediate risk. If a fight does eventually break out, though, your social media post will make it much easier for police to prove that you were involved. And if your post videoing the assault directly implicates you in a crime, that fact outweighs any context. If you're prohibited from owning a weapon due to your felony conviction, and you show off your gun collection on Instagram, you've pretty much done the police's work for them. It doesn't matter whether you were displaying your guns as a threat, as a joke, or as a prop for educating your followers about firearm safety.

It's a similar story with the data we share unintentionally via cookies and other advertising trackers. In the aggregate, our purchases offer real insight into our interests and activities—which can be very useful to someone who wants to investigate those interests and activities. We have trapped ourselves in these digital habits. There is no obvious reason to "like" a stranger's social media post, yet we do. There is no obvious reason to post Instagram photos of every bread loaf we bake, but we do. The companies monetizing these preferences are just repackaging information we gave them. And if we are willing to share our preferences with Target, why should they stay hidden from police? The simple truth is that we reveal ourselves because we like revealing ourselves. We like our likes and want to share them. The real problem is that the law does not allow us to choose how we expose our virtual selves, and to whom, leaving platforms and data brokers to capitalize on that exposure. At least for now, there are no secrets on social media—except maybe how much access police have to your data.

PART II

Consequences When Everything Is Evidence

7

Power Problems

At its core, policing is about power and social control.[1] Police enforce the laws written by those with political and economic power and have long punished those who deviate from social and legal norms. Legislators are responsible for passing laws that make it a crime to sleep outdoors even if you can't afford a home (and for maintaining an economic system in which some people can't afford homes.) But it is police who arrest the unhoused people sleeping in the park.[2]

Technology influences the amount of power that police have, how they use it, and whom they use it against. The digital surveillance methods discussed in the preceding chapters are not just enhanced or more efficient versions of traditional investigative techniques. They are categorically different, altering the very nature of what police can do. Their use represents a significant shift in the balance of power between citizen and state.

With more data available, police have more discretion to target individuals and groups for surveillance. Sometimes that targeting naturally arises from reported crimes, like when police search video feeds for a blue Jeep after one is reported stolen. But political, racial, and other societal pressures also shape these choices. Unfortunately, increased police power intersects with structural inequalities in the United States. The use of surveillance technology reflects and exacerbates existing power imbalances between the rich and the poor, white people and people of color, people with mainstream political views and those whose views are disfavored. To truly understand the power dynamics at play in our transition to digital policing, we must understand how these technologies reshape and reify existing inequality.

It is not just the police who gain power from the use of digital surveillance. The technologies discussed in this book all have one thing in common: They are created and operated by private companies. Inherent in police reliance on private technology is a dependence on technology companies and technologists. Highly sophisticated data-driven systems need highly educated and skilled data engineers and analysts to run them, which means that even as the use of these systems shifts power away from citizens and toward police, it also shifts power away from police and toward the corporations that control the data. How these systems are designed—by whom and for whom—will determine their priorities and therefore their outcomes. Whoever wins the race to become the "platform for policing" will gain an inordinate amount of power over society and over police departments themselves.

How Digital Policing Enhances Police Power

Traditional legal analysis sees little difference between human police officers patrolling public streets and 30,000 video camera feeds linked in a Real-Time Crime Center virtually watching those same streets, or between a citywide ALPR system and a police officer jotting down license plate numbers in a notebook. The thinking is that while the technology may increase the capacity, scale, and speed of such operations, it's still fundamentally the same kind of work that police have been doing for years.

This argument significantly undersells the power—and the danger—of digital policing. Today's technologies don't just collect data more efficiently than human police officers, they collect it differently. And this is true whether they are police-deployed technologies intended for evidence gathering (like video analytics systems and ALPRs) or consumer technologies that allow police access to their third-party data (like Ring doorbells and smartphone location trackers).[3] As will be discussed, digital policing turns surveillance into a superpower that should concern us all.

First, digital policing is largely *automated*. When searches are conducted by humans, you can analytically isolate the human act that precipitated the search (agents entering a home or snapping a photograph) and contest the legality of that act (Did the agents have grounds to enter the home? Was that photograph taken somewhere you had a reasonable expectation of privacy?). With digital collection methods, once the system turns on, it captures everything it is supposed to capture, and it doesn't have to knock on your door first. With the rise of artificial intelligence powered analytics systems, this data is not only collected and stored but also constantly sifted through as the system maps streets, energy grids, and social networks, transforming what used to be a singular action into millions of continuous searches.

Second, advanced data processing has enabled an *acceleration* of surveillance, allowing more information to be seen and analyzed more quickly and distorting the natural limits of time. With BriefCam's video systems, police can use video analytics to condense time periods, superimpose events, and travel back in time almost instantly.[4] The same is true of tools that allow police to sort through billions of messages on social media or weeks of geolocational clues. When police can be alerted instantly if a suspect shows up on a camera augmented by facial recognition or can gather a list of all the blue cars that have driven through a particular intersection in the past month, it doesn't just save police time; it changes what they can do.

Third, digital surveillance allows more data to be *accumulated*. The Internet of Things, citywide smart sensor systems, and digital devices produce a staggering amount of data, which is collected constantly. These always-on systems feed into virtually unlimited data storage systems, creating infinitely bigger, deeper, broader, and richer datasets. And because these systems are digital and automated, they aren't limited by the capacity of human personnel or the size of the evidence cabinet. If police can get access to a piece of data, there's no reason for them not to keep it.

Fourth, these rich datasets can be *aggregated*. Digital information can be coded and combined with information from other datasets, allowing artificial intelligence to discover patterns and connections across many different data streams. Consider how Real-Time Crime Centers not only allow police to watch the streets via surveillance cameras but also pull in information from other datasets and dossiers to swiftly identify individuals accused of crimes or vehicles that have been reported stolen—connections that would never have been made had all that information remained in siloed analog systems. In other words, digital surveillance is more than the sum of its parts. The aggregation of personal information from our smart homes, things, bodies, likes, and papers allows for patterns to emerge, exposing our private habits in new ways.

Fifth, digital policing can be more *accurate*. Certain kinds of pattern matching, such as facial recognition, can be done at scale while producing fewer errors than human analysts. Humans simply cannot scan through millions of photos or fingerprints and match them correctly without digital assistance. That said, digital technologies do not guarantee perfect accuracy; and in many cases, they can exacerbate error because people tend to blindly trust them. It is likely true that digital systems both provide better accuracy than humans and still get things wrong enough times for us to be concerned.

Finally, the data can be *actualized*—that is, the information can be coded, sorted, and made usable. In earlier eras, police may have collected a great deal of information via analog methods, but it would be stored in notepads, filing cabinets, or siloed computer systems. Lengthy audio or video recordings took even longer to review; doing so was expensive and time-consuming and rarely worth the effort. The usefulness of digital surveillance systems is that the information they gather can be broken down into sortable and searchable categories (such as type, object, or source) and stored in a database management system, allowing police to organize the data in new ways.

These six attributes—(1) automation, (2) acceleration, (3) accumulation, (4) aggregation (5) accuracy, and (6) actualization—distinguish today's digital surveillance methods from older forms of policework.[5] And different methods lead to different results.[6] Accumulated and aggregated datasets provide police with more insights. Accelerated and accurate searches provide better insights. Actualizable datasets provide more usable insights. Combined, these factors give police more control over the subjects of their surveillance. As we've seen, information about what we do and who we do it with, what we buy and from whom, who we love and who loves us can all be collected, sorted, and analyzed. The result is surveillance that doesn't just target individuals but expands to target everyone they associate with—friends, family, colleagues, neighbors, religious communities, civic groups. Innocent people and groups inevitably get caught in the net, and that is by design.

The final reason digital policing is different involves how quickly these systems can *scale*. The architecture of digital surveillance means that additional surveillance capabilities are just an upgrade away. The tens of thousands of cameras virtually patrolling Chicago would only need a software update to turn on facial recognition tracking technology. The hundreds of smart streetlight sensors in San Diego can add video or audio capabilities with ease. Companies like Fusus specialize in the kind of integrated interoperability that enables technological tools to be added to a centralized command system.[7] This kind of scalability was impossible in an analog surveillance system.

Digital policing supercharges police power.[8] Police can see into homes and hear sounds across a city. They can search billions of images with a single computer query. They can track the comings and goings of everyone who walks down the sidewalk in a particular neighborhood or drives over a particular bridge. For better or worse, these are superpowers that have never existed before and they need to be taken seriously. In the hands of the wrong people, they can endanger basic rights and freedoms.

How Digital Policing Changes Police Targets

Crime happens. People steal stuff. People assault other people. Good people do bad things. Bad people do worse things. Surveillance captures it all and stores it in databases, where it becomes potential evidence. But it's up to police and prosecutors to decide whether to dig deeper. In a world where everything is evidence, police have greater discretion to determine who they will target. If you trust that police will use their enhanced ability to monitor and investigate people to address societal harms, that might seem like a good thing.[9] But if you fear that police or the government will use their power in unequal, unfair, or political ways, such discretion is more troubling.[10] If the digital surveillance net captures everyone, then anyone is at risk of running afoul of law enforcement.

At various points in U.S. history, police have unfairly targeted religious minorities, laborers, protesters, immigrants, Native Americans, artists, LGBTQ+ people, comedians, civil rights activists, communities of color, gun owners, healthcare workers, students, musicians, political opponents, and pretty much anyone who stands a bit outside of mainstream culture.[11] Individuals on both sides of the political aisle worry about police being weaponized to silence their views. And rightly so. Politicians routinely use criminal laws as weapons in the culture war, which means that anyone can find themselves on the wrong side of a moral panic. In 2021, if your child decided to pursue gender-affirming healthcare in Alabama, they could do so under a doctor's supervision. In 2022, Alabama made that care illegal.[12] Similar laws targeting trans youth have passed in dozens of other states. For these children and their families, these legal shifts open a real risk of police surveillance. In Texas, all it took was an order from the governor for the state's child protective services to begin investigating families who supported their children's gender transitions.[13] Trans kids' social media posts, geolocation data from the cars their parents use to drive them to out-of-state gender clinics, smartphone apps that track medication doses—all of these could be used by investigators to enforce laws and policies targeting young people and their families. The surveillance infrastructure was always there. The only thing that changed was who became the target.

Members of marginalized groups are most likely to become the targets of police surveillance. But it's important to remember that the dangers of self-surveillance target everyone. Imagine being one of the most powerful people in the United States—an elected member of Congress—and deciding to take on the interests that control political or economic power in this country. Perhaps the congressperson openly attacks the sitting president, or the FBI, or Big Tech. Maybe they join a picket line, or fund a protest, or promote a boycott. While no one should feel sorry for the privileged, their digital exposure is as real as anyone else's. Want to take on Amazon? Amazon knows every senator's most embarrassing purchase. Want to take on Google? Google knows their most embarrassing keyword searches. Want to take on law enforcement, when they can direct all their surveillance power against you and your family—via pole cameras, social media searches, geolocational tracking? Any slip-up—a ten dollar Venmo for protest supplies, a perceived incitement to violence captured on video—could cross the line from protected First Amendment speech to material support of criminal activity, and the evidence will be there. Fundraising and lobbying contacts could be exposed as well as embarrassing family secrets that are irrelevant to the politician's work. This is likely one reason why certain powers get a pass in Washington D.C. If the tech giants holding our digital data wanted to play hardball, the secrets of the powerful could easily be exposed. That possibility is more than enough to silence criticism.

Of course, it is far more likely that police power will be directed against the less powerful. That has been the history of policing in the United Staes, and that will be its future.[14] The next two subsections examine two axes of marginalization—race and poverty—to demonstrate how digital policing will intersect with existing inequalities and exacerbate power imbalances.

Surveillance, Data, and Race

Policing in the United States has always been tied up with race. From slavery and Jim Crow laws to neighborhood segregation, the "war on drugs," stop and frisk, "quality of life crimes," mass incarceration, and now, predictive policing, police have served to reinforce racial hierarchies. Police did not make the laws—these were and are the societal and legislative choices of a racially unequal country—but as their enforcers, police have been the face of the racial inequality made manifest in law.

Many scholars have ably exposed the extent to which our systems of criminal justice, policing, and punishment more generally have been shaped by explicitly racist logics.[15] Surveillance technologies are no exception.[16] From 18th century lantern laws, which required people of color to carry a light source after dark so that they could be identified, to the FBI's wiretaps of Civil Rights leaders in the 1960s to various tactics used in the war on drugs, technology has been directed to investigate and control Black and Brown communities.[17] This targeting continues in the present day with social media surveillance of Black Lives Matter advocates, the installation of AI cameras in communities of color, and systems of predictive analytics collecting the names and criminal histories of Black men. It is likely not a coincidence that the first tests of the Persistent Surveillance Systems plane were conducted over Black and Brown communities in Compton, California, and West Baltimore, Maryland, or that the first five people falsely arrested based on facial recognition were Black.[18]

A world where your data will be used against you can only increase the likelihood that a racially biased past will be prologue to a racially discriminatory future. The warning signs are everywhere. Social media can be used to target anyone, but social media detectives in Chicago first targeted young men and women of color.[19] Gunshot sensors can be placed in any neighborhood, but they are disproportionately placed in low-income communities of color.[20] Person-based predictive policing algorithms designed to identify individuals likely to commit crimes targeted Black and Brown men at disproportionate rates.[21]

It is no wonder, then, that the most powerful critiques of digital surveillance have arisen from Black and Brown communities. Across the country, investments in public surveillance in the name of security have been met with community resistance. Black-and Brown-led research and advocacy groups like the Algorithmic Justice League, MediaJustice, Color of Change, the Lucy Parsons Lab, and Stop LAPD Spying continue to shine a spotlight on the role of police surveillance in maintaining and exacerbating racial injustice. Combining a historically discriminatory power like policing with a historically exclusionary industry like technology results in more race-based discrimination against communities of color. In doing so, it weakens those communities, reifying structural inequalities in society.

Surveillance, Data, and Capital

Police protect property. Think about it: Police officers spend much of their time responding to property crimes like burglary and shoplifting and patrolling to prevent such crimes. In doing so, they are safeguarding the capital investments of businesses and those individuals with property to protect. And the people they are safeguarding those assets from are typically those with less property or money. I imagine if you polled most police cadets, "protecting the interests of capitalism" would not be among their motivations for joining the police force, yet that is arguably their primary role.[22]

In affluent neighborhoods where violent crime is rare, police tend to do very little. They respond to property crimes like burglaries and car thefts, but their primary role is deterrence. They patrol the area to dissuade those who might invade these privileged spaces (namely, suspected burglars and car thieves). Self-surveillance technology dovetails neatly with this form of policing. Ring cameras, ALPR, and drones are just virtual watchmen protecting private property from others.

In poorly resourced communities, police respond to the gaps created by economic inequality by policing poverty itself. In these communities, theft, robbery, untreated mental illness, and substance abuse—all correlated with poverty—are more common. Police are tasked with bringing order and they work to establish social control through stop and frisk tactics, traffic stops, and heavy foot patrols. Surveillance systems dial up the level of control, policing poverty so it cannot escape its boundaries. Investment in high-tech systems aims to control the effects of economic inequality (which might not be the best investment available). One might well argue that investing to address the underlying structural inequality would be a better long-term solution than merely monitoring that inequality in high definition.

In urban business districts, police respond to quality of life concerns that interfere with commerce. True, urban areas have more violent crime, and police also respond to such crimes no matter the economic status of the victim or perpetrator. But as a percentage of their time, most of an urban police officer's job involves responding to calls about petty theft, stolen cars, mental health crises, drug dealing, overdoses, or unhoused citizens. The role of the police is to reestablish social order so that people with money to spend can work, shop, and dine free from interference. It is not a coincidence that business districts are building camera networks and partnering with police for more monitoring. It is in business's economic interest to keep poverty and disorder to a minimum in order to maximize their profits.

For people with capital and property to protect, this arrangement works well, which is why affluent communities are generally appreciative of police services.[23] Rich people see police cameras in their neighborhoods as protecting them from people without money, not as a threat to their privacy. And generally, police do respond to those with economic or social privilege in more respectful ways. Meanwhile, rhetoric around "public safety" elides the focus on private wealth.

The connection between police and capital is not a new insight. As sociologist Alex Vitale has written, professional police forces arose out of a need to protect private industry as it grew in unregulated ways, including by busting unions and maintaining control in factory towns.[24] The ties between police and economic power are clear, direct, and historically rooted. And as sociologist Simone Browne has written, this economic control has been intertwined with racial domination from the beginning.[25] Law enforcement in the South grew out of police surveillance of Black communities to maintain economic and racial control. And while obviously, police play many different roles today, it is not surprising that their investments in technology are guided by business interests. For many businesses, surveillance means security, which means sales. This convergence of interests protects the capitalist status quo, increasing the power of those with money and decreasing the power of those without. In other words, the growth of surveillance increases inequality and police power at the same time.

How Digital Policing Changes Corporate Power

While the police may be eager to invest in new technologies, they aren't building them by themselves.[26] They rely on outside technical experts and data engineers to make everything work. And deference to technologists means reliance on private companies and their agents. Even as the collection of data gives police more power over the people, the reliance on the technology that collects that data gives private companies more power over the police.

One of the earliest, and best documented, examples of technologists driving policing is the Los Angeles Police Department's relationship with the company Palantir.[27] Palantir manages and integrates multiple different data streams for its customers. Its Gotham platform, used in Los Angeles until 2021, allowed police to use social network analysis to track groups of potential suspects and clusters of reported crimes over time.[28] In her book *Predict and Surveil*, which discusses the LAPD's partnership with Palantir, sociologist Sarah Brayne observed how dependent police were on the technologists running the data-driven systems.[29] Police would upload details about individuals, cars, buildings, and reported crimes, along with other information about the city, which would be available for investigative queries when needed.[30] To gather this data, police would seek out people they considered most likely to be involved in criminal enterprises and stop them in order to record what car they were driving, who they were dating, and whether they were working, among other things.[31] Police officers were turned into data collectors to run the larger data-driven system, while at the same time police became dependent on the reliability of the data collected.

Technology companies influence public safety in more subtle ways, too. Tech companies based in the United States have a legal obligation to comply with lawful requests for data. However, companies also have a business interest in protecting their customers' data from overbroad or invasive police requests.[32] Responding to law enforcement is also time-consuming and costs the companies money. In other words, companies do not want to be seen as complying with law enforcement requests too easily, but when they must comply, they want to do so efficiently. All these competing interests have created a corporation-directed dance between platforms and law enforcement. Google's three-step warrant process for geofence queries is a prime example. The company's lawyers asserted a privacy interest in their customers' data, requiring police to narrow their requests via a series of particularized warrants. Private corporate lawyers directed law enforcement agents, and together they were able to come to a sort of compromise. The dance limits police power, but not by much. Usually, police can obtain anything they want after enough negotiation with the company's lawyers.

Other companies have been less protective of personal data. Many big technology companies have formal processes to streamline law enforcement requests, with some going so far as to set up dedicated digital portals for police. These processes make receiving and fulfilling the data requests more efficient and therefore less costly, but of course they also make it easier for police to get information. Amazon, for example, originally offered the videos captured by Ring cameras to police via a central portal, and only after negative news stories about the practice did the company began requiring police to get homeowner consent or an appropriate search warrant.[33]

Relying on technology companies to mediate police access to our data once again shifts power to the companies. If companies wanted to avoid complying with such requests, they could do so by using end-to-end encryption or other technical means to avoid possessing the data in the first place. Engineering choices to localize data inside a car (Tesla) or phone (Apple), and not in the cloud, require police to get access to the actual device they wish to search. Encryption, VPNs, and differential privacy designs can also minimize government access to otherwise sensitive data. Of course, these approaches run squarely into the business interests of many companies, whose business models involve monetizing the data they collect, including by selling it to others.[34]

Platforms of Police Power

Law enforcement's deference to technical expertise is only the first step toward a broader reliance on private technological companies for the purposes of public safety. The real change—involving an almost complete capitulation to corporate control—will happen at the platform level.[35] Think about the big tech platforms in your life. Apple, Google, Meta, Amazon—each controls an entire ecosystem of information. If you have an iPhone, you probably also use Apple apps and services to save your notes and photos and check the weather, store your files in the iCloud, and link your account to other Apple devices. Candidly, I can never leave the Apple platform because it would mean losing all my family photos, which are helpfully stored on a cloud service I pay for every month. For Apple, the money is not just in the hardware (the physical phone) but in the backend data services they can sell once they have a customer like me trapped in the platform.

Tech companies are vying to become the Apple of policing: A centralized platform combining data collection, analysis, and storage that could enter into contracts with city governments, like Palantir did with Los Angeles. And like Apple, some companies are using hardware as a hook to get access to police data. The company Axon provides an interesting case study. Axon (previously known as Taser) sells police-worn body cameras, which thousands of local jurisdictions have mandated as a mechanism of police accountability. While it remains unproven whether body cameras have in fact made police more accountable, there is little question that that they have generated a whole lot of video footage. All that video footage must be stored, and all that digital storage costs money. In addition, all that video must be made usable in cases involving people and incidents captured in the footage.

Axon quickly realized that significant money could be made from this data storage and analysis, so it created a platform to handle it. The economics are such that Axon can almost give away the cameras, knowing the money is in the back end. It is a familiar business strategy: The same logic is behind razor blade companies selling their razors below cost, knowing they'll make up for it with all the replacement blades they'll sell to the customers they've locked in.[36]

Axon's platform includes Evidence.com, a digital evidence management system that organizes video from multiple sources (including body cameras, in-car cameras, CCTV, interrogation room cameras, neighborhood-uploaded video, and soon all the Fusus data), plus still photographs from the crime scene, all in one place.[37] The database is searchable, so investigators can find an incident, officer, or location quickly and pull up videos from related cases. All the evidence can be mapped and organized over time. In addition, video scenes can be turned into demonstrative exhibits through augmented reality, so prosecutors can explain their theory of the case to the jury using images similar to old-fashioned crime scene photos. The database also feeds information into Axon Records, which offers a records management system for police, including automated prompts to allow officers to fill out police reports more quickly.[38] Axon Respond allows real-time data and video feeds to be sent back to a central command center. Axon Dispatch enhances the traditional 911 dispatch service.[39]

Rounding out the company's services is Axon Performance, which collects information on officers' actions, including inappropriate behavior or excessive use of force. With Axon Performance, supervisors can analyze audio transcripts for offensive words, search for Taser use, and discover when a firearm was unholstered. Axon Standards imports that investigative data into internal affairs reports for possible investigations of police misconduct.[40] As a final touch, Axon Justice allows prosecutors and defense lawyers to share discovery materials, connecting police investigation to the larger court system. Together, the Axon products create a platform for criminal justice data that links everything through the backend storage system, replacing many existing (and siloed) digital management systems with one that is fully integrated, and therefore far more powerful.

In similar fashion, the company SoundThinking (formerly known as ShotSpotter) uses the hook of audio gunshot detecting sensors to leverage the sale of other platform-related products. SoundThinking's SafetySmart platform links its sensors with other products, including a patrol resource system (Resource Router) that studies crime patterns in a jurisdiction to determine when and where police should be deployed—a form of predictive policing.[41] Other data-driven services include CrimeTracer (formerly COPLINK X), a Google-like service that allows police to query a billion law enforcement documents to obtain information, use social network analysis to uncover links between cases, and find related crimes across jurisdictions.[42] Officers can enter a partial license plate or suspect description and pull up leads. A service called CaseBuilder offers a data management platform to track gun recoveries and gun crimes and makes the digital evidence available to prosecutors and the courts.[43]

Axon and SoundThinking are not alone. Large tech companies like Microsoft, Accenture, and Motorola and small start-ups like Mark43 and Voyager Labs are also vying to provide the platform that powers policing. Microsoft created the Domain Awareness System in partnership with the NYPD with the express goal of selling the digital services platform to other cities (with the NYPD getting a cut of future sales).[44] Mark43 recognized that police officers hate paperwork so it offers streamlined digital reports as part of a platform of digital records management.[45] An officer can take a photo of an arrestee's driver's license, and the system will automatically populate the digital record, with date, time, and location already filled out. And once Mark43 controls the paperwork, it can make inroads into other parts of the data-driven policing market.[46]

When power shifts to digital platforms, the platform companies gain power over the police in two main ways. First, police become reliant on the data skills of tech company employees. Police departments can and do train in-house experts on these platforms, but those police experts often get hired away by tech companies that can pay them higher salaries (leaving police departments perpetually dependent on the platforms). The second problem is the lock-in effect. Departments cannot easily leave the vendor that serves as their digital backbone. Police departments are always dealing with ongoing criminal litigation involving real victims and perpetrators, and they can't take the risk of data getting lost in a vendor transition. All of this highly incentivizes sticking with the vendor you already know, which is why companies are fighting so hard to become the main platform.

The Costs of Privatization

Privatization of public safety has several other troubling consequences. First, private control over police data undermines democratic accountability. Even though police are public servants, legislators have struggled to provide public oversight of police departments. Adding in a layer of corporate secrecy and private data makes it even more difficult. And while citizens can band together to vote out their government, there might not be a direct way to vote out the company servicing the government. It may not be possible for individuals to escape a platform that has been designed in ways that are unaccountable or unfair.

Second, the incentives between private interests and public interests are not aligned. Private companies are legally accountable to their global shareholders, not to local citizens. If it makes financial sense to skimp on privacy audits, there might be pressure to do so, even if those audits are for the public good. In addition, companies must respond to stock market pressure to grow, expand, and sell more products, which often means adding more interconnected services to the platform, deepening the lock-in effect. Cities might prefer to skip newer services, but their technological dependency gives them weakened bargaining power. And when one company has significant market power, it crowds out competitors that might provide a better value to citizens or safeguard their data more carefully.

Third, it is unclear who owns the data that these digital policing systems collect and what they can legally do with it. One might assume that public data would be maintained only for the public good, but it is not clear that all the legal contracts cities have signed with these companies make that explicit. Could video from citywide camera systems be used to train the company's AI? What happens to police data when a company goes bankrupt or is sold to another company?

Finally, there is what I call the "who watches the watchers problem." What happens if a company (or its executives) uses their control over the platforms to get away with criminal acts? If all police files are controlled by a single platform, it wouldn't be hard for the people running that platform to erase evidence of their own wrongdoing. It is not difficult to imagine companies, or their executives, being corrupted by that power or by others interested in controlling the priorities of the police. It's difficult enough to prevent police from covering up evidence of their own misconduct. Adding a private element only makes accountability more elusive.

The power shifts brought about by digital policing have serious consequences for public safety. But the ability of police to choose their targets in a world of unlimited evidence, and the ability of private companies to influence those decisions, isn't the only problem. As the next chapter will reveal, digital policing is also a serious threat to our privacy.

8

Privacy Problems

Imagine digital records of these things:

- a cancer diagnosis
- an ovulation cycle or sperm count
- a suicide note
- an act of sexual intercourse
- a paternity test
- an admission of infidelity
- an office affair
- a stroke
- a family secret
- a confession
- a visit to a psychiatrist
- a prescription
- a poem about loss
- an email to your dying mother
- a video of you in your favorite spot in the park
- an expression of gender identity
- a bank statement
- a bankruptcy statement
- a group text chat with college friends
- a mean text about a co-worker or boss
- a photo of an ill-advised inebriated act
- a video of your bedroom
- an experiment with illegal drugs
- a prayer

If any of these records were relevant to a criminal prosecution, there is no legal principle that would prevent a judge from signing a warrant allowing police to obtain them. There is no mechanism for weighing the value of the evidence the records might contain against the loss of privacy caused by their disclosure. Prosecution always trumps privacy. In fact, the only intimate or personal digital facts that could not be revealed under these circumstances are those protected by formal legal privileges, such as the attorney-client privilege that applies when you talk to your lawyer, or the Fifth Amendment protection against self-incrimination.[1] Otherwise, your secrets are fair game. As we've seen, police would not even need a warrant to obtain many of them.[2]

This has not always been the case. Certain substantive Fourth Amendment limits were assumed at the Founding. Today, however, the default is to prioritize the collection of evidence over privacy, liberty, security, or autonomy interests. If you build a technology to capture digital clues, the police will come for the evidence. And the more data is available, the more vulnerable we become to police surveillance. As civil rights attorney Jennifer Stisa Granick wrote:

> Twenty years ago, we had a lot more privacy than we do today. Conversations vanished into the air as the very words were spoken. Only a time traveler could turn back the clock to learn whether we'd been at the scene of a robbery, a mosque, or an abortion clinic on any particular date—or who we were with. No one knew if we read the *New York Times* or the *Anarchist Cookbook*. The searches we made through the library card catalogs were known to us alone.[3]

Today's reality could not be more different. Whether you are the former president of the United States or a political protester, law enforcement can obtain your private messages, texts, geolocation, financial information, or anything else stored digitally, as long as they have a warrant.[4] This is the privacy problem.

The Three Privacy Conflations

There is a rich academic literature around privacy. Legal scholars, philosophers, sociologists, technologists, and those who have spent a lifetime studying the impacts of surveillance have offered numerous compelling perspectives on what privacy is and why it matters when it is threatened.[5] "Intimate privacy," "privacy-by design," "informational privacy," "intellectual privacy," "contextual privacy," and many other theories have been and continue to be debated and explored.[6] While this deeper philosophical and theoretical work is beyond the scope of this book, a common thread emerges from it: Privacy is intimately connected to human well-being. And so it is quite strange that the U.S. criminal justice system allows the desire to prosecute to overcome privacy at every turn.

This is, in part, because the Supreme Court and various legislative statutes have come up with their own ways of defining privacy. Unfortunately for those of us living under those laws, these narrow definitions have left us largely unprotected from law enforcement accessing our data. Current constitutional law is not able to effectively address the privacy risks inherent to the digital age. In particular, there are three areas in which Fourth Amendment doctrine falls short. I call them "the three conflations." First, constitutional law conflates expectations of privacy *in general* with expectations of privacy *from police*. Second, it conflates privacy with secrecy, essentially reasoning that unless one keeps something secret, it loses its constitutional protection. Third, it conflates collective privacy concerns with individual privacy concerns, failing to conceptualize collective harms—like the harm that occurs when an entire neighborhood is watched by private surveillance cameras. Together, the three conflations give broad cover to police and prosecutors who seek our personal information, to our detriment. Unravelling them may help us identify solutions to the privacy problem.

Conflating Privacy in General and Privacy from Police

As I detailed in Part I, much of the constitutional discussion about privacy arises from the Supreme Court's reasonable expectation of privacy doctrine which suggests that Fourth Amendment protections turn on "objectively reasonable" expectations of privacy. There are many problems with the expectation of privacy test (like the notion that "objectively reasonable" expectations can somehow be divined by nine Supreme Court justices after oral argument and legal briefing), but the part I want to focus on here is what I call "the who/whom question." Who is it that might get information about our lives that we don't want them to have? From whom do we expect privacy? The expectation of privacy test is clearly in relation to someone—privacy isn't a problem when you're alone on a deserted island—but whom? The police? A nosy neighbor? Anybody who might be around? Anybody at all? Because the Bill of Rights, and thus the Fourth Amendment, offers protection only against government actors, we might assume that the "who/whom" implied by our right to privacy refers only to government agents. But in the earliest cases involving police surveillance technology, the Supreme Court failed to offer a clear answer, instead conflating expectations of privacy in general with expectations of privacy from government surveillance.

Maybe it was an honest mistake, because at the time the Court was deciding these cases in the 1960s and 1970s, human police officers weren't any more capable of invading your privacy than anyone else.[7] That is why, for example, Justice John Marshall Harlan's opinion in 1967's *Katz v. United States*, a case involving the wiretapping of a public payphone, described the privacy in conversation or items exposed in one's "home or office" in terms of them being revealed to "outsiders,"[8] not just police. Similarly, in *California v. Ciraolo*, Chief Justice Warren Burger could analogize the police's use of a plane to take aerial photos of a backyard to passengers on double-decker buses who might also be able to peek over the defendant's ten-foot fences.[9] Putting aside the weirdness of the analogy (there were no double-decker buses around), implicit in the Court's reasoning was that any information that could potentially be exposed to anyone could be collected by police without implicating the Fourth Amendment. This logic carried over to the cases that established the "third-party doctrine" and it also finds support in cases involving public movements, eavesdropping, and open spaces around a home.[10] The Supreme Court routinely used exposure in general to anyone as a proxy for expectations of privacy from police.

To be fair, in the analog, human-centered world of the 1960s-1990s, this implicit assumption made good sense. The precautions a person might take to avoid being observed by a stranger would also protect them from being observed by a police officer, even one who carried some technical enhancement, like a flashlight or pair of binoculars. Basically, until the Court's 2012 decision in the *Jones* GPS tracking case, the benchmark for "expectations" of privacy was what humans could observe with their five senses. The technologies the Court was considering in these cases didn't give superhuman powers to the police; they collected the same kind of information anyone could, just perhaps less obtrusively.

The digital world changes that privacy calculus. Today's police surveillance technologies can do things that ordinary people cannot. Indeed, the collection and analysis of our personal data is not being done by humans at all. Sensors in cars and cities are automatically collecting more data than could ever be collected, much less interpreted, by a human observer. Video analytics software is pattern-matching millions of images a second. Artificial intelligence finds connections across vast datasets that are not otherwise observable. And unlike in previous eras, this data collection cannot be avoided.

Distinguishing our expectation of privacy in general from our expectation of privacy from the police in particular allows us a chance to preserve privacy even in the face of direct threats from law enforcement and indirect threats from consumer surveillance. In other words, instead of defining a Fourth Amendment expectation against what a neighbor might see, what your cell phone provider might know, or what your smart speaker might overhear, a better analysis would consider whether you had a reasonable expectation of privacy against government agents obtaining that information. We do not go about our lives thinking the government is surveilling our backyards, even though we know a nosy neighbor might. Similarly, we might rely on a third-party cloud service to store our communications but do not expect the government to have access to our racy emails or breakup texts. We do not expect police to have access to those private spaces of our lives (even if we expect or depend on others to have access to them.) And even with a warrant, we might want to claim some place of privacy that the government cannot reach. Defining privacy in relation to police power would allow us to do so, strengthening Fourth Amendment protections.

Conflating Privacy and Secrecy

"I have nothing to hide." It is a common response to concerns about police surveillance. It may even be true, but before making that claim so definitively, ask yourself the following questions:

- Would you be okay with turning over your Internet browsing history to your local police?
- Would you be okay with having a camera installed outside your home with a direct feed to the police station?
- Would you be okay with having a police officer follow you around everywhere you drive?

Even if the police promised they would not arrest you for minor things you might do—like the times you rolled through a stop sign or Googled whether the IRS could come after you for fudging a tax deduction—would you feel comfortable with this monitoring? If the answer is no, why?

According to the law, none of this information is secret. Police could obtain any of it from existing digital systems because you gave it to third parties. But just because something is not secret does not mean it cannot still be private. Sending a photograph to a friend, looking up a mysterious rash on the Internet, and saving a draft of a love letter to the cloud—is private, and most of us wouldn't want these things exposed. Under current law, that doesn't matter.[11] Our reasonable expectation of privacy does not cover that photograph, that Google search, or that love letter, which means police can get access to them if they so choose. Because the law conflates privacy with absolute secrecy, a whole world of data is exposed.

Prosecutors might argue that if Google knows about your criminal plans, why shouldn't the FBI? Why would we deprive law enforcement of this information when the suspect has already indicated a willingness to share it? Here, the operative question is not "From whom can I reasonably expect privacy?" but "With whom am I willing to share?" Personally, I am okay with Google using my keyword data in return for all the information it provides, but I still do not want the government monitoring my searches. I am fine sharing the details of my travel plans over email, but that doesn't mean I want the government seizing those digital papers to monitor who I am visiting. This is especially true if I think the government might not like me, my values, or my beliefs—or if I am existing in ways that challenge the norms the current government seeks to uphold. Under those circumstances, the ability to maintain privacy, even in the absence of complete secrecy, is vital.

Conflating Individual Privacy and Collective Privacy

Privacy is not only an individual right. It is also a collective good. But because so much of the U.S. legal framework is necessarily focused on individual rights, figuring out how to see privacy as both an individual and a collective matter can be conceptually tricky.[12]

There are two separate concerns here. The first involves the practical inability to challenge generalized surveillance without some individual cognizable harm. Under modern constitutional law, there is no legal recourse for non-individualized Fourth Amendment privacy harms.[13] The second is theoretical: We have no language for collective privacy violations.

First, in order to have what is called "standing" to bring a Fourth Amendment case, a defendant must demonstrate that they personally have had an individual expectation of privacy violated.[14] So, for example, I might care that your home was searched illegally by police, but because it is not my home, I cannot sue to show a Fourth Amendment violation. I have no privacy or property interest in the matter, and thus no standing to sue. Only the person who had their reasonable expectation of privacy violated (usually the homeowner or tenant) is allowed to sue to remedy the constitutional violation.

This judicially created limit can make it difficult to challenge today's digital surveillance programs.[15] For example, imagine there is a government agency that has the power to collect all our digital communications across the world. Perhaps this collection is done in the name of national security, to help the government to track terrorist plots and other threats to the nation. Now imagine that you are the type of person that might run afoul of this surveillance system because of your contacts with people abroad. Maybe you are a human rights lawyer who represents people who want to avoid being labeled terrorists. Or maybe you are a journalist or civil rights group investigating the living conditions of someone the government claims has engaged in bad acts. You might think it is very likely that your communications are being incidentally captured by this government agency. After all, you are speaking with people who you know have been targeted for surveillance. Do you have standing to bring a Fourth Amendment claim?[16] You can't prove your individual rights were violated, even though you know that some other people in your position have had their digital communications reviewed without a warrant. Or maybe you just think that this collection of personal communications is wrong as a matter of policy, and you want to challenge the practice independent of any harm to yourself.

A 2013 Supreme Court case addressed this exact scenario. Journalists, lawyers, and human rights groups like Amnesty International sued the National Security Agency (NSA) to challenge its bulk data collection of international communications, arguing that this collection violated the Fourth Amendment.[17] While it's likely that the plaintiffs' communications had been captured in this global surveillance net, none of them could prove it—because the targets of the surveillance were secret. And because the plaintiffs could not demonstrate that their individual expectations of privacy were violated by the NSA's bulk collection program, the Supreme Court held that they could not claim a Fourth Amendment privacy violation. Similarly, individuals alarmed by what they considered to be overbroad surveillance powers could not sue the NSA on behalf of those who were harmed or potentially harmed by the program. The plaintiffs needed to be able to show that the surveillance program caused them particularized, concrete harm, and they could not do so. The lawsuit was dismissed for a lack of standing because no privacy harm could be shown.[18]

The point here is not to critique the NSA program itself[19] but to show that even when a privacy threat is real—in this case, we know the NSA was collecting signals across the globe—there is no Fourth Amendment recourse because of the way we conceive of privacy as an individual harm. The collective privacy harm might be clear, but it will not be justiciable in court.

On a more local level, this conflation limits recourse for community-wide surveillance harms. Consider, for example, a person—let's call him Andrew—who lives surrounded by neighbors who own Ring cameras. Even if Andrew chooses not to install a camera himself, he has no claim to privacy against his neighbors. The neighbors' cameras watch him going to and from his home and maybe capture part of what happens in front and at the side of his home. Similarly, if the neighborhood homeowners' association buys an ALPR system to track the cars coming in and out of the neighborhood, then Andrew will be tracked, whether he agrees with the private surveillance plan or not (he does not). The footage or data will be available to police—probably by a simple request, since there is little reason for a neighborhood association to object to giving police information on someone else; after all, that is why they are collecting the information in the first place.

The Fourth Amendment analysis would begin and end with the fact that Andrew cannot show any expectation of privacy from nongovernment actors. Even if the video footage from those private Ring cameras ends up in the local sheriff's office so police could see Andrew pacing on the sidewalk (worrying about the rise of surveillance), there is no easy way for Andrew to demonstrate a privacy harm. Even though there are surveillance cameras everywhere in the neighborhood, there is no case to bring and no one to bring it against unless you can show an individual privacy violation. A generalized concern that too much surveillance is a bad thing is not a constitutional harm.

In addition, if anyone else should choose to walk or drive through the neighborhood, they could not escape the surveillance either. The delivery driver, friend, missionary, or salesperson, or just a person who wants to take a healthy walk in the area, gets captured by this collective surveillance net, without any remedy in law. The potential surveillance harms are not cognizable. How would you frame the complaint? What right do you have to walk down the street unseen by other people legally watching from their homes? None.

And yet, there is a privacy harm. Crowdsourced surveillance reduces your ability to do things around your home without worrying that someone is watching you. Such surveillance is also exclusionary. Video surveillance systems are meant to keep unwanted people out of the area, thereby maintaining a sense of security around certain property. Protecting the individual privacy of that homeowner undermines any collective sense of privacy outside the home. It turns public space into privately monitored space. If we can no longer find privacy from the eye of a camera lens, we have lost something of value.

The irony is that the Fourth Amendment was intended to protect a collective right. As legal scholar David Gray has argued, the Fourth Amendment speaks to "the right of *the people*" (not a person or persons).[20] The Founders' concern in drafting the amendment was that policing powers could be used against the entire community, which had happened under the British in the guise of general warrants. While it might be an individual (like Sam Adams) who was targeted by such a warrant, the harm was broader than the violation of a single person's privacy.

This is the second problem with conflating collective privacy and individual privacy. We have lost the theory that would give us the language for discussing and remedying collective privacy harms. Persistent surveillance planes recording entire cities, sensor systems tracking all cars, and any of the geolocational data streams discussed in Part I would all represent collective privacy harms even if no one were prosecuted as a result of the evidence they collect. The right of *the people* to be secure from unreasonable searches should reach government systems of surveillance—and yet that argument has largely been lost to history.

True, there are strong prudential reasons why a court system would want to limit the cases that make it to the federal courts to those with clear parties, clear harms, and a clear legal remedy. Courts refrain from issuing advisory opinions, and so our constitutional law has remained narrow and focused on particular cases and controversies. In addition, one could imagine the flood of cases from concerned citizens thinking something is unfair or wrong if standing rules were to be loosened for Fourth Amendment cases. After all, if anyone could sue for any Fourth Amendment violation against anyone, the courts would be overwhelmed.

And yet harms to *the people* are real. General warrants were harmful because they carried the risk of a privacy invasion.[21] The power of the government to grant arbitrary and unlimited search powers was the harm necessitating the drafting of the Fourth Amendment, and this would have been the case even if no individual colonist's home was ever actually searched. So, too, with systemic surveillance systems. If police suddenly announced that they had gained access to all the video cameras watching inside and outside your home but would not use the footage as evidence in criminal cases, there still would be a broad privacy harm, even if no single person could claim a specific privacy violation. That our current constitutional law has no way to remedy these harms is a real privacy problem.[22]

The Privacy Problem and Prosecution

Much more could be said about privacy in the digital age. The aim of this chapter is to show how the privacy problem enhances prosecutorial power. The prioritization of prosecution and the narrowing of Fourth Amendment privacy has allowed digital evidence to be easily collected and used against us. In essence, courts have enabled prosecutors to obtain digital evidence with very few (if any) legal constraints. Our desire for self-surveillance has worked hand in hand with the government's desire for better evidence, and while this is not normatively a bad thing, it does create a new privacy problem.

Constitutional law is just part of the puzzle of privacy in the digital age. In theory, statutory protections could do a better job defining what information should be private than vague constitutional interpretations. And a patchwork of legislative privacy protections for data does exist at a federal, state, and local level. For example, Illinois's Biometric Information Privacy Act (BIPA) expressly defines protected types of personal data, and regulates the use of facial recognition technology.[23] The California Consumer Privacy Act (CCPA) / California Privacy Rights Act (CPRA)[24] as well as similar statutes in nineteen other states, protects consumer data more broadly, defining what data is protected and what uses of that data are prohibited, and providing remedies for misuse.[25] But while privacy can be defined and protected through statutory law, each of the laws mentioned here allows police and prosecutors access to the protected data. Privacy laws do not mean privacy from law enforcement.

The upshot of the existing legislative privacy framework is that data has been deemed to be protected against some corporate misuses—but not from the government. Once again, the desire for prosecution has prevailed over considerations of privacy. As I will discuss in Part III, however, these types of legislative carve-outs for law enforcement could be changed—if there is the political will to change them.

9

Praxis Problems

"Praxis" is just a fancy word for practice, as opposed to theory. In theory, big data analytics can micro-target my interests to know my favorite morning Starbucks drink (venti dark with four sugars). In practice, it might get the order wrong when it matters—the day I cut sugar out of my diet. That's praxis.

The problem with policing technologies is that they get it wrong when it matters. And in the context of liberty and incarceration, it almost always matters. This is not to say that these technologies do not ever get things right. This book is full of stories where some digital technology helped capture someone responsible for a criminal act. Still, in a world filled with digital clues, there are also many opportunities for error.

This chapter explores a few of the problems with using surveillance technologies for criminal prosecution—problems that should have been addressed before these technologies were used in real cases involving real people. They include what I call "the six Ps": (1) the pilot problem, (2) the profit problem, (3) the probability problem, (4) the people problem, (5) the pressure problem, and (6) the process problem. These "Ps" create a real problem for prosecutors increasingly dependent on this type of digital evidence.

The Pilot Problem

How do you pilot new policing technologies in the real world without causing harm?

Whether we are talking about commercial surveillance of homes or government surveillance of populations, there is an inescapable problem: We are experimenting on real people. Both parts of this phrase are important. Our digital advances are still experimental. No one knows if wearing a smartwatch can really improve your health—it's an educated guess. No one knows if police can predict crime before it happens—it's a less educated guess. And these experiments affect human health and well-being. If your smartwatch misreads your blood pressure, your health might suffer. If a police department misinterprets a predictive policing algorithm, your community might suffer.[1]

One of the most striking trends from the first decade of big data policing is how many systems were rolled out as "pilot projects." Adopting the "move fast and break things" ethos of Silicon Valley, police departments introduced surveillance technologies ranging from spy planes to facial recognition systems without conducting a full risk analysis to understand how the technology would intersect with the real world.

This is the nature of pilot projects—they are, by definition, experimental. In the abstract, this is okay. You can't know if a theory will hold up until you test it. Yet the list of first generation policing technologies that had to be stopped in the pilot phase or ended in scandal—predictive policing, facial recognition, social network analysis, ShotSpotter, Dataminer, and others—is long enough to give serious pause.[2] In fact, it is hard to point to a single innovative policing technology that did not raise concerns around error, bias, or overcollection of data. Given how many pilot projects have stalled, it is strange to watch new ones launch every year. How did we get ourselves into a situation where citizens become test subjects for new policing technologies without adequate vetting or controls?

The answer is basically free money. The funding model for new surveillance technologies works something like this: Police departments want technological solutions to crime but have neither the technical expertise needed to come up with those solutions nor the money to buy such expertise. Tech companies have ideas for solutions to crime but need someone to purchase them. Federal grants bridge the gap. The federal government offers monetary grants to support research and development of new policing technologies through the National Institute of Justice (NIJ), which has given millions of dollars to such projects, including predictive policing, facial recognition, ShotSpotter, and ALPR.[3] The Bureau of Justice Assistance (BJA) gives billions more to police so that they can put the theories into practice.[4]

Wealthy individuals and their foundations have also invested in technological solutions to crime. For example, a foundation established by billionaires Laura and John Arnold helped fund the Baltimore spy plane,[5] and hedge fund billionaire Ken Griffin funded a predictive policing pilot program in Chicago.[6] Big police departments like the NYPD and Chicago Police Department have also used funds from civil asset forfeiture (which allows police to seize money or possessions they believe to be associated with a crime) to purchase new technology.[7] Whatever the source of the money, the fact is that local police departments are not always paying for new technologies out of their general budgets.

For local governments that want to buy surveillance technologies, this is a win-win. But what's being funded is often little more than an idea that someone hopes will work. An algorithm that can predict who will commit a violent crime by studying past behavior, a computer program that can scour social media for threats, and a video analytics program that can identify an anomaly in the footage—may all sound plausible enough to secure funding. If it turns out these systems do not end up reducing crime (or working at all), developers can always invent a new technology and go back for another round of funding to study it.

All the federal funding directed toward new policing technologies encourages private investment. Venture capital investors, recognizing that the surveillance market is global can gamble on a new technology with a fair degree of certainty that some country, somewhere will buy it, guaranteeing a return on investment. On the consumer surveillance side, the incentives to invest are even more obvious.[8] Data collection and monetization have been growth engines for many companies. Even legacy manufacturers are finding that data is their most valuable asset.

With so much free money sloshing around, companies are incentivized to build and test surveillance technologies as quickly as possible, which has meant few limits are placed on pilot projects. One might have thought that before green-lighting the Los Angeles Strategic Extraction and Restoration (LASER) person-based predictive policing program in Los Angeles, the BJA would have considered the implications for racial justice in a very unequal city. One might have thought that before funding facial recognition matching, the NIJ would have considered how facial recognition technologies normed on white men could result in the false arrest of Black men, who are already disproportionately represented in the criminal legal system. These harms were not unforeseeable. Critics have long pointed out the racially disparate impacts (both potential and actual) of new policing technologies.[9] But the grant process did not adequately take these concerns into account before the technology could be deployed in a real-world pilot program.

It does not have to be this way. At least at the federal level, grants can be conditioned on the completion of a risk analysis that takes civil rights, civil liberties, and privacy issues seriously. Recipients of many other federal grants are already required to test, evaluate, and audit programs to identify any racial justice or civil liberties concerns. When it comes to policing technologies, however, these concerns are put on the back burner.

The Profit Problem

How do you prevent corporate profits from driving local police priorities?

There is nothing inherently wrong with police departments buying advanced technology. When many private enterprises and other government agencies are investing in database management, sensors, and artificial intelligence technologies, why should law enforcement be held back by a fear of innovation? So long as society acknowledges the need for police, police officers will need equipment to do their jobs effectively.

The problem is the profit motive. As we've seen, the interests of private companies are not always aligned with the interests of the public. The pressure to generate profits may win out over addressing public concerns in ways that might limit growth. This is most evident in the case of publicly traded companies, which are required to prioritize shareholder interests, but it's also true for smaller private start-ups trying to grow their business in the face of competition. Companies cannot just "do the right thing" (or the cautious thing), because market forces continually push them forward into risk.

Take Axon, the company that started out selling Tasers and police-worn body cameras.[10] Both of these technologies obviously come with risks when used by police, but Axon sold them across the nation and quickly built market share. So, what happens when that market becomes saturated? The company had an incentive to come up with new lines of products to sell.[11] In the wake of several tragic school shootings, Axon began to consider how its products could be used as first responders in such situations and it came up with the idea of equipping drones with the company's video camera and Taser technology. Axon asked its AI

Ethics Board—a group of civil rights advocates, law professors, and technologists who gave advice about the legal and ethical impacts of Axon technologies—for its input on pursuing this new line of business development.

The AI Ethics Board had pushed back against Axon before. In 2019, it had convinced the company not to implement facial recognition technology on its police-worn body cameras despite the company's dominance of the body cam market.[12] It pushed back again this time, advising the company not to pursue selling Taser-armed surveillance drones to schools.

And here is where the profit problem arises. Clearly, deploying armed drones at schools sounds like a risky idea. But if the leading maker of body cams and Tasers does not enter the market, someone else might. Do you give up your position as an innovator in the policing tech space because of the worries of a bunch of academics? Axon rejected the advice of the AI Ethics Board and decided to pursue the Taser drones. In response, more than half of the board members publicly resigned in protest.[13] Axon eventually put the project on hold after significant public outcry, but it was more of a business decision than an ethical one.[14] The board members' very public protest had created bad optics, that threatened the bottom line.

Axon isn't the only company facing this dilemma. CEOs of public companies work for the shareholders, and it's not in their job description to walk away from potentially lucrative contracts on the basis of abstract ideals. All public companies face the pressure to be first movers, develop market share, and innovate, or be accused of failing in their fiduciary duties to shareholders. Addressing civil rights and privacy concerns, or even plain moral choices ("Do we need to build that armed robot?"), only slows companies down. In today's uber-competitive market-driven system, the profit problem is hard to avoid.

The Probability Problem

How can we apply generalized algorithmic insights to individual real-world cases?

AI-enhanced data-driven systems are accurate much of the time. This is genuinely impressive. It's remarkable that, under certain conditions, a facial recognition system can use a predictive algorithm to identify a single face from a dataset of billions of images. The fact that a Real-Time Crime Center with video analytics can use a pattern matching system to identify every object passing by is just dizzying. But just because these systems usually work doesn't mean they don't make mistakes. For some tasks—like sending an online promotional coupon, for example—an imperfect prediction might be harmless. I can easily ignore the "50 percent off" deal sent to me based on the probability that someone with my Internet browsing habits is looking for a new age-appropriate multivitamin. When it comes to police investigations, though, the consequences of an error are much harder to ignore.

To understand how the probability problem arises, it is helpful to examine the limits of computer vision. Computers do not "see" like humans do. They identify shadings, patterns of light and dark, all converted into 1s and 0s.[15] If you want a machine learning algorithm to recognize "man," you show it lots of pictures of men, and eventually, certain visual patterns will emerge from the training data. The computer will then be able to identify "man-like" objects in its system with a high degree of probability.[16] If it is part of a video analytics system, it will attempt to match any "man-like" object that passes in front of the camera lens.[17] But when an image doesn't match the pattern well enough, the computer won't be able to recognize it.[18] Machine learning algorithms commonly misidentify men with long hair, short builds, or thin faces, and they get confused by floppy hats and makeup. The algorithm may successfully identify men most of the time, but in some situations, it might not. It's a risk based on probabilities. It might be a risk we are willing to take. It might be a risk that can be mitigated by human intervention (a person tasked with reviewing the matches for accuracy), but it is still a risk.

Now multiply that risk across billions of images. It is hard to put a human in the loop when you are watching an entire city through your cameras or scanning all of social media for threats. And even when humans are in the loop, our deference to machines can prevent us from recognizing their mistakes. The few cases of proven erroneous facial recognition matches make this clear.[19] In each of these cases, the computer generated the original probabilistic match, but a human police officer looked it over and decided it was a good-enough basis to arrest someone.[20] The influence of the computer match overcame any human cautiousness about whether they had the correct person.

The other probability problem with machine learning algorithms is that they tend to zero out anomalies. Video analytics systems, for example, are trained to recognize defined objects: man, woman, car, bicycle, dog, cat. This works well enough most of the time. But new things get invented every day. People reject binary status. Patterns change. And because machine learning algorithms make predictions based on what they've seen in the past, they don't know how to deal with people (or things) that don't "fit."[21] When a machine learning system is training itself to identify men or women, for example, it might simply erase trans or nonbinary faces.[22] People outside the norm are literally not seen.

This is troubling for obvious reasons, but it also highlights the inherent weakness of AI pattern matching systems: They can only identify what they are trained to recognize. In his book *Four Battlegrounds: Power in the Age of Artificial Intelligence*, Paul Scharre recounts how members of the U.S. Marines Corps outsmarted an AI targeting system created by the Department of Defense's Defense Advanced Research Projects Agency (DARPA).[23] The DARPA robot was designed to scan and identify people on the battlefield and had been trained on lots of footage of people in a military context. In a test of the robot's defensive capabilities, the marines easily bested the system using three unconventional tactics.[24] Two marines somersaulted toward the device for 300 meters. Another hid in a cardboard box and approached the robot while wearing the box. Another group—borrowing from *Macbeth* and the Birnam Wood—cut down some trees and approached hidden by tree branches. All the groups easily got past the AI sensor, which was still looking to target the people it had been trained to identify.[25]

For police, the problem of probability offers reason for caution, but perhaps little reason for practical concern. Most Fourth Amendment laws are based on probability. To search your backpack, for example, a police officer must have probable cause—which is essentially a prediction that the search will uncover evidence of a crime. Courts have been tremendously forgiving when these predictions don't pan out.[26] Police can believe they have probable cause based on false or incomplete information and still continue with a search. They can fail to uncover evidence in most of their searches and still be allowed to perform searches or make arrests, even though their internal prediction algorithm is clearly faulty.[27] While judges are loath to put an exact percentage on what "probable" means when it comes to probable cause, it's pretty much accepted that it's less than 50 percent, so police can expect to guess wrong more than half the time. That's a big range for mistakes.[28] We can only hope that such a low Fourth Amendment bar is raised when it comes to policing technologies, or we'll have many more errors on our hands.

The People Problem

What do we do when the people using the technology don't understand how it works?

Sometimes errors arise from technology itself, and sometimes they arise from the people using it. When someone's liberty is at stake, human error can have devastating effects. *Wired* magazine reported on such a failure related to a surveillance app called Covenant Eyes.[29] Covenant Eyes is an app for smartphones and computers used to monitor someone's online activity and block them from accessing certain content. It's primarily marketed to people who want to stop watching online porn, or want to stop their spouse or child from doing so. The app takes screenshots of the device, which it sends it back to a server (and an "accountability partner," if desired) on a regular basis. The screenshots are blurred, but an alert is generated if inappropriate content is detected.

Covenant Eyes is marketed to families and churches, and the company explicitly discourages its use by law enforcement.[30] Nevertheless, the pretrial and probation department in Monroe County, Indiana, (and several other cities) decided to use the app to track the online habits of defendants awaiting trial. In the case that *Wired* wrote about, a man had been charged with possession of alleged child sexual abuse material.[31] As a condition of his pretrial release, the Covenant Eyes app had to be put on all the devices in his home. This meant that the phones and devices belonging to his wife and two kids were also monitored every second of the day. Even if the app worked perfectly, requiring this level of surveillance as a condition of pretrial release is problematic. Everything on the family's devices was sent back to the pretrial services department, including private texts, YouTube videos, and conversations with a therapist. While presumably the family wanted their loved one to remain out of jail, this is a high cost to pay for that freedom.

The problem for the husband was that the app does not distinguish between a user's attempt to view a website and a network request made by a browser as part of a background refresh. Browsers can automatically refresh commonly visited websites so that they load more quickly—think weather and traffic reports, or breaking news. In this case, the Covenant Eyes app alerted to a visit to Pornhub, a popular pornography website, which would violate the conditions of the husband's pretrial release. The family denied viewing Pornhub and demonstrated to *Wired* that the Chrome browser refreshed to various websites that were stored in the browser's memory without any action on their part.[32] Unfortunately, the people at the pretrial release department did not understand (or did not care) how the technology worked. Despite being shown their error, the judge remanded the husband to jail pending trial.

In the Indiana case, the technology worked as designed; the issue was how people interpreted its output. It could be true that the husband's computer was contacting a forbidden website without him having initiated that contact. The problem wasn't the app but the pretrial services people, who mandated the use of an app that they didn't themselves understand. This is the risk for all surveillance technologies; people must use them correctly, and many times they don't.

The Pressure Problem

How do we address the pressure to make surveillance data fit a desired narrative?

Police are judged on the number of arrests they make. Prosecutors are judged on the number of convictions they secure. It makes sense that these are the metrics by which we measure their performance. Whenever there's a crime, victims, community members, politicians, and the media demand action, and that action usually comes in the form of an arrest and conviction. Police work to gather evidence, and prosecutors use that evidence to prove their theory of the case and bring the wrongdoer to justice. So there's a lot of pressure to make sure the evidence that's collected tells a particular story.

This is not a new problem. Criminal casebooks are filled with examples of shady forensic science being used to convict people. Forensic evidence may seem "scientific," but some of it is really junk science, that is unproven and at times actively misleading.[33] And yet unscientific "bitemark evidence," "shoe print evidence," and arson investigations have been used to convict people of serious crimes.[34] In 2009, the National Academies of Science issued a scathing report about the lack of scientific reliability behind many common forensic techniques. In some cases, prosecutors used bogus experts to strengthen their cases.[35] In other cases, legitimate, well-meaning scientists allowed biases to sway their judgment and made claims about evidence that exceeded the bounds of scientific certainty. Testimony about ballistics—whether a particular bullet was fired from a particular gun—is a common source of dispute, for example. And as one recent study found, digital forensic examiners might make the same types of bias errors[36] for many of the same reasons.[37]

Sometimes the pressure to make digital evidence fit a particular narrative leads to complications. A shooting case in Chicago set off allegations of technological manipulation, a multimillion-dollar defamation lawsuit, and a national debate about the reliability of surveillance technology as evidence in criminal cases. From beginning to end, the case was afflicted by a series of understandable, but very real mistakes—not because of the technology itself, but because of its centrality to the prosecution's narrative.[38]

It began with a shooting in May 2020.[39] At the time, twenty-five-year-old Safarain Herring was on the run. He had been shot at two weeks earlier, and a relative had relocated him to a different part of Chicago for his safety. It was a difficult moment for the city: George Floyd had been murdered by Minneapolis police less than a week before, and people were angry.[40] Protests had resulted in the destruction of businesses, and everyone was on edge. On the evening of May 31, a man named Michael Williams went out to buy cigarettes at a local gas station but found that rioters had destroyed the store, so he headed back home. On his way, he saw Safarain Herring looking for a ride and in an act of neighborly kindness, Williams picked up Herring to drive him to the place where he was staying. When the car stopped at a light, another car pulled up next to it. Someone in that car shot Herring through the window. Williams immediately drove Herring to the hospital, where he later died.

The police had a murder, but no motive or suspects other than Williams. But Williams—a sixty-four-year-old grandfather who lived with his devoted wife—seemed to have no reason to harm Herring.

He had reported the drive-by shooting and cooperated with the police investigation. No gun or bullets were found in his car. Yet Williams was arrested and held in jail for eleven months as the prosecutors and defense argued about the evidence against him. That evidence was weak and largely depended on the ShotSpotter data. ShotSpotter had detected what police believed to be the gunshot that had killed Herring; the alert recorded the time and location of the alleged shot. Police also had a silent video of Williams's car and one other car driving through a red light around the time of the ShotSpotter alert. That other car had its windows up, which police said proved the shot couldn't have come from inside it. There was no evidence tying the crime to Williams, except for the fact that Herring had been riding in his car when he was shot.

In preparing for trial, defense lawyers keyed in on two discrepancies in the ShotSpotter report. First, the audio system initially had flagged the sound as a firework, and it was only after human review that it was determined to be a gunshot.[41] Second, the address initially listed for the shot was a good distance away from the location of the actual shooting; but the address was later manually changed to match the correct location.[42] Both alterations in the report seemed suspicious to the defense lawyers because the changes matched the prosecution's theory of the case. It sure seemed like prosecutors had pressured ShotSpotter to manipulate the evidence, changing the facts around to support their theory of the case.

While skepticism of police technology is warranted in general, in this specific case, the changes also matched Williams' own story. Williams admitted there had been a drive-by shooting at a particular location at a particular time and that he had been present in his car. It was a gunshot, not a firework, that killed Herring. The analysts were thus correct to change the audio sound after reviewing it. They had also been correct to change the address of the alert. ShotSpotter's data-driven system had defaulted to the "official" business address of a large nearby park rather than the actual location of the shooting, on the other side of that park. The precise location of the shot, as calculated by ShotSpotter, hadn't changed between the two reports, and they were consistent with both Williams's and the government's theories of the case. The changes hadn't been made with nefarious intent, and they only made the report more accurate.

Despite this, the Williams case was used to attack ShotSpotter in the media. National news stories were written about the unreliability of the technology, and the company itself was portrayed as a villain that had manipulated data, resulting in the wrongful arrest of Michael Williams. In response to the media claims, the company filed a $300 million defamation lawsuit against Vice Media,[43] which had published a story about how the gunshot data had been changed to support the prosecution's case. Community groups began advocating for a ShotSpotter boycott. But in focusing on the technology, critics disregarded the real problem: prosecutorial error. The issue was not that ShotSpotter alerted to the sound of gunfire (both sides agreed there was a fatal gunshot), but that the ShotSpotter report was being used as evidence to bolster a weak murder case. Both sides told the same story of a gun being used at a particular time and place. The contested issue was who pulled the trigger, and the audio sensor couldn't answer that question. Yet the prosecutors used the fact that a ShotSpotter report existed to place suspicion on Williams.

Ironically, the defense counsel's focus on ShotSpotter (although misplaced) caused the prosecutors to rethink the strength of their case. They dropped the charges against Williams—but only after he had spent almost a year in jail. A court later dismissed ShotSpotter's defamation case, but not before putting journalists on notice about the potential consequences of any reporting that is critical of tech companies.[44] The prosecutors never had to explain why they had targeted Mr. Williams.

That's not to say the technology was without blame. The automated audio sensor was initially inaccurate. It took a human to override the algorithm. The address of the gunshot was also initially wrong because the system had been programmed to default to an official business address. Automation led to error, algorithms led to error, and defaults led to error. But the far bigger mistake was made by the prosecutors, who used technologically impressive (but actually inconclusive) evidence to convince a judge to put an innocent man in jail awaiting trial.

The Process Problem

How do we ensure that defendants have equal access to digital evidence before trial?

Geolocation data can be inculpatory, putting a suspect squarely at the scene of the crime. But geolocation can also be exculpatory, showing that someone other than the suspect was at the same place at the same time. You might think that defense lawyers would be able to access this exculpatory information rather easily. You would be wrong.

When it comes to digital evidence, three related problems combine to stack the deck against defendants. The first is an asymmetry in the statutory law that allows the government, but not defense attorneys, to issue subpoenas for data. The second results from the fact that digital evidence is often used for investigative leads, but not as evidence in trial, which shields the collection process from judicial scrutiny. The third involves the way data-driven systems are designed with the needs of prosecutors—not due process—in mind.

The Asymmetry Problem

Prosecutors have many ways to obtain digital evidence. They can issue grand jury subpoenas, obtain judicial warrants, or sometimes simply request data as relevant to a criminal case. As we've seen, a company faced with a lawful request for data must comply. Statutory laws like the Stored Communications Act (SCA) explicitly grant government access to emails, text messages, and other sensitive information.[45]

The problem is that most of these laws—including the SCA—make no provision for defendants to access the same material. In *Privacy Asymmetries: Access to Data in Criminal Defense Investigations*, legal scholar Rebecca Wexler explores this asymmetry in data access. She writes,

> [P]rivacy asymmetries generally arise from statutory texts and legislative histories that are silent as to criminal defense investigations. For instance, . . . the Postal Accountability and Enhancement Act, the Stored Communications Act, the Video Privacy and Protection Act, Section 6103 of the Tax Code, the Right to Financial Privacy Act, the Family Educational Rights and Privacy Act, the Wiretap Act, and the Computer Fraud and Abuse Act all contain privacy asymmetries disadvantaging defendants that arise from similar textual structures. These statutes first provide a broad confidentiality protection against disclosures of sensitive information; they then enumerate express exceptions for law enforcement investigations but remain silent as to defense investigations.[46]

In other words, even if a defense attorney thinks a piece of third-party data might prove their client's innocence, there's no legal mechanism by which to compel a company to hand it over.

In addition to the silences of the privacy laws, legal doctrines protecting corporate interests have been used to thwart defense access to information about technologies that prosecutors rely on.[47] In cases involving predictive policing, DNA matches, and computer searches, defense lawyers have had difficulty challenging the technologies in court because the companies objected to revealing their trade secrets. After all, if your company is valuable because of its proprietary algorithm or machine-learning model, revealing its inner workings at trial will aid your competitors. But without access to such information, it's hard for defense attorneys to argue that the algorithm is getting it wrong.

The "Only an Investigative Lead" Problem

Not all digital evidence ends up in court. Sometimes, surveillance provides the initial clue that helps investigators narrow in on a suspect, allowing them to get better evidence (like DNA or a confession) to use at trial. In fact, tactics used by police early in an investigation, like social media searches or ShotSpotter alerts, often will not even be mentioned at trial because prosecutors do not want to spend time litigating the technology. And if the evidence from policing technologies is not introduced at trial, there is no process by which defense lawyers can challenge its admissibility, reliability, or impact on police investigators.

Facial recognition is a clarifying example. Police investigators begin thousands of cases by running a photograph or surveillance camera image through a facial recognition matching system.[48] The system attempts to match the "probe" photo to the database of stored photos and produce a name.[49] Investigators then follow up by going to the named person's home, interviewing witnesses, and searching for digital or forensic evidence. Often, once investigators identify a potential suspect, they're able to find better evidence (surveillance tapes, an eyewitness, or a confession), so the initial facial recognition process does not have to be admitted at trial—meaning that there will not be a court proceeding to adjudicate the technology's admissibility or accuracy. The accused may not even know that facial recognition played a role in their arrest. Legal scholar Elizabeth Joh calls this the "surveillance discretion" gap.[50] As mere investigative tools, surveillance technologies fall into a constitutional gap. In that liminal space, they remain in use, but largely unaccounted for by the criminal legal system.

The surveillance discretion gap is exacerbated by two other aspects of the modern criminal legal system: pleas and prosecutorial charging decisions. As Justice Anthony Kennedy once wrote, ours is a system of pleas, not trials.[51] Almost 97 percent of federal criminal cases and 94 percent of state criminal cases are resolved by plea bargains, meaning there is no trial and therefore no adversarial process to challenge the digital evidence.[52] If a person initially identified through facial recognition pleads guilty to the crime, there is no way to challenge the process. The source of the evidence no longer matters once the defendant has admitted guilt. Prosecutors can also prevent dubious digital evidence from being litigated by dismissing cases that rely on it. If a prosecutor does not want to defend the accuracy or reliability of a facial recognition system (or ShotSpotter) in court, she may drop the case rather than risk a negative ruling that might affect other cases down the line. Sometimes the two powers work together, with a prosecutor offering a defendant a very lenient plea bargain they're almost certain to accept, knowing that otherwise she might have to defend how her office obtained the evidence.

So, what should we do about a technology that might not be examined in the ordinary course of trial or pleas, and yet has real implications for the accuracy, fairness, and justice of our criminal legal system? It is a hard question, but also one we've considered before in the context of a different technology: DNA testing.

While DNA evidence is routinely interrogated at trial, it also encourages a lot of defendants to take plea deals. And, like today's digital technologies, DNA evidence can be exculpatory. The legal system learned this lesson the hard way after numerous defendants were exonerated, because the biological material recovered at a crime scene did not get tested or examined before trial—and when it did finally get tested, it wasn't a match. But it took years to establish the right to test recovered DNA evidence after conviction. This cost money and time, and it meant the real perpetrators were free to commit other crimes while innocent people spent years in prison.

In Washington, D.C., where I practiced as a public defender, the city council addressed the problem of untested DNA evidence by passing the D.C. Innocence Protection Act (IPA), which requires a pretrial hearing about the existence and potential use of recovered biological material (DNA).[53] If biological material is recovered as part of the investigation into a violent crime—then whether or not the government chooses to test it—the defense is given notice of its existence and offered the opportunity to have testing done independently. If the defense waives this pretrial access, they forfeit the ability to raise DNA as an issue post-conviction. The IPA takes seriously the power of forensic science and says that it is better to litigate it before trial, not after.

Practically speaking, as a defense lawyer, if you know your client's DNA is going to be on the knife, you waive the hearing. If you don't think the DNA will match your client or want to challenge the government's evidence, you do the test. The IPA serves as a forcing function, requiring prosecutors to reveal whether DNA evidence exists and allowing defense attorneys to consider it themselves.

You can probably see the parallels to digital evidence. Like DNA evidence, forensic identification methods like facial recognition or geolocation also need to be forced out into the open. The D.C. law might serve as a model for how to do it, requiring the prosecution to explain in open court how digital forensic identifying technology was used in the case as an investigative tool, independent of whether prosecutors plan to rely on it at trial. The court hearing would provide notice that digital technologies played a role in the case and give the defense the opportunity to request an independent test of the identification algorithm and underlying data.

In such a hearing, the prosecution might, for example, provide evidence that police used facial recognition to identify the defendant, which they later corroborated with other information. The defense would be given the opportunity for independent examination of the evidence—in this case, information about the facial recognition match to see if the process was done correctly. If there is reason to question the accuracy of the match or the process, a hearing could be held before trial. If the defense found no issue with the process, the matter would be considered settled and could not be brought up again postconviction. A "Digital Forensic Identification Act" would serve a forcing function, making sure new technologies do not create bad outcomes. And by requiring courts to consider these issues before trial, the law would save time and money that might otherwise be spent on appeals.

The Brady Problem

The technologies described in this book all began with a series of design choices. Product managers, software engineers, and coders sat down to figure out how to achieve a certain goal through digital means. Perhaps the goal was monitoring the number of times a "smart" pill bottle was opened or identifying who rang the video doorbell. Perhaps the goal was recording a license plate from a distance or identifying objects on a city street. Whatever the goal might be, the technology had to be designed, tested, and deployed with it in mind.

A number of scholars have revealed the ways biases can be embedded in digital design. Sociologist Safiya Umoja Noble exposed the racism encoded in search engines in her book *Algorithms of Oppression.*[54] Sociologist Ruha Benjamin explored the racial bias in criminal justice technologies in her book *Race After Technology: Abolitionist Tools for the New Jim Code*, which likens discriminatory surveillance technology to Jim Crow laws.[55] Data journalist Meredith Broussard wrote about the ways technology can erase race and gender differences and exacerbate bias in her book *More Than a Glitch: Confronting Race, Gender, and Ability Bias in Tech.*[56] Perhaps not surprisingly, when technology is created by overeducated, affluent white men, systemic racial and gender biases get baked into the design. As we've seen, these race, class, and gender inequalities are replicated and reified in various policing technologies.

But there is another design bias that has not gotten as much attention: law enforcement bias. When a company's customers are police and prosecutors, their goals take precedence in the design process, sometimes with problematic results. The design problem is not necessarily nefarious, just myopic, as both developers and customers do not always think about the larger systemic issues they should be considering.

For over a decade, my scholarship has focused on how police use data-driven systems to predict crimes. So, I was surprised when I saw a posting for a symposium at John Jay College of Criminal Justice about something called "intelligence-driven prosecution," which billed itself as a new form of data-driven, cutting-edge prosecution.[57] The symposium was hosted by the Manhattan District Attorney's Office under then-district attorney Cyrus Vance Jr., and it was promoted to prosecutors from across the country. To me, it looked like predictive policing for prosecutors, and I was curious.

Fortunately for me, they posted the PowerPoint slides of their plans on the Internet for a brief time—just long enough for me to download them and start studying the promised "innovations."[58] The presentation proposed three major changes to traditional prosecution. First, prosecutors would use data to isolate, on a granular level, the places and people driving violent crime.[59] Second, the NYPD and Manhattan District Attorney's Office would link up their datasets—which contained vast amounts of personal data on suspected criminal actors in Manhattan—so that all the information would be in a central data center in the cloud.[60] Clues that used to be scrawled on a detective's notepad (witness notes, interviews, tips, gossip) would be uploaded to the cloud, connected to police, prosecution, and court data about crimes, and searchable by event, person, witness, or any other category defined in the database.[61] The goal was to operationalize that data to target "priority offenders" for more aggressive prosecution in the hopes that incarcerating them would reduce overall crime.[62] It was a form of "predictive prosecution" designed to incapacitate these young men using the existing criminal justice system. Manhattan DAs had a list, they had checked it twice, and they were going to take out those bad apples from the Big Apple.

The prosecutors who ran the program swore they were getting the worst of the worst off the street. Others, including me, worried that proactive prosecution distorts the traditional role of prosecutors—to seek justice for crimes that have been committed, not those that might be committed in the future—and could lead to abuse since there is almost no check on prosecutorial discretion.[63]

A system that links up all the policing and prosecutorial data generated in a jurisdiction as big as Manhattan is precisely the endgame for a world of your data being used against you. My focus here, though, is on the design choices behind this data-driven innovation. The engineers built these digital systems with the goal of allowing prosecutors and police to share data—after all, they were the customers. But because of that law enforcement bias, they didn't think about how that system would intersect with the larger criminal legal system, which of course includes the defense. More specifically, they didn't think about *Brady* evidence.[64]

"*Brady* evidence" refers to evidence that prosecutors are required to share with the defense under rules laid out in a 1963 Supreme Court case, *Brady v. Maryland*.[65] The basic idea is pretty simple: If police or prosecutors have evidence that calls the government's case into question or might exonerate the defendant, they have to turn it over to the defense. If an eyewitness described the perpetrator as having blue eyes, but the defendant has brown eyes, the defense is entitled to that information.[66] If a witness is getting paid to testify or has made a deal with the prosecutor to testify in exchange for a lesser sentence, the defense is entitled to that information, too.[67] Importantly, the prosecutor doesn't have to personally be aware that impeaching or exculpatory evidence exists. If the police possess such evidence, the prosecutor is still obligated to turn it over. If they don't, they've violated the defendant's right to due process.

After reading about the intelligence-led prosecution symposium my question was: What about *Brady*? The slides were filled with images taken from the database.[68] Police and prosecutors had recorded information about gang affiliations, past arrests, notes about suspected motives and grudges, and more.[69] Interviews were uploaded chock full of information about the history of violence in a particular community. It felt like something you'd see at an intelligence agency, not a DA's office: All of Manhattan's criminal patterns in one place, searchable, and available to prosecutors for prosecution.

It's an incredibly powerful system for prosecutors who want to identify people and groups who might be involved in crime. But what happens when a victim in one case is a defendant in another? Or a cooperating witness? What happens when interview notes from one case provide impeaching evidence in another case? Prosecutors have the information—it is in the central database—but they have no way to find it. It was almost like they had forgotten how interwoven crime is in a community. Today's victim is tomorrow's suspect. But when I asked the data engineers at Palantir who helped build the system if anyone had mentioned the term "*Brady*" to them, they answered no. They had made no attempt to link different facts across different cases over time, or to make it possible to find impeaching evidence about a witness in the database. No one had thought about how the different people in different cases might interrelate or have different interests depending on the case. This super powerful database had been built to allow prosecutors to prosecute priority offenders, but its designers failed to understand that sometimes prosecutors have to turn over impeaching or exculpatory information. This isn't a criticism of the engineers themselves, who explained that the database could have been designed to trace these connections. That just wasn't the goal they were given.

The Real-Time Crime Center is another example of a system built according to the needs of police, and without *Brady* protocols in mind. As designed, a Real-Time Crime Center receives video feeds from city cameras, private cameras, police body cameras, and information from other sources, including 911 calls, ALPR hits, gunshot sensors, and crime data.[70] Again, this centralized hub for data offers a powerful weapon for criminal investigators. Perhaps ShotSpotter alerts to a shooting on a particular corner. In surveillance footage, police identify a suspect, who hops into his car and drives away. Police might know this is a high-crime corner associated with a particular gang, and the camera angle gives them a pretty good picture of the tall, male suspect, wearing a blue hat, white shirt, and blue jeans, holding the gun. For police and prosecutors, collecting these digital clues will be an ordinary part of preparing a case.

But what if a city camera across the street captures a different angle of the scene? Maybe there are multiple tall men wearing blue hats, white shirts, and blue jeans. Maybe more than one of them has a gun. What if the ALPR data points to a Toyota, but the man police arrested drives a Ford? What if other ALPRs in the area point to other suspects? What if the gunshot sensor alerted, but the location it identified was a block down the street, putting in question where the shot actually occurred? What if the gang members interviewed on the scene suggest a rival gang member's assault as a motive for the shooting, and historical arrest data backs up the tip? All of these facts are captured digitally in a large Real-Time Crime Center, but unless a prosecutor affirmatively searches through the clues, there will be no way to find the inconsistencies that must be turned over to the defense. The only data that will matter will be what is seen through the prosecution's lens.

As a final example, think about facial recognition technology.[71] The algorithm does not "see" a face; it matches the likelihood that two faceprints represent the same person by comparing patterns of pixels. This likelihood is expressed as a percentage. A detective can put a probe photo into the database and get back anywhere from five to one hundred matches with accuracy rates ranging from 85 to 99 percent. (The threshold for accuracy and the number of possible hits depends on the software used.)[72] From a police perspective, facial recognition is a great shortcut for finding a suspect. A probe photo taken from the scene can be run through a dataset of millions of DMV photos (including yours), and a match will be made very quickly. It can seem almost magical.

But—and there is always a but—the process also creates impeaching evidence. Yes, the algorithm found a 96 percent match, which seems pretty convincing—but it also provided different potential matches at 92 percent and 94 percent certainty, and on down the line of the other hundred matches. If the detective thinks the more accurate match is correct, what to do with the others? In the analog world, if the detective spoke with three witnesses on the street and got three different descriptions of the suspect, it would be quintessential *Brady* evidence. What about the three strong matches revealed by the facial recognition algorithm? And what if the detective thinks the real suspect is the guy with a 94 percent match? This can happen when, for example, the detective already knows that the suspect matched at 94 percent is involved in similar criminal activity, or that the higher matched person is already incarcerated. In those cases, the detective might rightly override the algorithm—but what to do about the better match? Again, in an analog world, this would be *Brady* evidence. An officer can't ignore a clear witness identification of another suspect just because their gut told them it was someone else. They would need to turn that information over to the prosecutor, who would need to turn it over to the defense as impeaching or exculpatory evidence. Why would facial recognition evidence be different? The answer is that it's not. Yet prosecutors have not recognized this as a *Brady* problem.

Policing technologies may provide more and better data to police, but that doesn't mean they only capture evidence that fits the prosecutors' narrative. The more clues that are available in general, the more that will be useful for the defense. For prosecutors with access to this amount of evidence, turning over all potentially impeaching or exculpatory material is a tough ask, especially when the systems were not designed to identify that information. One of the most obvious and unanswered praxis questions about new digital evidence is how process problems like these can be solved. Thinking through *Brady* issues before rolling out citywide systems or new identification technologies is a necessary first step.

PART III

Responses When Everything Is Evidence

10

Judicial Responses

Judges are the least obvious artists in our society. They may look like bureaucrats in robes, but underneath those robes are creative figures who paint with words. A judicial opinion begins on a blank canvas, onto which is sketched the structure of a story and an argument. The final image will be recognizable, borrowing as it does from other artists who came before, but the choices of color, depth, shading, and symbolism, even the mistakes evident in the brushwork, are the artist's own. Those less familiar with the craft of judging might see a judicial opinion as a fixed and perhaps inevitable distillation of set principles. But for those in the know, the work is as imaginative as any other art form—distilling a vision, yes, but one that could look very different in the hands of a different artist.[1] While judges may protest that they are "just following the law" or "just applying precedent," in truth they are no more bound by those constraints than a painter is bound by primary colors or types of paint. An opinion, especially about constitutional law, is always creative, contingent, and crafted.

When judges apply precedent from an analog era to cases involving digital evidence, the result, as we've seen, is a dramatic shift in power toward the government and away from citizens. But as artists, judges have the power to interpret the law around digital evidence differently. This chapter considers three ways judges should respond to Fourth Amendment questions in the digital age. The goal is to future-proof the Fourth Amendment so that it can effectively deal not only with today's digital surveillance threats, but also with those that have yet to be invented.

First, judges should internalize the fact that *digital is different*. For judges to address the constitutional gaps discussed throughout this book, they will need to recognize the distinctions between analog and digital technologies in terms of the evidence they allow police to collect and the ways they are able to use that evidence. Second, judges should upgrade the Fourth Amendment search doctrine. This chapter offers three theories I have developed to address smart data, persistent surveillance, and the harms of digital rummaging. Finally, judges should rethink the search warrant. As we've seen, the current understanding is that police can collect any evidence they want, provided they obtain a warrant for it. In the digital era, this reading of the Fourth Amendment practically invites police to engage in overbroad or invasive searches. Judges should consider whether some data should simply be off limits to police, no matter how useful it might be to an investigation.

Modernizing Fourth Amendment doctrine will require courage and creativity. Judges will need to be both artists and statesmen, channeling their inner John Adams by taking seriously the threat of tyrannical government oppression via digital surveillance. But if they are willing to internalize these shifts in perspective, there is nothing preventing them from implementing solutions right away.

Digital Is Different

If you are a judge tasked with figuring out how the Fourth Amendment should apply to geolocation (or any new surveillance technology), you won't find existing law much help. The text of the Fourth Amendment has not changed since 1791 and most of the Supreme Court cases that address surveillance date to the 1970s–1990s.[2] Think about what computers were like in the 1970s—huge, dumb, and low on storage space. They certainly did not fit in your pocket and let you order food to your door. The surveillance technology that centered *Katz v. United States*—the case that gave us the "reasonable expectation of privacy" test—involved a reel-to-reel tape recorder, that had to be manually affixed by FBI agents to the top of a coin-operated telephone booth and turned on and off before each recording.[3] Anyone born this century would need to consult the Internet (or an AI model) to even visualize what such a setup might look like. Technology has advanced considerably, but the law is still stuck in the disco era.

The cases discussed in this book have wrestled with how to apply Fourth Amendment analysis to a world of digital surveillance. One part of the puzzle is technological. Is a plane flying over a single backyard and taking a photograph the same thing as a "spy plane" flying over the entire city of Baltimore and recording everything below? Is tracking a suspect with a beeper during one trip the same thing as tracking Antoine Jones's car by GPS continuously for a month? The intuitive answer is no—they are different. But why are they different, and what does that mean for the Fourth Amendment?

The second part of the puzzle is about the capacities of humans versus digital systems. Any debate over new surveillance technologies must confront the question "Couldn't police do this before the technology was created?" Is an eighteen-month-long pole-camera surveillance operation the same as a stakeout involving human police officers? Is an automated facial recognition matching program the same as police officers reviewing a physical book of mugshots? Again, the intuitive answer is no, but why? What makes digital different as a constitutional matter?

As discussed in Chapter 7, automation, acceleration, accumulation, aggregation, accuracy, and actualization make surveillance technologies powerful tools for police. These tools don't just make policing more efficient or effective; they fundamentally alter the nature of police work.[4] In a digital era, police are performing a different act and getting a different result. The ability of these technologies to scale is different, too. Fourth Amendment law needs to respond to these differences.[5]

If judges accept that digital is different, they can reject analogies to out-of-date cases and think from first principles. In fact, they must—allowing a "future-proofed" Fourth Amendment, responsive to these changes, to emerge. The Supreme Court has already hinted at this possibility with its decisions in *Riley v. California*[6] and *Carpenter v. United States*.[7] The legal question in Carpenter—whether the government had violated Timothy Carpenter's reasonable expectation of privacy by acquiring cell site location information (CSLI) that revealed his location at the time of the robberies—could easily have been resolved following traditional precedent.[8] This was, in fact, Justice Anthony Kennedy's argument in dissent.[9] The CSLI records were shared with a third-party, private cellular provider, which shared them with the police. The evidence came from corporate records, not Timothy Carpenter's records, and they revealed not what he did in private, but where he went in public.

Following older Fourth Amendment cases, Carpenter should have lost under the third-party doctrine. Yet, the majority of the Supreme Court recognized that a technology that could track a person's movements in detail over a long period of time required a different Fourth Amendment response.[10] The logic behind the *Carpenter* decision involved many potential privacy threats that went beyond the facts of the case. After all, Carpenter's location data didn't actually expose many revealing or intimate details about his life. Instead, the Court focused on the potential for CSLI to act as a retrospective "time machine" and the danger this presented to everyone with a cell phone. The Supreme Court recognized that digital was different and creatively responded to the challenge.

Or compare how the district court and the *en banc* appellate court approached the Fourth Amendment harms in the Baltimore spy plane case. As discussed, community groups like the Leaders of a Beautiful Struggle sued to enjoin Baltimore's use of persistent surveillance planes, that recorded the entire city from above in twelve-hour bursts.[11] When the district court judge initially considered the case, he applied the analog Supreme Court precedent and refused to enjoin the PSP program. The *en banc* appellate court, however, recognized that there is a world of difference between flying a single plane over a single property to look into someone's backyard with one's own two eyes and flying multiple planes over an entire city, recording everything with the highest tech cameras available. The scale, scope, and privacy considerations in the latter case necessitated a different Fourth Amendment approach.[12]

The past need not control the digital future. If judges are to have any hope of addressing the problems of digital surveillance, we must first create space for a new understanding of what Fourth Amendment privacy means in the digital age.

Seeing a "Smart" Fourth Amendment

Recognizing that digital is different opens the door for courts to take a more modern Fourth Amendment approach. What should that approach look like in practice?

As discussed in Part I, our digital things, homes, bodies, papers, and likes are open to warrantless collection because private third parties mediate the digital communication or storage of our data and thus undermine a reasonable expectation of privacy. Similarly, our smart cities have become surveillance cities because there is little expectation of privacy from persistent sensor surveillance in public. As should now be clear, without such an expectation of privacy, the Fourth Amendment does not protect from such government sensorveillance. At the same time, these forms of evidence gathering entail obvious privacy harms. Accounting for these harms requires a new approach to the Fourth Amendment search doctrine. In the following three subsections, I offer three theories of how the Fourth Amendment can fit the digital age, focusing on smart data, persistent surveillance, and the harms of rummaging. The goal is to offer judges a different way to think through the puzzle of digital evidence.

Theory One: Smart Data and Informational Security

From a constitutional perspective, what types of data should require a warrant before collection? We know smart data emanating from the Internet of Things reveals very personal habits and patterns of daily life. Although it's exposed to third-party companies, the digital information from your home, wrist, or car is probably not something you expect to share with police or the FBI.

If you are a judge puzzling through a case regarding police access to a smartwatch, what does the Fourth Amendment protect? The physical watch? That's just a plastic band with a few computer chips inside. The data the watch collects is clearly where its real value lies for users and for prosecutors. But while the watch itself is clearly within the possession of the person wearing it, its data has been shared with a third party—otherwise, it wouldn't work as intended. What should we do about that third-party exposure? A Fourth Amendment that protected only "things" and not the data from those "things" would be fairly meaningless in a digital age. A Fourth Amendment that protected only information that had never been shared with third parties would also be fairly toothless. So, how should the Fourth Amendment apply to the personal data originating from smart things but mediated by third-party entities?[13]

The history of the Fourth Amendment offers some insight. If Thomas Jefferson had crumpled up an early draft of the Declaration of Independence and thrown it in the corner, what he would have cared about protecting were the words on the paper. The reason personal papers were so valuable in the eighteenth century—the reason they received specific protection in the Fourth Amendment—had nothing to do with the quality of the parchment, but with the thoughts and ideas reflected there. Similarly, the amendment's protection of the home was not about the physical walls providing shelter from the elements, but rather the private space within those walls, which allowed residents to attend to personal matters without fear of discovery. It has always been the information *inside* those constitutional interests of homes, persons, papers, or effects that the Fourth Amendment intends to secure from government collection.

Such a theory of informational security allows judges to respond to the problem of third-party data by focusing on the source of the data.[14] Under this theory, if police wish to collect the data from a smart device (such as a Wi-Fi-enabled air conditioner or a smart pacemaker), they must get a warrant to do so, just as they would need a warrant to search the actual device. In a digital world where "our" things are dependent on third-party technology to function, it is unreasonable to use that exposure to justify warrantless collection. By applying to homes, effects, persons, and papers, and their digital equivalents, the theory of informational security respects the limits of the Fourth Amendment text as well as its intent, which always been to protect information.[15]

As an example of how the theory of informational security would work in practice, consider a new car with the latest in vehicle telemetry. I happen to have a car like this, and I have a complicated relationship with it. It's modern and electric, and it has more sensors than any car I have ever owned. It is also spying on me, which is somewhat awkward given that I'm writing a book on self-surveillance. Because it is electric, my car keeps close tabs on where I am going and whether I have enough battery power to get back home. It remembers things, too. It knows what music I like (or at least what music my kids like) and records my driving patterns. It prompts me to confirm which soccer field I am driving my children to and has suggestions for how to minimize the time it will take to get there. If I wanted to rob a bank and use it as a getaway car, I would be in trouble, because the car's mapping technology is constantly collecting data and sharing it with the car company.

Under a traditional analysis, police would need a warrant to search inside my car and download the maps and driving history via the actual car computer. However, they would not need a warrant for the information I knowingly shared with the third-party car company (or the maps company, or the infotainment company). The theory of informational security would require police to obtain a warrant for the geolocational data from my car (my effect) even if the data also exists with the third party (the car company and anyone to whom they have sold the data). In other words, my car's data would be treated as a part of the car, even if it also lived in the cloud.

The theory of informational security finds support in many Fourth Amendment cases.[16] The protection of a suitcase is never about the outside shell, but what that shell contains, a logic extended to various containers (briefcases, backpacks, bags) under what's known as the "container search doctrine."[17] We require a warrant for containers because we protect what they hold. Similarly, bodily fluids are protected from unwarranted searches because of the information contained in the biological material. It's not like we want our urine back after a drug test; we just want the information in our body to have some constitutional protection. Accepting the logic of informational security is a good next step for judges faced with overseeing a Fourth Amendment update in a world of smart devices.

Theory Two: The Problem of Persistent Surveillance

The ubiquity and inescapabilty of sensors and cameras—those we carry in our own pockets, as well as those that watch us from atop streetlights and commercial buildings—also presents a problem for the Fourth Amendment. When a citywide video analytics system is always on and always tracking the people it "sees," it is hard to determine at what point the system meets the threshold for a "search" in Fourth Amendment terms. In finding that police acquisition of cellphone location data required a warrant, the Supreme Court in *Carpenter* reimagined the Fourth Amendment to protect against certain kinds of pervasive data-collecting systems. But what kinds? If you were a judge sitting down to evaluate citywide ALPR databases, or networked facial recognition systems, or smart city sensors, how would you know when a warrant is required?[18]

In my view, a judicial response to the problems of persistent surveillance would build on the reasoning in *Carpenter*, *Jones*, and *Riley*,[19] updating the Fourth Amendment to protect citizens against certain types of systemic surveillance technologies (like CSLI and GPS). This kind of "future-proofing" theory requires some difficult decision-making. It's easy (relatively speaking) to determine that the search of a home began when police officers crossed the literal threshold. It's much harder to determine the metaphorical threshold at which a surveillance technology becomes equally invasive. But drawing such lines is what judges do. And in *Carpenter*, *Jones*, and *Riley*, the Supreme Court identified several characteristics of pervasive surveillance technologies that judges might take into consideration when making these determinations.[20]

First, the Court has expressed concern with *aggregated* data collection. The harm of CSLI and GPS tracking involved the collection of disparate bits of information that, taken together, could reveal something deeply personal. For example, GPS data that regularly captured you stopping at the liquor store on the way to work, then returning home by way of two bars and a nightclub, might signal that you have an alcohol abuse problem. A late-night trip to a bar, followed by a few hours in an apartment that isn't your own, followed by a morning trip to a pharmacy could reveal an unplanned intimate encounter. In *Carpenter* and *Jones*, the Court recognized that the mosaic of our lives could be pieced together through digital clues. Surveillance systems that allow for the easy accumulation of this kind of data raise a Fourth Amendment concern.

Second, the Supreme Court expressed concern with *retrospective* search capabilities, which allow investigators to go back in time and search for clues. In *Carpenter*, the ability to track anyone caught in the digital net for weeks using CSLI was, in the Court's eyes, a dangerous power when unregulated. After all, police could investigate the travel patterns of anyone within the CSLI network—judges, journalists, ex-wives—because no warrant was required to query the data.[21]

Third, the Supreme Court recognized that the *scale* and *scope* of the system matter when evaluating surveillance harms. In two opinions, the Court used the term "too permeating surveillance" to describe the type of surveillance that would create a Fourth Amendment search problem.[22] While the Court did not define this term of art, large-scale video and sensor systems that capture the movements of people throughout a city seem to qualify. CSLI tracking captured almost everyone. GPS tracking captured almost everything. Both the scale and the scope troubled the Court.

In addition, the Court has long expressed concern about the government using its powers arbitrarily and recognized that warrant requirements can serve as an important check on these powers. Without judicial processes for regulating access to and use of data collection systems, these systems can easily be misused. And systems that allow for constant searching or unlimited access to information are especially ripe for abuse. After all, it would be quite tempting for government agents to use them to investigate hunches, satisfy curiosities, or target persons critical of the government. Judges faced with ruling on such systems should take into account whether these systems are *permeating* or *arbitrary*.[23]

Finally, the Supreme Court has recognized that the Fourth Amendment exists in part to protect other constitutional rights, including the rights to association, assembly, and free expression. Mass surveillance systems obviously chill these *associational* First Amendment protections. You are less likely to attend a protest against police brutality if the police are collecting personal data about all those who attend. In fact, even the threat of government access to your data can chill dissent or criticism of an authoritarian-minded government.

The closer a system of surveillance gets to creating aggregated, retrospective, permeating, arbitrary surveillance powers that impact associational freedoms, the more likely courts will find that the government acquisition of data from that system violates a reasonable expectation of privacy.[24] In other words, a police officer pulling data from such a system would be considered a search requiring a judicial warrant.

Under my future-proofing theory, facial recognition tracking with real-time identification would be the type of superpowered surveillance system that should require a warrant to access (assuming it should exist at all).[25] A citywide video analytics system that allows users to search for a particular person would yield *retrospective* insights about that person, *aggregate* data points to reveal information about who they are and what they do, and map their *associations*. Such a system would be *permeating* and could be used *arbitrarily*. For those reasons, any search through the stored database of images (that is, any attempt to match a face within the system) would require a judicial warrant.

On the other side of the continuum, a smart streetlight sensor that provides data about electrical use and traffic patterns might not require a warrant.[26] The information from the sensor is limited (with few aggregation problems) and, while retrospective, would not be permeating or revealing of associational details. Police might therefore be able to search the dataset without violating the Fourth Amendment. A network of smart streetlights, however, might be a different story, particularly if they had object recognition tracking capabilities (such as ALPR).

Judges tasked with determining whether a challenged surveillance system violates an expectation of privacy might consider the following five questions, which take the Supreme Court's factors into account:

1. Does the system collect data that can be aggregated to reveal patterns of daily life, or is the data siloed?
2. Is the surveillance "too permeating," or is it limited in scope?
3. Does the system allow for arbitrary data collection, or is it targeted to a person or place?
4. Does the system allow retrospective searches, or just ephemeral monitoring?
5. Does the surveillance impact associational freedoms?

Surveillance systems that are aggregating, permeating, arbitrary, or those that allow for retrospective searches that could chill associational freedoms would fall on the "search" side of the line, requiring a judicial warrant, because otherwise they would violate a reasonable expectation of privacy under the logic of *Carpenter* and *Jones*. If a system does not raise these concerns, police can use it without a warrant. In either case, these future-proofing principles allow judges to respond to the threat posed by new persistent surveillance technologies while remaining consistent with existing doctrine and Fourth Amendment theory.

Theory Three: Digital Rummaging

As might be evident by now, one of the difficulties in applying the Fourth Amendment's "reasonable expectation of privacy" analysis to the reality of ever-present digital surveillance is that our expectations are ill-defined. Everyone sort of knows that Google has access to our search history, but we still consider what we type into the search bar to be private.

In the face of this confusion, some legal scholars have offered suggestions about how to rethink the Fourth Amendment to better fit the problem of digital surveillance. One of the ideas I have championed has been to examine the harm of "rummaging."[27] As I define it, digital rummaging involves the harm of police searching through our personal data in an arbitrary, overbroad, intrusive, and embarrassing way, and which should be considered its own Fourth Amendment violation.[28]

Rummaging has been a key concern of the Fourth Amendment since it was drafted. After all, members of the Founding generation had experienced British customs agents going through their homes and barns and seizing what they pleased, all justified by general warrants and writs of assistance.[29] Early Fourth Amendment cases like *Boyd* directly acknowledged the harms of allowing government agents to rifle through personal papers as they had in the *Wilkes* and *Entick* cases in Great Britain.[30] As Chief Justice Roberts once wrote, it was this fear of rummaging that gave rise to the Fourth Amendment: "Our cases have recognized that the Fourth Amendment was the founding generation's response to the reviled "general warrants" and "writs of assistance" of the colonial era, which allowed British officers to *rummage* through homes in an unrestrained search for evidence of criminal activity."[31] In fact, one of the most consistent throughlines in constitutional interpretation from the Founding to the present day has been a concern about giving the government the power to rummage through things, papers, and homes—even to look for criminal activity.

For example, one way of understanding the "particularity requirement" in the Fourth Amendment's warrant clause ("particularly describing the place to be searched, and the persons or things to be seized")[32] is as an anti-rummaging rule. Even with a warrant, police must specifically describe what they are seeking and limit their search accordingly. Similarly, the search incident to arrest doctrine, which allows police to search a person or place after an arrest, has been interpreted to protect against rummaging, limiting the scope of the search to evidence directly connected to the crime of arrest and areas in the arrestee's immediate control.[33] Otherwise, as Judge Learned Hand once wrote, "After arresting a man in his house, to *rummage* at will among his papers in search of whatever will convict him, appears to us to be indistinguishable from what might be done under a general warrant;

indeed, the warrant would give more protection, for presumably it must be issued by a magistrate."[34] Other doctrines like the inventory search doctrine and the plain view doctrine are also cabined by a fear of rummaging.[35] Even in old-fashioned analog cases, judges raised the concern that police might justify a search on one basis (say, checking an arrestee's glove compartment for a weapon) only to look for other incriminating information outside the bounds of their suspicion.

In the digital age, government agents with broad legal authority to arbitrarily sift through our smart homes or locational data would be able to turn up a great deal of private information about us. Without a warrant requirement, this type of rummaging is very possible. In fact, this is one way of looking at the *Carpenter* case. Remember, if *Carpenter* had been decided the other way, police would have been able to sift through all of Carpenter's cell site location data without a warrant. Reshaping Fourth Amendment analysis to focus on rummaging rather than expectations of privacy would ask courts to consider whether the government was intruding into personal data arbitrarily and in an overbroad fashion.[36] If so, the police action would fail the rummaging test and violate the Fourth Amendment. A particularized warrant would mitigate fears of arbitrary, overbroad searching while allowing police to obtain the data necessary for their investigation.

A Fourth Amendment test that focuses on whether police have exceeded their power to sift through personal data may be easier to evaluate than one that requires divining societal expectations of privacy. The former focuses on government actions, whereas the latter is always a guessing game—where only judges (who are hardly representative of the general public) seem to know the answer. Best of all, the rummaging theory is more consistent with the original understanding of the Fourth Amendment. The fear of government agents going through our private things has remained constant from the Founding to the present day.

For judges, it might be liberating to have another Fourth Amendment test in their analytical tool kit to help them to think through the privacy harms of digital surveillance systems. An opposition to rummaging provides that principle, and it is well-grounded in Fourth Amendment history, case law, and theory.

A Substantive Fourth Amendment

New legal theories around informational security, persistent surveillance, and digital rummaging allow for a forward-looking judicial response to warrantless searches. But what about searches conducted with a judicially approved warrant? Are there any categories of data that should be secured against government collection under any circumstances?

As a matter of constitutional law, warrants that are unparticularized or overbroad are unreasonable, as are those issued without probable cause or unconnected to a crime. But as long as police can show probable cause of a crime and identify what in particular they want to search or seize, there is no category of evidence off limits to them. In almost all cases, a search with a warrant is considered reasonable because the process of getting the warrant makes it so.

My proposal here complicates this traditional analysis. It asks whether courts should consider another factor when determining the reasonableness of a search: the type of data sought. Perhaps a digitally aware Fourth Amendment will recognize that some intimate information cannot be obtained, even with a warrant, because it is too personal. After all, at the time of the Founding there was no way to collect information about what was happening inside a person's (literal) heart and use it against them. That's no longer the case.

Questions about substantive restrictions on police access to data create hard questions without good answers. As we've seen, personal data has been used to solve very serious crimes. Was solving those crimes worth using the data in that way? Should police be able to get access to our genetic secrets? What about our virtual diaries? Should police—even in dutiful pursuit of a criminal case—be able to listen to our bedroom conversations or extract the data from our smart beds? As the data trails of our lives get more personal and revealing, the question of whether certain kinds of information should be kept from police will only grow.

Unreasonableness and Warrants

In rethinking reasonableness, the first thing to remember is that for much of U.S. history, police could not obtain deeply personal information even if they wanted to. British customs agents might have wanted to watch what was happening in Sam Adams's Boston home, but they could not listen at his window without being noticed. They could not track his nighttime habits or monitor his heartbeat. Even if they could, and even if the agents believed such information would uncover evidence that Adams was committing a crime (treason, domestic violence, tax evasion), it is hard to imagine that an eighteenth-century judge would have approved a warrant allowing them to collect such private information.

Because of the practical limits on collecting personal data at the time the Bill of Rights was written, the Fourth Amendment is largely silent on what unreasonableness means beyond the requirement to get a warrant. Largely, but not completely. In addition to the rummaging harms just discussed, the Founders were quite concerned with protecting papers and the thoughts and ideas they contained.[37] While courts have moved away from the absolutist protection originally granted to papers, some aspects of those protections could and should be reimagined in the digital world.

Substantive Limits: Papers and Beyond

On what basis is the government entitled to everything you have written, or thought, or possessed, just because that information may reveal evidence of a crime? Stepping back, it seems odd that a group of Founding Fathers who very much distrusted government, and who worried about a government criminalizing their political speech, would carve out such a broad exception to privacy protections ("Oh, well, if you're investigating a violation of the law, of course you may read my diary about fomenting sedition"). It seems unlikely, too, that they would consider the idea that government authorities could snoop in their bedrooms or rummage through their desks anything other than an offense to civility and a betrayal of liberty.

To be clear, except for the Fourth Amendment's mention of "papers," there is little direct support for the idea that certain categories of evidence should be off-limits to the government. The strong protection that safeguarded Entick's and Wilkes's treasonous papers in the eighteenth century and John Boyd's papers covering up tax evasion in the nineteenth century has been hollowed out in the modern era. Papers—as the repository of so much criminal guilt—are no longer protected in absolute terms. Forbidding police from collecting them with a probable cause warrant would be a radical step, unlikely to gain favor in the courts today. And, of course, when police suspect they will uncover evidence of a crime, homes, effects, and persons are even less protected than papers.

At the same time, the status quo—which allows police to obtain all data with a warrant, no matter how private or secret—is also ripe for abuse. A world in which all searches of all datasets are allowed as long as police have a warrant is a world in which even our most intimate moments could be captured and revealed. For example, police investigating a woman suspected of seeking an abortion could—with a warrant—access smart video cameras in her home, read her virtual diary, access her period tracking app, and get her blood pressure and pulse readings from her smartwatch (or the digital equivalents). There has been an alleged "crime" and with a warrant, there is potential digital evidence to be uncovered—but there are also countervailing values that should make that warrant unreasonable.

Figuring out what those countervailing values are, and how to weigh them, requires going back to why papers were protected in the first place. The justification for a strong constitutional protection of papers turned on conceptions of privacy, property, and practicality. First, papers are filled with private thoughts, which are not less private simply because they've been memorialized in writing. As legal scholar Craig Bradley once reflected,

> The most private matters are one's own thoughts and the physical embodiment of those thoughts in the form of communications solely to oneself. These would include a diary, a reporter's notes of an interview or of a news event, and a doctor's tape recording of his or her thoughts and diagnoses following examination of a patient. Such matters, as long as they are not passed to another to read or transcribe, are nothing less than the record of one's own thinking and should be considered as private as the thoughts themselves. Whether they are kept for personal or business reasons is irrelevant. It is the individual's expectation of privacy which is at issue, not a judgment as to the nature of the thoughts.[38]

According to this logic, thoughts need not stay secret to be private. Communications with trusted loved ones and friends, or within certain legal or societal confidences, could remain just as secure.[39] Understanding the Fourth Amendment's protection of papers in this way would shield conversations, communications, and ideas from government inspection even when police believe that a person is involved in criminal activity. Again, a clear example of this principle in practice can be seen in *Wilkes* and *Entick*, both of which involved defendants literally in the process of publishing ideas that broke the law. In a famous dissent in *Warden v. Hayden*, Justice William O. Douglas wrote:

> Privacy involves the choice of the individual to disclose or to reveal what he believes, what he thinks, what he possesses. . . . Those who wrote the Bill of Rights believed that every individual needs both to communicate with others and to keep his affairs to himself. That dual aspect of privacy means that the individual should have the freedom to select for himself the time and circumstances when he will share his secrets with others and decide the extent of that sharing. This is his prerogative, not the States'.
>
> The Framers, who were as knowledgeable as we, knew what police surveillance meant and how the practice of rummaging through one's personal effects could destroy freedom.[40]

Justice Douglas did not win that argument, but as we think about how to protect papers—including digital papers—we should reflect on how the drafters of the Constitution would have felt about their letters and missives (many seditious) being subject to search.

The second justification for returning to a Founding-era understanding of the protection of papers centers on property. In eighteenth-century America, papers were considered a form of "dearest property"[41] that held a heightened position of importance. Legal scholar Morgan Cloud has artfully examined how modern courts have failed to see the content of private papers as a form of valuable property because courts (and all of us) have forgotten that "property," as defined by the influential Enlightenment philosopher John Locke, included liberties,[42] rights,[43] and the product of labor (including expressive labor).[44] Property was not just a thing or a place; it could also be intangible. Locke's conception of property matters because James Madison, the author of the Fourth Amendment, borrowed his ideas in crafting the constitutional text:[45]

> Madison embraced Locke's broad understanding of the nature of property. A man's ideas, beliefs, abilities, and the opportunity to exercise them were his most treasured property. For example, "a man has property in his opinions and the free communication of them," and also "has a property of peculiar value in his religious opinions, and in the profession and practice dictated by them." The "safety and liberty of his person" is "property very dear to him." And a "man is said to have a right to his property, he may be equally said to have a property in his rights."[46]

While this phrasing may sound a bit old-fashioned (it is old-fashioned), it is also quite revolutionary to see property as including ideas. Building on these insights yields a strong argument for disallowing the government to sift through papers considered to be expressive property.[47] As Professor Cloud concludes, "Madison emphasized that the most important kinds of property government must protect were not tangible things, but rather a person's thoughts, opinions, and rights."[48]

Finally, as to practicality, the reality is that police cannot uncover incriminating materials in papers without also reviewing innocent materials.[49] If you're looking for a gun in someone's glove compartment, you don't need to go through the wallet they also keep there. But if you're looking for evidence in someone's personal diary, you won't know which entries are relevant to the investigation without reading (or at least skimming) all of them. As the *Wilkes* court recognized "some papers, quite innocent in themselves, might, by the slightest alteration, be converted to criminal action."[50] The concern was that in searching through papers, police might incidentally (or intentionally) discover other incriminating evidence.[51] Remember, Wilkes and Entick actually were guilty of sedition, and yet the courts rejected the searches into their papers despite the likelihood that evidence would be found there.

These arguments still hold weight. At a minimum, the Fourth Amendment should offer some substantive protection against searches of digital papers that reveal ideas that are deeply personal, political, or religious in nature. This idea tracks back to *Entick* and *Wilkes* but expands the protection of papers to include those that cover personal matters, not just political ones. Of course, some of those ideas might be criminal, heretical, dangerous, or treasonous. But as ideas—expressed on paper or in digital form—they should remain out of the government's reach, even with a probable cause warrant. A sympathetic case might involve a teenager's diary idealizing youthful rebellion. A less sympathetic case might involve a madman's manifesto ideating mass murder. Because the definition of digital papers can be expanded to include health data, family data, and other personal information, courts could expand this substantive Fourth Amendment protection to cover certain private details captured by our smart devices.

My suggested test—such as it is—simply adds a substantive step to the Fourth Amendment warrant process. In addition to ensuring that a warrant complied with the requirements of probable cause, particularity, oath, and so on, a judge would also have to conduct a substantive reasonableness analysis. In performing this analysis, the judge would have to evaluate whether the sought-after data was too private for police to access, a category that would include digital papers involving beliefs, health, family, or other personal views. For example, in the insurance fraud case where police sought data from a suspect's smart pacemaker, a judge might look at the kind of information that was being requested and reject it as unreasonable—despite being provided probable cause that a crime had occurred and that the smart heart data might be evidence of that crime. In a case involving the mental health of a murder suspect, a judge might reject prosecutorial access to a mental health app, even given probable cause that information about the suspect's *mens rea* (mental state) would be found there.

As a final example, recall David Riley and the incriminating photos found on his smartphone incident to arrest. In the *Riley* case, the Supreme Court held that searching the smartphone required a warrant because of the quantitatively and qualitatively "different" nature of information that can be found on smartphones. It was a win for David Riley, but it's important to remember that if police had simply taken the time to get a warrant—which, with the evidence they already had against Riley, would not have been difficult—he would have had no good way to contest the search, despite how invasive it was.

I propose adding another step to this process, requiring the judge approving the warrant to consider whether searching through the collected photos and images of this young man's life is reasonable in the face of the suspected crime. Consider the photos on your phone. What do they reveal about you? Your birthday party, your college friends, your weekly soccer matches, your nights at the bar, your flirtatious selfies, all tagged with date, time, and location—together, these images offer a detailed portrait of your life to anyone who views them. Out of thousands of photos, a few might reveal incriminating information, but is it reasonable to expose all the others to get at that information? The answer to that question might be yes, but it is an important question to ask, and judges can do so without any change in the doctrine. After all, by signing the warrant, judges are implicitly stating the search is reasonable. Adding this substantive step would merely require that implicit determination of reasonableness to be augmented by explicit written findings. In a *Riley*-like situation, a judge would have had to agree that the privacy harm of exposing thousands of innocent photographs is worth potentially finding evidence of illegal gun possession.

There are two benefits of adding a substantive reasonableness determination to the warrant approval process. First, the rule would require a court to balance the government's request against the individual's interest. Even in cases where the individual loses the balancing test of reasonableness, the process would provide some protection. Second, in a select few cases, judges will be able to reject a warrant as requesting digital information that is too personal or papers that are too private. The point is that if substantive reasonableness is accepted as a limiting principle, then in order to get a warrant, the government will need to articulate a reason (besides that a crime was committed) for accessing otherwise private information.

The drawback of this substantive test is obvious: Good evidence about bad acts will be kept from government investigators. In almost every mass shooting, the perpetrator leaves behind some diatribe of hate and ignorance explaining why they felt justified to do their horrible act. This rule might limit access to such expressions of hate if finding them required investigators to read through a shooter's digital diary entries. It would not limit access to all digital clues (manifestos posted publicly online, for example, would still be available to investigators), but it might preclude investigations of pure belief (no matter how inculpatory). The rule might also preclude automatic access to digital information about physical and mental health or other intimate information not directly connected to the crime. Digital clues might exist, but a court should not grant access to them until prosecutors have proven a nexus to the crime and offered a reasonable justification for reviewing such personal data. Just because someone has committed a crime does not mean their entire digital life should be exposed.

Courts willing to impose a substantive limit on government access to digital papers and personal data must be willing to accept that some evidence will be lost. Ideas that might help prove a suspect's guilt, even confessions or incriminating photos, will not be able to be obtained, even with a warrant. Without access to a mass shooter's diary, for example, prosecutors might not be able to prove that the shooting was a hate crime. But the history of the Fourth Amendment makes clear that just because something is available does not mean it should be in the government's hands. A rule requiring a substantive determination of reasonableness would help bring that logic into the digital age.

A Judge's Task

Judges are not technologists, and many do not have the time or inclination to rethink foundational theories of constitutional law. Yet, without a judicial response to a world where everything is evidence, the Fourth Amendment, and therefore our individual rights, will continue to weaken as digital surveillance intensifies. It is not beyond the role of judges to ask how the Fourth Amendment should apply to new forms of data collection and surveillance. We need answers to questions about whether digital is different and how to think about smart data, persistent surveillance, and digital rummaging harms. Judges have the artistic tools and legal talents to make the Fourth Amendment fit the digital age. They just need to sketch out a response.

11

Legislative Responses

When it comes to data privacy, constitutional law provides the floor, but it is the responsibility of legislatures to build on that floor. The previous chapter detailed the minimum constitutional protection digital evidence should receive, not the maximum statutory protection it could receive. And indeed, legislatures have passed numerous laws in response to court rulings or ambiguities in existing Fourth Amendment law. The Wiretap Act was a federal response to the *Katz v. United States* decision, which protected against police collection of private telephone conversations.[1] The Electronic Communications Privacy Act (ECPA) addressed the electronic communications that fell outside the Wiretap Act.[2] Other federal laws like the Health Insurance Portability and Accountability Act (HIPAA) and the Genetic Information Nondiscrimination Act (GINA) have added protections around certain types of data.[3] Simply stated, Congress has a great deal of power to prevent the government from gaining access to personal data—if it chooses to do so.

Unfortunately, the legislative efforts so far don't inspire a great deal of confidence. A comprehensive federal privacy law giving consumers the right to their personal data would solve many of the problems set forth in this book. Europe's General Data Protection Regulation (GDPR) and the European Law Enforcement Directive offers potential models for such legislation, but they have not been adopted beyond the European Union.[4] As of 2025, several U.S. states have passed laws addressing data privacy, data protection, or data security, but these laws have tackled only a small part of the problem.[5] This is not entirely the fault of legislators. Conceptualizing digital rights is hard, and sometimes the project of securing them feels overwhelming, encompassing debates about governmental data collection, corporate surveillance capitalism, and the global commoditization of our lived experiences though data. More importantly for our purposes, all the existing data protection laws carve out exceptions for law enforcement access, making even the strongest of them unresponsive to the concerns discussed in this book.

My goal in this chapter, therefore, is to focus not on legislating *data* as a whole, but on legislating *digital evidence*—a problem that can be solved much more straightforwardly. At a minimum, legislation can keep everything from becoming evidence that can be used against us in court. Governments can limit their own power to collect, purchase, or use the data that exists about each of us. Legislators can require warrants, policies, audits, or any other check they see fit to adopt. They can even enact a wholesale ban on governmental use of a particular technology if they desire; there is no countervailing right of the police to surveil you. The federal government can limit federal law enforcement authorities by statute and can condition state and local grants of federal funds on following the same rules. State governments can similarly limit state police to certain categories of evidence by statute.[6] The chapter addresses how we should think about government access to digital evidence by proposing two alternatives—one weak and one strong. Both are preferable to the status quo and offer realistic pathways for adoption.

None of the rules I propose would affect the ability of private companies to collect data. In theory, the most absurd extremes of surveillance capitalism can coexist with a strict ban on police use of captured data in court. We could live in a world where Google still knows all your secrets but the police could never legally get access to them. Before exploring what such laws might look like, let's take a moment to digest the underlying point—one that runs counter to our current assumptions about police power, data collection, and privacy. With legislative action, society could have unfettered digital innovation *and* protection from government misuse or abuse of the data produced by that innovation. There is no reason the data we produce must be available to police and prosecutors. That is just the present reality in the absence of legislation or clear constitutional protection. We can embrace both digital tools and digital privacy.

Of course, there is a reason that legislators—even those concerned with growing digital surveillance—default to granting law enforcement access to data. Data helps solve crimes, which most legislators want to do. Balancing personal privacy with the need to collect evidence for criminal prosecution is a significant challenge, especially when there are real victims demanding accountability. But it is the job of legislatures—representative, legitimate, diverse bodies of decision-makers—to perform these balancing acts, taking the collective and contested interests of the community into account. Presently, however, they do not seem up to the job, so until they are willing take up that challenge, I've taken the liberty of offering my own suggestions.

A Weak WALL to Protect Personal Data

This book is filled with stories of police using digital tools to solve cases of murder, arson, and sexual assault, and other serious crimes. Assuming we want police to keep catching folks who harm others, we need to allow them to acquire at least some digital evidence. But assuming the current status quo—in which our digital data is protected either not at all or solely by judicial warrant—is insufficient, we need to create ground rules that place limits on data acquisition by the police. Those limits must be defined legislatively.

One option would be to draft a law allowing police access to private data with restrictions. The easiest parallel for this kind of "weak" regulation is the Title III Wiretap Act of 1968.[7] Wiretaps are very invasive surveillance technologies that allow police to listen to the conversations inside your home. In fact, they share many similarities with digital mass surveillance—including the danger of unregulated collection and law enforcement abuse, paired with real utility for evidence collection. In his book *The Listeners: A History of Wiretapping in the United States*, Brian Hochman makes the case that the historical battles around wiretaps, which pitted privacy concerns against corporate surveillance and government spying, can help inform today's debates about government surveillance in all its forms.[8] But as Hochman points out, while the Wiretap Act of 1968 did place clear restrictions on law enforcement use of the technology, it was a decidedly law-and-order statute that permitted police to use invasive surveillance techniques so long as certain procedures were followed.[9]

The rules governing modern wiretaps impose real procedural and substantive limits on the practice.[10] With limited exceptions, wiretaps are allowed to be used only to investigate specific serious felonies.[11] Before obtaining a wiretap, investigators must show that there is no other way for them to get the needed information,[12] and they must submit a formal and written Wiretap Act warrant application to a federal judge for preapproval.[13] They must establish probable cause that the wiretap will reveal information related to a criminal case.[14] They must delimit the scope, time, and targets of the surveillance.[15] They must minimize unintended collection of personal data from the target and their interlocutors, and from anyone else who uses the phone.[16] They must report back to the judge who signed the probable cause warrant on the success or failure of their collection.[17] Finally, they must regularly publish a public report disclosing the frequency of wiretap requests.[18] The report is published on the U.S. Courts website each year.[19]

Distilled to its idealized core, the Wiretap Act model of legislation imposes the following seven restrictions on police capture and use of surveillance data: (1) use limits (applicable to only certain types of serious cases); (2) exhaustion limits (there must be no other way to obtain the information); (3) justification limits (probable cause plus particularity); (4) notice limits (written documentation and accountability); (5) scope limits (specificity as to timing and subject matter); (6) minimization limits (reducing collection by subject matter and target identity); and (7) transparency limits (public accounting). These rules recognize the inherent privacy harm of this type of surveillance and raise a legislative barrier preventing unfettered access to personal information. In addition, the statutory check has the added benefit of involving all three branches of government: The legislative branch writes the limits; the judicial branch approves the limits; and the executive branch honors the limits.

The model I propose would apply those core limits to all police requests for personal information, whether derived from consumer data or from government surveillance. I call it a Wiretap Act-Like Law ("WALL"). A statutory WALL would be more restrictive than the status quo, but not so onerous as to be rendered unusable. From a privacy perspective, this legislative proposal still creates real concerns, but it also mitigates the worst abuses. WALL is a compromise, an attempt to balance competing interests, with all the inherent tension that implies.

Applying this proposed WALL framework to consumer data and policing data in turn demonstrates that a legislative response to surveillance can work—while also suggesting that different sources of information might require slightly different rules governing access.

WALL and Consumer Surveillance Data

Imagine the police believe an individual, Johnny Smith, is distributing oxycontin, a legal but addictive narcotic, illegal to resell. Smith came to the attention of police after an informant's tip. However, a pharmaceutical database also reveals an unusual number of prescriptions were filled using his cell phone number. Although different names were attached to the prescriptions, the fact that they all listed the same phone number was suspicious. In addition, each of the smart pill bottles that contained oxycontin had been opened frequently, which is consistent with drug abuse or distribution. Police arrest Johnny Smith with a month's worth of legally prescribed oxycontin but want to pursue criminal drug distribution charges based on the digital evidence they uncovered. The government's theory of the case is that the database of prescription purchases and the digital clues from the smart pill bottles reveal that Smith was not taking the oxycontin as intended, but rather fraudulently acquiring prescriptions under various names in order to sell the pills.

Under the status quo, all the prescription and smart pill data would be available to police without a warrant. There is no federal law preventing police access to a private prescription pharmaceutical database, and lower courts have found no Fourth Amendment protection in statewide prescription databases—which means police can get access to information about the medicines you're taking to treat your addiction or anxiety disorder without much difficulty.[20] The data from the smart pill bottle is not protected by federal law or the Constitution because it has been shared with a third-party provider. And, even if the third-party problem weren't in play, police would have a suspect and an alleged crime, so obtaining a judicial warrant for that data would not be difficult.

Requiring a WALL warrant would limit police access to the prescription database and the data from the smart pill bottle without precluding it entirely. Following the seven Wiretap Act considerations discussed above, we can see how the requirement to obtain a WALL warrant would change the case against Johnny Smith.

Use Limits: First, the use of personal data would be narrowed to certain types of cases. If WALL warrants were limited to serious *violent* felonies, police would not be able access the prescription information in the oxycontin case. If you expanded the scope to serious felonies, the oxycontin distribution case might be pursued, but an oxycontin possession case (a misdemeanor in most jurisdictions) would not be. If I were writing the law to create WALLs, I would limit their use to serious violent felonies, especially given that police and prosecutors often have a loose interpretation of "serious." This is not to say that illegal oxycontin distribution is not important just that the benefit of stopping it does not outweigh the harm of giving police too much power to expose our digital trails.

Exhaustion Limits: Exhaustion limits would perhaps be the biggest change from the status quo. Under the Wiretap Act, agents must explain "whether or not other investigative procedures have been tried and failed or why they reasonably appear to be unlikely to succeed if tried or to be too dangerous."[21] In the WALL context, this would mean police would have to explain why other more traditional investigative methods failed before resorting to digital searches. Data grabs would be the last resort for police, rather than their typical first stop, which would force police to investigate as they did before digital clues existed. In the drug case, for example, police could have relied on numerous traditional methods that exist for investigating oxycontin distribution, like talking to witnesses or checking surveillance tapes at the pharmacies to see who picked up the prescriptions.

Justification Limits: The requirement of probable cause would also serve as a limiting factor. Articulating probable cause requires identifying three distinct proofs. First, police must demonstrate a nexus—a close connection—between the person and the alleged crime (individualization). Second, police must demonstrate a nexus between the crime and the evidence they seek (particularity). Finally, police must make sure the request is not overbroad. The probable cause requirement necessarily limits what can be searched or seized. For example, the police would be hard-pressed to uncover all suspicious sales at a store, or all drug refills of any kind unrelated to their particularized suspicions about oxycontin and Johnny Smith.

Notice Limits: A WALL would require a formal written warrant, adding elements of solemnity, requiring police to sign an oath, and saving a record of the request. These are minor differences compared to normal warrants, but they are still important because they provide notice to the target that surveillance has occurred and memorialize these types of government actions. Without such a process, police would be free to search pharmaceutical databases, or rummage through any other digital trails on a whim. Resource constraints might keep police from abusing the process too frequently—but they might not, or not always. With a warrant, police are held accountable both before the search, when they obtain the warrant, and after the search, when they return the warrant to the judge. These forms of notice are valuable because they restrain police use of otherwise easy-to-access datasets.

Scope Limits: A WALL warrant would require that requests for data be as narrow as possible, reflecting the particularity of probable cause. Like the Wiretap Act, which requires a "particular description" of both the "nature and location of the facilities from which or the place where the communication is to be intercepted" and "the type of communications sought," the WALL warrant would need to be specific about the data sought.[22] Searches would be limited by time and content and targeted to particular places or devices. Prescription data may not be fully analogous to voices on a wiretap, but in both cases it is imperative to only collect what you need, and nothing more.

Minimization Limits: Minimization is another big difference between a wiretap warrant and a traditional warrant. The minimization requirement acknowledges at the outset that the form of surveillance in question is inherently overbroad, invasive, and violative of other people's rights. For example, wiretapping a target's home is going to mean hearing voices of family members who are not the target. It's the same with personal data. When accessing a prescription database, agents might uncover potentially illegal prescriptions written to other customers who are not targets of the surveillance. Or, perhaps Johnny Smith's secret heath issues will come to light. Requiring police to delete data not responsive to their inquiry and data recovered outside the scope of the warrant is one way to protect information in such databases from overcollection and misuse.

Transparency Limits: Finally, just as wiretaps must be publicly disclosed and accounted for by the government, so would WALL warrants. Every year, a public report counts each instance of Title III surveillance, which includes wiretaps, cataloging the length and method of surveillance. The goal is to provide a check on the potential abuse of this invasive surveillance technique. And indeed, one result of the public reporting mechanism is to keep the overall number of wiretaps relatively low (for example, 2245 in 2021).[23] The same kind of public reporting can happen with WALL warrants, recording the number and nature of the requests and the legal basis for the surveillance.

WALL offers a workable legislative response to the growing bounty of consumer data that might be helpful for police investigations. In the absence of constitutional limits or self-regulation by technology companies, the best way to balance the needs of police with individual privacy is a federal or state statute modeled on the Wiretap Act. While not perfect, and perhaps not sufficient, this compromise is straightforward and could be applied to data arising from our smart things, smart homes, smart bodies, and social media posts. WALL would also work for searches of computers, tablets, and smartphones. And with WALL warrants protecting personal data from police acquisition, the Fourth Amendment debates about expectations of privacy, third-party data, reasonableness, and other legal uncertainties surrounding digital evidence could be largely set aside.

WALL and Government Surveillance Data

Laws can also restrict the use of data from government surveillance technologies, whether these are cutting-edge smart city systems or more ordinary police technologies like ALPRs, Real-Time Crime Centers, or drones. The federal government can always limit its own ability to collect and use surveillance data, and because so many states rely on federal funding for law enforcement, Congress can condition grants on following federal rules.[24]

This section explores how a WALL statute would limit police use of surveillance technology. As we'll see, the WALL proposal works well when talking about retrospective investigatory searches—but less well when the government is in the business of real-time monitoring.

Imagine that Johnny Smith—our oxycontin dealer—was caught on a surveillance camera handing some pills to an individual in return for cash. Police take a still photograph and want to run it through a facial recognition system to find the suspect's identity. There is currently no federal or state law forbidding this process. Police can run any face through a police database of images—sometimes including the state

DMV dataset that contains your photo—for any reason.[25] A WALL statute for facial recognition matching systems would limit this investigative use, once again borrowing from the logic of the Wiretap Act to craft statutory limits around use, exhaustion, justification, notice, scope, minimization, and transparency. The focus here is on facial recognition, but this statutory framework could apply to any investigative search into a police database, whether it contains retrospective ALPR data, video surveillance footage, smart sensor data, or stored drone footage.

Use Limits: Facial recognition is a powerful technology, and its use could be limited by the severity of the crime being investigated. If a crime did not meet a particular threshold (whether that threshold was set at a serious violent felony, a serious felony, or any felony), facial recognition would be disallowed. A framework that restricted use of facial recognition to the most serious violent crimes would prevent the technology from being used to identify Johnny Smith. Drug dealing may not rise to the level of severity that would justify using a technology that so seriously erodes our privacy. The same logic might preclude a search through a video analytics system to capture footage of the hand-to-hand deal, or other invasive data dives.

Exhaustion Limits: A second barrier might be exhaustion limits. Police have a photograph of their suspect at a particular location. There are many ways they could investigate his identity—showing his photograph to shop owners in the vicinity of the alleged drug deal, for example. Facial recognition is far from the only option, but it might well be the easiest one, which makes the exhaustion limit especially important. Any photograph can be used to identify anyone in the database. Without exhaustion limits, police might simply run every photograph they capture through the system because the process is so effortless. A WALL-like system that requires exhaustion attempts via traditional investigatory means might limit police reliance on the technology.

Justification Limits: Probable cause exists to run Johnny Smith's name through the facial recognition system. Police can articulate their rational belief that the transaction observed was a drug transaction and thus a crime. Probable cause is a low standard, and the apparent transfer of pills for cash, while possibly innocent, is likely enough to suggest a crime may have occurred and thus meet that standard. One can easily imagine a judge signing a warrant to allow this facial recognition search.

But imagine that instead of running the photo of *the suspect* through the facial recognition system, police wanted to run the face of an *innocent bystander*. This potential witness would be helpful to speak with, and facial recognition could provide a clue to her identity. In a situation where no law prevented use of facial recognition, police could run the face and find the name of the bystander (or anyone else). However, with a probable cause standard, police would be prohibited from using the technology to find the witness because there is no reason to believe she committed a crime. In this case, probable cause would be a barrier to this overbroad search.

Notice Limits: The formal notice process parallels a traditional wiretap warrant, requiring a written, sworn statement. Again, while this formal warrant will not be an issue for police investigating Johnny Smith, it would be an issue if they wished to use facial recognition to identify the witness. If they are required to write down their probable cause, swear to it, and submit it to a judge, police will not be able to make the requisite finding that the witness was involved in criminal activity, and thus facial recognition could not be used.

Scope Limits: In the context of facial recognition, scope limitations may not have much impact. Generally, the request is to search through a particular facial recognition database (such as DMV records, arrest records, or social media) with the understanding that the search will be relatively limited in time, place, and focus. Facial recognition datasets are limited in content and generally unrevealing—unlike, say, a geolocational search, which might expose someone's secret associations and thus should be carefully cabined by time, place, and content. The scope would need to be addressed in the warrant, but likely would not cause any issues. On the other hand, if police were seeking access to the city's video analytics system in order to find video evidence of the hand-to-hand transaction (or perhaps other drug deals), then scope might matter. Legislatures could require that police narrow their request to look through citywide footage to a particular time or place or person. Again, the bar is not high. A judge would have little concern signing off on a warrant requesting to look at a specific location of the city around the time the suspect had been observed.

Minimization Limits: Because the content of the information in a facial recognition database does not reveal much more than identity, minimization practices should be considered but might not be an issue. Of course, if police wanted to search a database of geolocation information or the collected video in a Real-Time Crime Center, the situation would be different, because such a search could expose a significant portion of the lived experience of the target and others represented in the database. In that case, minimization requirements would be necessary.

Transparency Limits: Finally, publicly disclosing the number of times facial recognition technology is used, the types of cases in which it is used, and the results is an important step for transparency. At some regular interval, police should be required to explain their practices and provide an accounting of their successes or failures with a particular technology.

Legislative Checks on Mass Monitoring

The digital technologies used for police investigation inevitably collect more information than needed. And when it comes to surveillance technologies that monitor the streets in real time (like video analytics or ALPR), WALL warrants—or any warrants—are of little use. Because the searches are constant and continuous, there is no opportunity to go to a judge for approval beforehand. ALPRs automatically alert for an identified license plate.[26] Video analytics systems detect anomalies without any human intervention or approval.[27] These technologies turn everything into potential evidence, without any check on the process. A WALL warrant might provide added protection in cases where police want to introduce evidence drawn from a monitoring system, but a broader legislative response is required.

One way for legislatures to check mass monitoring systems would be to make sure they are thoroughly vetted and debated before installation. As Barry Friedman and Maria Ponomarenko have explained, policing technologies should not be implemented without democratic accountability.[28] Buying an ALPR or Real-Time Crime Center is a democratic choice. Someone used tax dollars to buy a camera system and pay the digital storage bill. That someone (or group of someones) is usually either directly or indirectly accountable to voters. It might be the city council, or a chief of police appointed by the mayor, or a federal law enforcement agency overseen by Congress. The problem is that most of these procurement decisions do not require public approval.[29] For decades, society has deferred to police to buy whatever surveillance toys they desired without any process for vetting the technology.[30]

At a minimum, legislation should require public approval of public surveillance technologies. Such laws already exist in dozens of jurisdictions. For example, the ACLU has been involved in a national campaign to require Community Control Over Police Surveillance (CCOPS) statutes, which give citizens an opportunity to learn about the technology under consideration and weigh in on its approval.[31] CCOPS statutes also provide governments with information about the technologies they are purchasing. Without a public feedback and approval mechanism, even local politicians may be unaware of the technologies being used, or their costs.

Systems of democratic accountability can also involve a deeper investigation into the technology. For example, legislation can require audits focused on civil rights, civil liberties, privacy, and racial justice risks to be conducted before and after a technology is adopted. Facial recognition systems can be audited for racial bias. ALPRs can be audited for error. Video analytics technology can be audited to check the assumptions behind their anomaly detection alerts. All of this can be done via the legislative process.

Democratic accountability and transparency alone, however, may not provide an adequate check on constantly monitoring surveillance technologies. Democratic appeals to safety are often the driver of surveillance, not a mechanism to limit it. After all, most existing surveillance systems—from drones to ALPR—have been implemented with public knowledge and implicit democratic support. For this reason, and for reasons that I'll elaborate below, a more absolutist legislative prohibition on new surveillance technologies may be required.

A Strong Legislative Limit

Walls are great for keeping things out, but they're not foolproof. You can always go over a wall, or around it, or knock it down. Sometimes it is better to address a threat directly than try to build a wall against it. The ability of police to access digital clues from commercial and public sources presents a grave threat to privacy and liberty, and the protection provided by a legislative WALL compromise may be too weak. Again, if one of the primary concerns about your data being used against you is that the government can access all of our data just by getting a judicial warrant, imposing a slightly stronger warrant requirement is not a satisfying solution.

Four limitations of the WALL approach suggest the need for a stronger, more absolute form of legislative protection for personal data. One is that wiretaps themselves have been abused, and the narrow scope of their original use has been expanded over time. As just one example, the definition of "serious felony" that was meant to confine the use of wiretaps to only a small number of crimes has been broadened to include many, many more crimes, undercutting the notion that wiretaps are saved for the worst of the worst.[32] Such definitional limits can easily expand in response to political pressures.

A second limitation is that use restrictions do not do anything to stop systems of data monitoring. Requiring a warrant to search for a car in a video analytics system offers some level of protection, but it assumes that the system of surveillance exists and has collected video of the car. Once you have built the architecture of surveillance (even with use limits baked in), it is hard to go back. From a privacy perspective, it would be safer to not build a citywide camera system in the first place.

A third limitation has to do with power. As we've seen, the definition of crime shifts over time. Once you have built a system of surveillance, you are at the mercy of those in power and however they choose to define "crime." Today, protest is allowed: Tomorrow, protest is criminalized. Today, the unhoused are treated with empathy: Tomorrow they are targets for prosecution. The footage of the protesters or people in need exists regardless. How, and whether, it's used is entirely dependent on the politics of who is enforcing the criminal laws.

Finally, sometimes people mess up and fall prey to corruption. Systems fail to do what they promised. The history of police technology is a history of scandal, error, and abuse. Things go wrong all the time, and if the past is prologue, they will still go wrong with a WALL system in place.

Strong Legislative Prohibitions

A strong version of a legislative response to surveillance would involve walling off entire areas of data collection from police use. For example, just as HIPAA protects health data from being shared or resold (although it does allow access by law enforcement), a data privacy law for health information might forbid police from using data from a smart pacemaker or smart pill bottle in court at all. Similarly, a ban on police use of geolocational data as evidence would allow you to use Google Maps without worrying that it could be used as evidence against you in a criminal case. Almost any of the digital clues discussed in Part I could be kept out of the hands of police and prosecutors if legislatures so desired. There is nothing stopping Congress or a state from banning law enforcement use of video analytics technology or drones or spy planes as evidence in court.

Enacting a strong legislative prohibition on certain forms of surveillance evidence may be politically challenging, but proposing it at least forces a conversation about the appropriate balance between enabling prosecution and protecting privacy. Allowing police 24/7 virtual access to a video camera system inside a home might help solve a murder, but it would also reveal everything else that happened there. If we were forced to choose between either granting police virtual access to every home because doing so might one day catch a murderer or denying police such access, knowing that a murderer might get away with the crime, it's not at all obvious that we would choose the surveillance. We might decide that the privacy invasion is too great, even if it means some crimes go unsolved. Facial recognition is another technology that, on balance, we might choose to ban in criminal cases. Maintaining our sense of autonomy and liberty, not to mention our values of free association and dissent, requires a level of anonymity (even in public). Facial recognition at a mass scale destroys any ability to exist free from government oversight. Again, the fact that we invented a technology doesn't mean that we must use it for criminal prosecution.

A strong legislative response would ban police from using certain technologies and forbid use of certain private data in court. The cost to law enforcement and criminal prosecution of such an approach would not be insignificant, but that cost must be balanced with other concerns—including the fear that new technological power will be abused by those in power.

A Digital Communications Privilege

Another strong legislative response might involve the creation of an evidentiary privilege. Evidentiary privileges arise from statutory law and create strong prohibitions against using certain information in court.[33] Privileges can be topical or based around certain valuable communications.[34] The three best-known communications privileges are attorney-client privilege, spousal communications privilege, and the Fifth Amendment's privilege against self-incrimination.

These privileges generally protect private communications. Often, those communications reveal facts of a crime (which is why the prosecutor wants to introduce them at trial). Despite their usefulness to prosecutors, the Federal Rules of Evidence and state laws protect those communications because of other countervailing societal values. Essentially, lawmakers made an *ex ante* judgment that it is more important for spouses to be able to speak freely to each other during their marriage than for the government to be able to use evidence from their conversations in court. The same holds for lawyers. If, for example, a criminal defendant admits her guilt to her defense lawyer, that communication cannot be obtained by the prosecution. A confession of guilt would be quite useful in proving guilt at trial, but protecting the attorney-client privilege is more important. Prosecution does not overcome privacy in all situations.

A digital communications privilege could bar certain forms of data from being used in court. As with other more traditional state evidentiary privileges (doctor-patient privilege, journalist-source privilege, priest-penitent privilege, psychologist-client privilege), a space could be carved out to protect digital data from becoming inculpatory evidence.

How would such a privilege work?

When I began thinking through this question years ago, I thought a new evidentiary privilege best paralleled the self-incrimination clause and the line of cases arising from the Fifth Amendment, which have held that we are not required to testify against ourselves in a court of law. To my thinking, if my smart heartbeat created a digital trail that was used against me in court, that seemed like self-incrimination deserving of protection. Similarly, if I wrote an electronic diary entry intended only for myself, even if I saved it to the cloud, that felt private enough that use of it against me in court seemed like a Self-Incrimination Clause problem. It was not a bad theory, but it has one problem: The Supreme Court has only protected "testimonial" statements under the Fifth Amendment.[35] "Testimonial" here refers to a kind of statement, like sworn testimony, given under coercive governmental pressure.[36] The government had nothing to do with compelling you to reveal your heartbeat to your smart device or your diary to the cloud, so both would fall outside of the privilege. Without a broader rethinking of the testimonial line of cases, the tell-tale heartbeat would not be considered self-incriminating.

I was puzzling through this question during a classroom discussion one day when a student named Matt W. piped up. One of the best parts of being a law professor is the students, who sometimes come up with insights that change the way you think. As we worked through my privileges theory, Matt W. commented that he felt like he was *communicating* with his digital devices. His smartphone was like a close friend whom he trusted with his secrets and questions, and who constantly provided him with information. He was communicating health data to his smartwatch, which was communicating information back. As a digital native, he considered those devices a part of his life, and he was in dialogue with them as he went about his day. In the context of rethinking privileges, this emphasis on *communication* was an important point. The law routinely protects privileged communications, so why shouldn't the smart heartbeats or keyword search questions that we depend on also be considered communications? Put another way, if your body "talks" to a smartwatch, and you literally ask questions to your Echo device, why can't the law protect those communications between you and your device the same way it protects the communications between you and your spouse, or you and your priest?

From a theoretical perspective, there is nothing inherently more private about a conversation between spouses than a smartwatch recording someone's blood pressure. Both are private, just in different ways, and both can be defended as necessary in a digital society. Just as we need protected lines of communication between lawyers and their clients for the legal system to work, we need protected digital communications for our smart things to work. The value of smart things is in the communication between person and thing. If—and it is an "if"—you see the transfer of data between you and your devices as a communication, then you can see why a legal system might protect the private nature of this information, even at the expense of prosecuting cases.

Theory only gets you so far, however, because there are some practical lines to be drawn. Unlike the relationship between two spouses or a lawyer and their client, the connection between ourselves and our digital things is not settled. There is no formal, legal relationship that could be defined between me and my phone. My relationship with Google, my smart car, and my AI-enhanced digital life is determined by companies' terms of service, which have never established a privilege. But they could.

Establishing a digital privilege would require two things. First, one would need an agreement between the user and the digital provider establishing that the information shared between the two parties was a communication and meant to be private. This agreement could be made part of the company's terms of service. Second, one would need a law establishing that this communication should be considered privileged, akin to other recognized evidentiary privileges. Some smart devices might be easier to protect than others. Biometric communications shared from a body to a device seem like obvious candidates. Our relationship with other smart devices might be harder to define. My car is communicating my location to a digital provider, but that information feels less personal than my heartbeat. Still, there is something communicative happening between me and my devices. Those communications are private. They are important. Why not make them privileged?

To play out the practical reality one step further, assume that society agrees that our reliance on digital technology is a relationship equally as important as marriage, a lawyer-client relationship, or any of the other recognized privileged relationships under state law. This analogy may not be too far off—your smartphone probably does know more of your secrets than your spouse (and certainly more than your priest). If one can establish a protected communication between a person and their digital device, information shared between them can claim a privilege (and not be turned over to the police or used in court).

For example, imagine that one Friday morning, I look at my Outlook calendar and see I have scheduled an event: "Friday, January 2, 10 a.m.: Time to steal a car." I pick up my smartphone, strap on my Fitbit, and grab my car-stealing tools. I locate a nice car, break into it, drive it away, and sell it for a few hundred bucks at a local garage. All in a day's work—except the car had GPS tracking and was reported stolen almost immediately. The police find the car and notice me nearby, carrying some suspicious tools and a whole bunch of digital clues. In a world where everything is evidence, police can obtain a warrant to search my smartphone and find my calendar entry. Police can issue other warrants to access the geolocation data from the apps on my phone or my Fitbit. With those pieces of evidence, police can line up the stolen car's GPS with my location data and trace a perfect match. Case closed. Convicted.

A digital communications privilege would complicate the prosecution significantly. I communicated with my calendar. It was a communication I created for my own purposes, using a digital repository (my papers). If Outlook and I have agreed in the terms of service that this data is private, and if the legislature has recognized this digital communication as privileged, then it would not be available to the prosecution. In similar fashion, if my Fitbit data is deemed privileged because the legislature determined that the privacy of personal health data is too important to risk it being revealed to police, it could not be used as evidence. Same with my smartphone data, although the arguments there seem a little weaker, since my location data isn't as obviously communicative.

If you recoil from the idea of undermining law enforcement in this way, ask yourself whether you would have the same reaction if, instead of referring to car theft, the Outlook reminder read: "Friday, January 2, 10 a.m.: Time to meet clinic doctor regarding abortion." In a state that had criminalized abortion, that calendar event could be evidence of a crime. Or imagine it read "Friday, January 2, 10 a.m.: Time to buy a gun," and you lived a state with restrictive gun regulations that criminalized such a purchase. Without an evidentiary privilege, these scheduled events could be used as evidence just as easily as the calendar entry for my planned car theft.

The idea that evidentiary privileges might be applied to data is not new. Legal scholar Rebecca Wexler proposed an "abortion data privilege" in testimony to the House Judiciary Committee in 2022,[37] an idea she later refined in a law review article co-authored with Professor Aziz Huq.[38] The Wexler/Huq privilege is a "topical" privilege, not a communications privilege, meaning that it covered the topic of abortion data (and was not dependent on communications).[39] It would entail a narrow but absolute ban on the use of data relevant to abortion (which might encompass health data, Internet search data, geolocation data, and other digital clues), but only in a specified range of cases, namely "proceedings to hold a person criminally or civilly liable for seeking, obtaining, providing, or assisting in seeking, obtaining, or providing abortion services."[40] Though their specific proposal focuses on a single topic, as a concept, the Wexler/Huq privilege can be applied to any case in which digital evidence is weaponized to target specific crimes.[41] Unlike Fourth Amendment search rules, an absolute evidentiary privilege protects information throughout the entire criminal and civil investigatory process. As a creature of legislative rulemaking, it can be designed however the legislators deem best. It can exist via state law or federal law or both.

In a world where everything is evidence, the scope and strength of a digital communications privilege would be significant. Considering everything digital to be a privileged communication would radically undermine current law enforcement practices. Legislatures considering taking such a step would need to balance the privacy harms that would result from the disclosure of different types of digital information with the needs of law enforcement and consider when, if ever, the privilege should be lifted. But even if legislatures decide against a strong privilege for data, framing the conversation around such a privilege reverses the default assumption about who has access to intimate information about us. Perhaps the onus should be on the government to justify its acquisition of personal data rather than vice-versa.

Legislating Digital Rights

Beyond the problem of data *as evidence* is the problem of data *as data*. Just because our digital technologies currently double as surveillance technologies doesn't mean that they must. But capitalism, consumerism, techno-solutionism, and corporate capture of industry, along with racism, colonialism, and failures of the democratic process, have yielded a system in which companies extract value from the data we produce while the government uses it against us in court.

This situation, too, could use a legislative response. State and national legislatures should aim to pass a comprehensive data privacy law that includes meaningful checks on government access and use. There has already been some progress in this direction. Thoughtful privacy and data protection laws have been drafted and debated in the halls of Congress. Model laws protecting personal data exist in several states.[42] Illinois passed legislation protecting biometric data, for example.[43] And there are many other ways legislatures can protect our data if they so choose. Unregulated data brokers can be regulated.[44] Facial recognition can be regulated or banned.[45] Congress can fund institutions modeled on the National Institute of Science and Technology (NIST) to regulate and audit algorithms or fund independent institutions through the National Institute of Justice or Bureau of Justice Assistance that would regulate police surveillance technology.[46] Legislators at the state and federal level could establish a right to control our personal data, as well as remedies for its misuse or misappropriation. Control over data is neither a Democratic or Republican issue, with both sides having a reason to fear that their data will be used against them.

Legislation can achieve all the goals discussed in this chapter, in theory. But over the last decade, we've seen that even bipartisan support for data privacy regulations fail to curtail police access to data. It might, therefore, be easy to conclude that implementing these protections can't be done. But that isn't true. Big things can be done. All it takes is the political will (or at least the cynical recognition that if steps are not taken even legislators will be at risk for digital exposure).

12

Individual Responses

As the saying goes, before you can change anything in life, you have to recognize the problem. Unfortunately, when it comes to digital surveillance, we are the problem. We have been seduced into revealing our data by the promise of convenience. Buying into the myth that surveillance equals safety, we have traded away the anonymity that allows us to live our lives with a sense of freedom. We set the trap of digital surveillance ourselves—and then got caught in it.

How do we escape the trap? This is in many ways the hardest chapter to write, because the answers are so deeply unsatisfying. The obvious one—disconnecting from the digital things we need to thrive—is unworkable for most people. And even ditching your smartphone for a payphone (assuming you could find one) won't save you from being filmed by your neighbor's Ring camera as you walk past his door. Most of us cannot escape the digital world and wouldn't want to. But whether you were seduced into revealing your data or made the target of policing surveillance, the reality is that you cannot escape on your own. This is a collective problem, and individual solutions can only go so far in combatting it.

That said, there are small, constructive steps we can take to limit the power of digital surveillance in their lives. This chapter details five of them: (1) *see* the trap of digital surveillance; (2) *strengthen* community efforts to challenge digital surveillance power; (3) *sabotage* your data, seeding error and confusion throughout your digital trails; (4) *support* the most digitally secure devices available by buying them and rejecting the others; and (5) *select* elected representatives (federal, state, and local) who will prioritize privacy over profits and policing. These steps can't save us from digital threats entirely, but if enough of us take them, they'll help us push back.

Seeing the Trap

There is a reason seduction works: It feels great until you realize you've been deceived. If consumer data companies were up-front with us, explaining that they wanted to commodify our data and sell it for an obscene profit, we might not tolerate them. But the companies hide their true intentions, giving us the attention we crave, the things we want to hear or feel. When we start to realize what we're giving up in exchange, we might tell ourselves that the privacy risk is not so bad, that the relationship is worth it. But we also know that the longer we stay, the more we'll end up hurting ourselves.

Once you recognize the seductions in your life, you can act accordingly. Do you really need a cloud-connected camera in your living room so you can watch your cat while you're at work? Pets did just fine without cameras. Do you need a smart toothbrush? Do you really get that much value out of knowing that you're getting an A+ in dental hygiene? Sure, these things are cool, and maybe insightful, but are they worth the power and privacy distortions that arise from giving private companies (and thus the police) your data? When we're talking about a toothbrush and a cat cam, probably not. In other cases, you might decide that the trade-off is worth it. But before you make that call, ask yourself what you're giving up for the promise of something better.

As a simple framework for evaluation, you might think about the data in your life in three buckets: (1) necessities; (2) luxuries; and (3) conveniences. Necessities you need. If you're hoping to break into comedy, you should probably keep your social media accounts, despite their terrible collective privacy record. Luxuries you do not need. It's important to stay hydrated, but you don't need a smart cup to track your water intake.[1] Without meaning to deride anyone who has embraced a "quantified life," the reality is that such enlightenment comes at a significant surveillance cost. Like the special operations forces who accidentally revealed the location of a top-secret U.S. military base by running laps around the compound with their Strava fitness bands enabled,[2] sometimes we should just stay fit without recording every step. Conveniences are the hardest to evaluate. It is super handy that my car remembers the way home and that I can order a pizza with my preferred toppings in one click.

Shutting those features off feels like harming myself to spite the data harvesters. And yet this is one of the few things we can control on our own.

When it comes to conveniences, the most you can do is ask yourself, is this worth it? The answer may well be yes, and that is okay. The fact that you buy the same pizzas every Friday isn't terribly revealing and saving that order in your delivery app is probably worth avoiding the hassle of selecting the same toppings again and again. Even more significant privacy disclosures might be worth the trade-off. If you have ever gone through the process of getting TSA PreCheck so that you can speed through the airport security line, you have bought into a great example of convenient self-surveillance. For the price of handing your personal information and your travel plans straight to the federal government, you get to skip through airport security. PreCheck, like Google Maps and online banking, is a convenience that you might well find worth any privacy cost. What's most important is to recognize that these choices *are* choices, and make them with our eyes open, rather than allow ourselves to be seduced into them.

Seduction, of course, also happens at the societal level, as some people buy into the idea that surveillance equals safety and then impose that logic on everyone else. In order to fight that logic, we have to understand democratic self-surveillance for what it is—an attempt at social control.[3] The push often comes from business interests, which help fund and promote the growth of surveillance systems in commercial districts. In other areas, property owners, community groups, or the police themselves advocate for greater surveillance. Exposing the financial interests of those selling the promise of surveillance technology is important. But so is seeing the technology's impact on those who did not fund or ask for surveillance in the first place.

Recognizing that public surveillance is not public safety opens the door for a political response, but at an individual level, there is little you can do to opt out. Unless you're able to pick up your life and move elsewhere, you won't be able to avoid the cameras (and even then, there's no guarantee that your new location won't adopt a surveillance system soon.) Individuals can no more say no to having a surveillance camera installed on their street than say no to other democratically imposed limitations on freedom, like traffic laws or taxes.

Once you notice this trap, you can also see why claims that self-surveillance is a matter of "consumer preferences" or "personal choice" sound so hollow. True, no one forced you to buy a Ring camera. In fact, you bought it knowing it would limit your privacy and expand Amazon's power. It was your choice. But only a small part of that choice was under your control. You chose the Ring camera, but cannot control what happens to the video data. You chose your Prime purchases, but cannot control who else gets to know about them. The data is available to the companies and the police, and you cannot do anything about that. If you use the product, you become the product.

The deception of consumer choice is that it isolates the purchase from the broader question of who controls the system (and the data in the system). Maybe you were willing to buy a smart pacemaker, but you did not choose to give the data to the police—even if you technically "consented" by signing a legal document agreeing to some law enforcement access in return for not having your heart stop. Individually, you cannot stand up to either Amazon or the police. You have no more ability to dictate the terms of a legalistic privacy policy than to order the police chief to turn off the ALPR cameras on your block. As an individual, you remain fairly powerless.

Supporting Resistance

It's useful to educate yourself about surveillance and recognize your personal role in allowing it, but the ability of individuals to resist surveillance *as* individuals is limited—which is why it is so important to support organized, collective efforts. Community-based activism has won some important battles against police surveillance. For example, community opposition to facial recognition technology convinced some localities—including San Francisco, Boston, and Springfield, Massachusetts—to ban police from using it.[4] In Detroit, the group Our Data Bodies successfully argued against implementing live facial recognition in police camera systems.[5] In Chicago, local advocacy groups like the Lucy Parsons Labs convinced the mayor to cancel contracts with ShotSpotter (now SoundThinking) over concerns about how the technology impacts communities of color.[6] In Seattle, concerns about surveillance led to the installation of a chief privacy officer for the city, whose office reviews surveillance technologies before and after implementation.[7] In Oakland, a privacy advisory board weighs in before any new policing technology is implemented.[8] In Los Angeles, the Stop LAPD Spying Coalition's protests against predictive policing systems forced the police to initiate an inspector general's investigation, which eventually led to the dismantling of the programs.[9] Each of these local movements only succeeded because individuals worried about surveillance in their communities banded together to take action.

One thing these successful organizing efforts have in common is that they were all local movements that arose organically in response to a particular problem. This is, in part, because decisions about policing are made at the local level. But having a concrete problem to organize against—a specific technology identified as problematic—also helped focus advocacy on a particular solution: banning or limiting the use of that technology.

The flip side is that successes have also remained local. Many have also been temporary; some of the limitations have been reversed, including a few of the facial recognition bans. But even given the setbacks, these examples show us that collective action works, offering real resistance to digital surveillance. Which means that one of the best ways for individuals to escape the digital surveillance trap is to support those seeking to change the status quo in their city or town. As an individual, you might be unable to stop a citywide surveillance project on your own, but you can contribute financial support, mutual aid, social media promotion, time, and energy to a broader effort. If there's a protest, you can show up; protests only work if people are willing to put their bodies on the line. In any case, you'll be more successful when you band together with others.

Supporting National Advocacy

Marching alongside these local organizers, and often supporting them logistically or financially, are national advocacy groups. Organizations including the Electronic Frontier Foundation, the American Civil Liberties Union (ACLU), the Brennan Center for Justice, the Center for Democracy and Technology (CDT), NYU's Policing Project, the Algorithmic Justice League, the Georgetown Law Center for Privacy and Technology, the Electronic Privacy Information Center (EPIC), Fight for the Future, the Cato Institute, the Lawyers Committee for Civil Rights Under Law, Secure Justice, Color of Change, the National Association of Criminal Defense Lawyers (NACDL), the Surveillance Technology Oversight Project, and the NAACP Legal Defense Fund have all highlighted the risks of data-driven surveillance in reports, testimony, and advocacy projects.

These national advocacy groups—staffed by lawyers, technologists, and other subject-matter experts, in addition to lobbyists and policy professionals—have almost leveled the playing field against better-resourced corporate and governmental opponents. Their fingerprints are on almost every bill, policy proposal, and white paper that has shaped the privacy debate. They also only exist because people support their efforts financially. As nonprofit organizations, they are dependent on the generosity of those who sympathize with their cause, but do not have the time or capacity to become legal or technological experts on the subject matter. It is hard for an ordinary person to pursue impact litigation or testify before a legislative body, but these experts can, because of the support of donors.

For this reason, it is critical to support their advocacy, especially in areas that require technological or legal expertise. The folks making the technology will always be able to pay for lobbyists to argue their side, and the government that writes the privacy laws will always have an incentive to exempt itself from the rules. Nonprofit groups ensure that the voices of those impacted by surveillance are heard. If you think about it, you are already subsidizing the tech companies by giving them your data to monetize—and you are literally paying taxes so the police can surveil you on the streets. It only makes sense to give some money to those fighting on the other side.

That money will go to support efforts to change the discussion around police surveillance technology. One such effort is the Atlas of Surveillance, a project created by the Electronic Frontier Foundation (EFF) that seeks to identify all the police surveillance technologies being used in the United States.[10] It is an open-source project, largely run by volunteers and students, designed to help individuals learn about surveillance tech in their cities. Users can search by city, state, or technology and inform themselves about the technologies that are being used near them, from drones in Anchorage, Alaska, to body-worn cameras in Zephyrhills, Florida. EFF offers many such citizen-focused anti-surveillance projects.[11] You can take a virtual tour of a city to spot the surveillance devices and read excellent blog posts about why certain types of government surveillance impacts civil liberties. For decades, EFF has pushed back on government access to private data, with a high level of technological sophistication and policy nuance.

Another organization whose work is worth highlighting is the Algorithmic Justice League (AJI). The AJI is a nonprofit organization founded by computer scientist Joy Buolamwini to raise awareness about the inequitable and unaccountable impacts of artificial intelligence, including its use in facial recognition.[12] Dr. Buolamwini conducted some of the most impactful early research studies demonstrating the racial and gender bias inherent in modern facial recognition technologies.[13] She and her collaborator at the time, computer scientist Timnit Gebru, demonstrated that some facial recognition systems could not accurately recognize women, and especially women of color.[14] Yet, unlike many other MIT scientists, Dr. Buolamwini goes beyond statistics and research studies to engage audiences with poetry, art, and multimedia performances. Describing herself as "the Poet of Code," Dr. Buolamwini has reshaped an understanding of civil rights advocacy around technology.[15] She starred in the Netflix documentary *Coded Bias*,[16] and her work has been featured in congressional hearings on facial recognition.[17] Her organization has reshaped the debate around AI and racial justice, bringing in a new generation into the arena.

These are just two examples of the many national organizations doing excellent work to raise awareness around police surveillance technologies. If you care about resisting the unchecked growth of these technologies, these organizations and others like them deserve your support.

Supporting Journalism

Journalists have also played a critical role in exposing the impact of digital surveillance. While community groups, experts, and advocates have been organizing for a less surveilled future, a handful of tech journalists have completely reframed the debate. These journalists have filed Freedom of Information Act (FOIA) requests, uncovered government contracts with tech companies, and exposed the privacy risks of new technologies. Almost every week for the last fifteen years, technology journalists have exposed some scandal involving policing, privacy, and technology.

As someone who has followed surveillance news for years, I believe it is no understatement to say that a few journalists have radically shifted awareness about the extent to which technology companies have gained power at the expense of our privacy. Established newsrooms like *the Washington Post* have supported reporters like Justin Jouvenal, Geoff Fowler, and Drew Harwell, who have exposed the rise of surveillance technology in local police departments in dozens of stories.[18] Brand-new entities like *404 Media*, led by Jason Koebler and Joseph Cox, have matched these scoops with regular investigative bombshells about surveillance.[19] *NBC News* reporters Jon Schuppe, Cyrus Farivar (now at *Forbes*), and Oliva Solon (now at *Bloomberg*) have broken dozens of stories about police technologies and the scandals that surround them.[20] *Wired*'s Dell Cameron has spent years doggedly tracking down the financial and carceral connections between surveillance technology companies and law enforcement.[21] Garance Burke and her team at the *Associated Press* have tracked surveillance technologies across the globe.[22] Avi-Asher Shapiro exposed the growing role of start-ups like Fusus that have entered the surveillance market.[23] The magazines and institutions that supported these journalists' work—some of which have since shut down—need financial and popular support.

If I oversaw the Pulitzer Prize for journalists covering surveillance technologies here are my top nominees for articles that have been especially impactful:

Kashmir Hill broke a major story on Clearview AI and changed the national debate around facial recognition. Hill has been a groundbreaking tech reporter for years, and her article "The Secretive Company That Might End Privacy as We Know It" in *the New York Times* revealed the power of Clearview AI's facial recognition technology and the company's freewheeling agreements with police.[24] The article drew national attention to the growth of unregulated facial recognition technology, essentially halting future partnerships between Clearview AI and U.S. police forces and spurring congressional hearings and greater oversight.

Jennifer Valentino-DeVries and a team of *New York Times* reporters exposed the importance of location data in dramatic fashion in "Your

Apps Know Where You Were Last Night, and They're Not Keeping It Secret."[25] Using images and multimedia to show the power of advertising trackers, the article provided an interactive demonstration of how easily geolocational data could be used to identify individuals and track their every move as they went about their lives. It sparked a national conversation about the unregulated nature of location tracking.

Caroline Haskins, then at *Vice*, and Alfred Ng, then at *CNET*, exposed the relationships between Ring and police departments, including the novel financial arrangement under which police were incentivized to improve public relations for Ring.[26] These unusual relationships and financial incentives drew scrutiny and changed the public's perception of the technology.

Ali Winston, writing for *The Verge*, exposed Palantir's use of social network analysis in New Orleans.[27] His article, "Palantir Has Secretly Been Using New Orleans to Test Its Predictive Policing Technology," drew national attention and caused such an uproar that the city council soon backed away from the company and predictive policing in general.

Sidney Fussell at *Gizmodo* was the first journalist to expose how video analytics might be integrated with police body cameras. In his article "The New Tech That Could Turn Police Body Cameras into Police Surveillance Tools," he identified the risk of AI enhancements years before the AI hype began to build.[28] The article had the effect of slowing down the adoption of video analytics in body cameras and creating an early debate about new forms of surveillance.

Finally, Julia Angwin, a pioneering investigative journalist and founder of the nonprofit journalism outlet *The Markup*, supported Dhruv Mehrotra, Aaron Sankin, Surya Mattu, and Annie Gilbertson to conduct one of the deepest data dives into predictive policing to date.[29] The reporters analyzed over 5 million predictions from thirty-eight police departments and found systemic racial biases in the analysis. It was, and remains, one of the most comprehensive studies of the inequality baked into predictive policing. The article detailing the results of the study, "Crime Prediction Software Promised to Be Free of Biases. New Data Shows It Perpetuates Them," was the nail in the coffin for the first generation of predictive policing companies.[30] Soon after the article was published, PredPol, the company that had led the push toward this type of data-driven policing, announced it was shutting down operations.

Each of these articles had a direct influence on the trajectory of surveillance technologies. Some provided the impetus for shutting programs down. Others opened a debate. All of them, along with many others, helped push back on the growing adoption of digital surveillance tech. And while many tech journalists have been justly celebrated for their work on digital policing—Kathleen McGrory and Neil Bedi at the *Tampa Bay Times* won an actual Pulitzer Prize in journalism for their investigation into Pasco County's predictive policing surveillance strategy.[31] Journalism is a huge part of exposing how your data will be used against you, and supporting newspapers, magazines, and independent writers helps ensure that journalists can keep holding tech companies and police departments to account.

Sabotaging Surveillance

Digital self-surveillance has one fundamental flaw: It is dependent on a constantly flowing stream of accurate data. If that data stream is disrupted or corrupted, it becomes unreliable. One way, then, to respond to the problem of self-surveillance is to sabotage your own data stream. Digital sabotage can involve seeding errors in collected data, creating gaps in collection, or purposely thwarting collection efforts. If it's done on a large enough scale, such sabotage makes reliance on the data risky and unhelpful, especially in criminal prosecutions.

Seeding errors simply means adding inaccurate information into systems of data collection. The digital profiles being created by data brokers and others reflect your choices. Some data points are passive (the geolocation on your phone shows you going to church). Some are active (you agree to share purchase and location data with CVS or Walgreens in exchange for a coupon you always forget to bring with you). Here is where you can be creative. You should not be giving Starbucks your actual birthday, so make one up. Maybe invent a fake name or hobby. You would be amazed at how easily data can get mixed up. I once ordered an actual arrow quiver from an actual hunting company. The quiver was for a child's Halloween costume—but it was enough to get me coded as a hunter by the data brokers. I have never gone hunting in my life, but every time I get a hunting catalog in the mail I smile at the error.

Sabotage can take many forms, some more extreme and time-consuming than others. One can, for example, create multiple digital personas to hide personal data. There is no reason why you must use a real name or the same email address to sign up for most of the things you sign up for online. Just as you might have a different password for each digital account, you might create a different email for each thing you do. Digital aggregators are looking for points of connection—like the fact that you used the same email to purchase a gym membership, a pair of running shoes, and an over-the-counter remedy for athlete's foot. Creating new names and email addresses makes it harder for aggregators to find those connection points. When your data does get sold, this (admittedly inconvenient) tactic will also reveal which company sold it.

An easier task would be to turn off many of the tracking apps on your phone and refuse to press "I agree" when websites inevitably ask for your permission to track you. You could also take two minutes to delete data that is stored for no reason except that the company wants to keep it around. If you choose privacy at every turn, you weaken your data trail and create gaps.

Of course, it is not that easy to sabotage things you love (or need). It would be unwise to sabotage the smart pacemaker that records your heartbeat for your doctor. If you turn off GPS in your car, you might get physically lost. If you disconnect your phone, you might feel emotionally lost. As the stories in this book make clear, there are limits to individual resistance.

Buying Smart

The smart devices changing our lives did not just show up on our nightstands one day. We bought them, and in doing so, we often made a choice between multiple options, some more privacy-protective than others. Of course, "choice" is a bit of an unfair word here, because any choice we have is constrained by what's on the market and what we can afford. Privacy-protective devices are often more expensive devices. The reason Android phones are cheaper than iPhones is that Google isn't making money only from the phone, but also from selling your data.[32] Apple iPhones protect your data more, but they also cost more. The privacy choice is only a choice for those with the financial means to choose.

Consumers aren't the only ones making choices about privacy. When you study police surveillance technologies, you discover something ironic: Tech companies—which are largely responsible for creating the problems enumerated in this book—have been far more responsive to privacy concerns than judges, legislators, or consumers. It was Google's lawyers who invented the three-step geofence warrant protocol. It was Ring that shifted video storage to the device rather than the cloud. It was Apple that encrypted the data on its devices. These companies, and others like them, have taken numerous privacy-protective stances because their lawyers and technologists made the decision to do so (in response to sustained public pressure). If tech employees had not fought from the inside to protect user data, the problems of surveillance capitalism and police access to our personal data would have been a whole lot worse. The companies that listened to those cautious voices should be rewarded by consumers demanding even more caution. Those companies that prioritized the financial gain of exploiting data should be rejected.

Of course, choices to protect privacy can always be undone, and tech companies have a habit of walking back initially protective design decisions when they have a financial incentive to do so. We can't trust that companies will prioritize customer privacy over government interests when billions of dollars hang in the balance. And even companies with good policies could go bankrupt and end up selling their data at fire-sale prices. Cynicism, greed, and power will always pull toward exploiting data for profit. Still, when given the choice to financially reward a company for doing the right thing, it makes sense for individuals to do so.

Voting for Privacy

As we saw in the previous chapter, the history of legislative action around data and surveillance is short and sad. Nevertheless, some exemplary leaders have tried to tackle the problem. Senator Ron Wyden has steadfastly demanded accountability from technology companies. He has asked government agencies to illuminate how they use personal data. In hearings on technology issues, he asks sophisticated questions that reveal issues that would otherwise be hidden or go unremarked.[33] He is able to do so in part because his staff is known to be the most technologically literate on Capitol Hill. Such literacy could be the norm if voters prioritized leadership on issues around technology, surveillance, and privacy when considering legislative candidates. If voters voted for people who promised more protection for our personal data, we would have more protection.

Privacy is not necessarily a partisan issue. In 2019, I had the privilege of testifying before the House Oversight and Reform Committee on the issue of facial recognition.[34] This was one of the first big congressional hearings on the subject under the leadership of the late congressman Elijah Cummings. As I sat listening to the Congressmembers speak, I was a bit shocked to realize how much hard-right Republican Jim Jordan and progressive Democrat Alexandria Ocasio-Cortez agreed on this one issue. Both expressed support for restrictions on facial recognition, and it was honestly hard to figure out which of them thought the technology was more dangerous. Their colleagues, too, had similar worries. Their specific concerns may have taken on a partisan flavor, with some members hypothesizing about Christian churches being surveilled via facial recognition while others railed against the racially biased systems used in public housing complexes. But they agreed that facial recognition technology was dangerous and one could see a common bond emerging around the dangers of surveillance.

Voting for privacy is one of the easiest things an individual can do to push back against surveillance. If we had more Ron Wydens in the Senate (and more technologically savvy congressional staff that looked like his) we would have more accountability from both tech companies and government agencies. If we voted for more skeptical representatives who asked hard questions about how technology was being used, we might have more protective laws, or at least better information about how our data was being used. A vote for privacy-focused representatives is a vote for legislative solutions to the problems outlined in this book.

Conclusion

The Tyrant Test

Big challenges require bigger responses. The growth of digital surveillance threatens traditional notions of American liberty. The right to live free of government oversight, the right to dissent and protest, the right to be our own weird selves—all of these are existentially challenged in a world where everything is evidence. We've seen ways that judges, legislatures, and citizens can push back against digital surveillance, and some are already doing so. But the dark secret is that most of us—even those with the power to personally influence law and policy—are not. We are building the tools of tyranny, and do not seem to care enough to do anything about it.

The word "tyranny" might draw eyerolls (though perhaps fewer than it once did in our age of authoritarian posturing), but a future of absolute digital control is not too far off. Imagine a city with hundreds of thousands of government surveillance cameras that can monitor movements on the streets and in office buildings, identifying every individual who passes by—a system of facial recognition combined with ALPR and video analytics. Now imagine that the same government entity tracks your smartphone, not simply the location data, but also the information about your purchases and interests. This entity knows when you travel home to visit your family and whether you have paid your bills on time. It provides a credit score that unlocks not just better payment options, but upward social mobility. Now imagine having all that information linked to the information collected about your family, friends, and colleagues to create a detailed map of your life. Finally, imagine that government entity also controls which sources of information you can access and which you cannot, while also monitoring what you are viewing. You can call this tyranny, digital authoritarianism, or something else. What it is not is futuristic or fictional—it is modern-day China, whose surveillance capabilities are only growing.[1]

Consider the following scenario: A U.S. president identifies a perceived threat to the nation. Maybe it is a traditional enemy, like an international terrorist organization or transnational criminal enterprise. Maybe it is a less traditional enemy, like a deadly drug or virus. Maybe it is an idea, like communism or gender theory. Maybe it is the presidents' detractors, an "enemy from within" he accuses of conspiring against him. In any case, the president convinces the nation that it must use all the law enforcement surveillance power available to combat this criminal concern. The tactics of the "war on drugs" or the "Red Scare" can easily map onto some other type of national threat. What would limit the collection of personal information about the people in the disfavored group—whether they are immigrants or transgender people, the vaccinated or unvaccinated, gun owners or opioid users? The data exists. It is sitting on a cloud server or smart device somewhere. Constitutional theory, statutory protections, and community resistance can offer only limited protection in this scenario. If the government designates something a "crime," warrants will provide access—not protection—to data that may help prove that crime. Executive power will be used to target those people supporting that crime. Cameras will track them. Geolocation will find them. Smart data and social media will reveal them. Any behavior, ideology, or identity can be targeted. All it takes is a label, and the political will to use police power.

So far, the United States has avoided the tyranny of political dictatorship, but not the tyranny of overcriminalization. In the last decade, we have seen the passage of laws targeting people seeking abortions, trans youth, and undocumented asylum seekers, as well as threats to prosecute political enemies, journalists, and leaders of civil society. In our darker past, we saw criminal laws targeting racial minorities, immigrants, women, the wider LGBTQ+ community, people with AIDS, religious minorities, and political dissenters. It would be foolish to think this kind of persecution couldn't happen again, and next time, it will be supercharged by technology. The desire to channel hate against members of less powerful groups is a powerful force in the United States, and politicians know they can manipulate that rage to gain more power.

Given this knowledge, how should we proceed in the face of the growing digital surveillance threats discussed in this book? How do we exist in a world where everything is evidence? My advice is to assume the worst. Assume power will be misused. Assume the tyrant will gain access to your data and proceed accordingly. This is what I call "the tyrant test."[2]

A Framing Fear

The tyrant test begins by assuming that your personal data will be misused by a metaphorical (or actual) tyrant and asks what structures you would put in place to protect against that misuse before the tyrant gets the upper hand.[3] What data would you protect through laws or other regulations? What data would you refrain from creating in the first place? What data would be completely off-limits?

The tyrant test recognizes that the harm of digital surveillance is the power it gives the government to monitor and control people, and that structural limits must be implemented to restrain that power. Those limits would put power in the hands of the people, establishing overlapping checks and balances, as well as rights and remedies established by *ex ante* enforceable rules to make sure that data is secured before it can be used against us.

If this approach sounds familiar, it is because the United States, itself, was built on the tyrant test.[4] We have—as you will remember from your high school history lessons—faced the problem of the potential tyrant before. Only a few years removed from British monarchy, the drafters of the U.S. Constitution knew that if they didn't do their job carefully, they would have escaped one tyrant only to hand power to a new one.[5] Their specific concerns were varied but included worries about political repression, confiscation of goods and monies, arbitrary and abusive investigations, and government surveillance.[6] They designed the U.S. legal system to ensure that a would-be tyrant could never gain enough power to do the things they feared. The tyrant test borrows the spirit and structure of the U.S. Constitution and applies it to the digital world.

Four points are worth emphasizing at the outset. First, the tyrant test requires a distrustful attitude toward power[7] and recognizes the current tendency to trust tech companies, judges, and the police with personal data (because, after all, we have nothing to hide) is misguided. Second, the tyrant test is not just a thought experiment or a metaphor about power, but addresses a real threat, just as it was for the Founders.

Third, the tyrant test does not trust any branch of government as a sole check on abuses, instead, it relies on overlapping structures to provide protection. While it involves aspects of the judicial, legislative, and individual solutions to digital surveillance discussed earlier in this book, a satisfactory response to the tyrant test requires a holistic approach, not just piecemeal improvements. Finally, the tyrant test is informed by the United States' long history of racial tyranny and draws lessons from the events leading to the passage of the Fourteenth Amendment. Reconstruction-era policing offers egregious examples of search and seizure violations against newly freed, formerly enslaved persons. What historians now call the "second Founding" was shaped by a reaction to petty, arbitrary, and racially discriminatory police surveillance and informs the protections needed to avoid such surveillance.[8]

Trust No One

Having read an entire book about creepy surveillance technologies and their impact on privacy, autonomy, and power, you might think it unnecessary to highlight again the importance of distrust. But trusting and hoping remain our society's dominant approach to personal data protection. We view data breaches and exposures as rare exceptions, not the foreseeable result of data creation. We have put our faith in corporate policies rather than federal laws to protect our data. Instead of fearing the worst, we have largely trusted that judicial warrants and constitutional law will protect our privacy. Indeed, one way to interpret our current apathy when it comes to personal data collection by companies and the police is that we trust that our information will be used wisely and be protected. In some ways, it is a touching indication of faith in our legal system; but it's naïve and dangerous.

To be clear, this trust is not shared by everyone. Communities that have long borne the brunt of heavy-handed policing are very aware of the dangers of new forms of surveillance power. Scholars like Simone Browne, Ruha Benjamin, Chris Guillard, and others have drawn connections between technologically enhanced surveillance and the history of racial oppression in the United States.[9] Surveillance has always shadowed Black lives from before the Civil War to after the civil rights movement.[10] A Black man trying to ignore the racially discriminatory laws of the Jim Crow South faced a form of legally sanctioned tyranny enforced by community surveillance and police force. There was no trust, only oppression. But because Black and Brown Americans are so often politically disempowered and ignored, and their testimony so often not believed, white Americans have managed to ignore the warnings from those who have long lived under a form of carceral tyranny.

Even for the privileged, trust is not always an option. Sometimes there is no way to opt out of surveillance. When you buy a new car, it is difficult if not impossible to avoid having location and driving data shared with your car company (and whoever else they choose to share it with). And of course, self-driving cars will require connections to many other systems to allow for seamless and safe navigation. To say that you are trusting the technology suggests a choice that you no longer have. You are bound by the design decisions, data privacy policies, and financial incentives of the companies producing the tech. Although it would be a terrible business decision, a vindictive car company owner could essentially turn a vocal critic's car into an expensive brick or surveillance trap. Billionaire CEOs with visions of grandeur are not the most stable group, and they have been known to act like digital tyrants.

Yet by and large, the self-surveillance stories in this book arise from a certain trust in data collectors and digital providers. It is an orientation that must change. The digitizing of our lives has happened far in advance of rules or laws concerning our digital trails and it will continue to outpace judicial or legislative protections. Our response must be to picture the tyrant reviewing our Google search history and to act accordingly.

America's Anti-surveillance Attitude

It's hard to get more American than rebelling against a tyrant. It happens to be our origin story and one that should resonate today. And it was not just tyranny in the abstract that the Founding generation feared, but a particular form of government surveillance.[11] While today we talk about digital tyranny in a metaphorical sense, at the time of the American Revolution, British surveillance power was quite real, with deadly consequences. Customs agents and government ministers policed what the colonists were doing, utilizing broad search powers to monitor goods and people.[12] General warrants authorized searches against everyone, everywhere, all at once. As the Supreme Court once said, "It is familiar history that indiscriminate searches and seizures conducted under the authority of 'general warrants' were the immediate evils that motivated the framing and adoption of the Fourth Amendment."[13] Writs of assistance provided unbounded power to seize personal papers and thus spy on holders of unconventional (even radical) ideas.[14] In his 1761 speech *Against Writs of Assistance*, James Otis declared, "Every one with this writ may be a tyrant."[15]

Such concerns did not go unnoticed. A young John Adams happened to be in the audience during Otis's famous Boston speech and he incorporated its sentiment when drafting the search and seizure principles in the 1780 Massachusetts Declaration of Rights, on which the Fourth Amendment was modeled.[16] The origin story of the American origin story can be traced to that Boston square—and to the direct rejection of tyrannical powers and the arbitrary use of policing power. At risk of speculation, I can't imagine James Otis would have trusted the government with facial recognition or drones.

In this way, it can be argued that the Fourth Amendment was drafted to prevent a tyrant from abusing their power. Yes, the Founders' concern was partly about protecting political activity and expression, but it was also very much about criminal law. Agents broke into houses, offices, and farms to investigate tax evasion and sedition. Homes, persons, papers, and things were targeted for exposure as a way of manifesting social control over the colonists.[17] Imagine John Adams and the people who risked everything to push back against growing British surveillance giving the green light to video cameras on every block, listening devices in every home, agents recording every traveler, and a centralized record of purchases or goods bought and sold. Those liberty-minded people would have been horrified at the idea that much more invasive surveillance powers were being handed over to a potential tyrant called the federal government.[18] They, like you, would see that the appropriate response to such tyranny is to resist and rebel—and definitely not to sign up for a home doorbell camera accessible by the local night watchman.

Structural Responses

Tyranny exists as an all-encompassing, structural system. Any response to tyranny must therefore also be structural. This was the lesson of the

Founding: No branch of government can be trusted. Early American history is quite clear that the Founders designed a constitutional structure marked by checks and balances and the separation of powers, with an eye toward thwarting a tyrant. The fear was not a foreign despot taking the country by force, but a tyrant from within, being granted too much lawful power in a governmental system.[19]

It was quite clear to the Founders that the executive branch, as the democratic equivalent of a monarch, could not be trusted. A president could act like a king if not checked by other branches and the people. The drafters of the Constitution were particularly focused on restricting executive policing powers for this reason. As legal scholar Laura Donohue wrote in *The Original Fourth Amendment*,

> The Founders' concern went beyond the amassing of tyrannical power in one place to the impact such an accumulation of power would have on the separation of powers. General warrants gave power to the executive branch, without constraint on how the power could be used. General warrants amounted to the proverbial fox guarding the hen house.[20]

That the president could not be trusted did not mean the legislative branch could. Although "we the people" elected members of Congress and empowered them to write laws, the Founders recognized that Congress should not be given unchecked policing powers. In addition to specifically prohibiting "ex post facto laws" and "bills of attainder," the Fourth Amendment was meant to prevent the legislature from approving laws akin to general warrants. As legal scholar Thomas Davies has written:

> [The Framers] were concerned about a specific vulnerability in the protections provided by the common law; they were concerned that legislation might make general warrants legal in the future, and thus undermine the right of security in person and house. Thus, the Framers adopted constitutional search and seizure provisions with the precise aim of ensuring the protection of person and house by prohibiting legislative approval of general warrants.[21]

Lawful but oppressive policing was just as much a fear of the Founders as rogue agents acting arbitrarily. Tyranny can come from laws, and legislatures must be prevented from enacting such laws.[22]

Finally, the judiciary could not be trusted. Judges were the bad guys in many colonial dramas, acquiescing to British governors who wished to prosecute colonists. Famous cases like the seditious libel prosecution of John Peter Zenger, a publisher of a local paper critical of the king, underlined the dangers of politically affiliated judges.[23] Indeed, one reason why juries play such a central role in the legal system is that the Founders trusted citizen-jurors more than judges.[24] Jurors were heroes of American revolutionary lore, acquitting colonists of their illegal actions while judges sought to enforce tyrannical laws. In fact, it was King George III's decision to shift more power to judge-dominated admiralty courts from jury-dominated civil courts that inspired one of the grievances in the Declaration of Independence, which accused the king of "depriving us . . . of the benefits of trial by jury."[25] Juries were the final piece of the Constitution's protection against tyranny. They stood alone in the structural balance of power, able to reject the laws passed by the legislature, enforced by the executive, and overseen by the judiciary. Juries at the time of the Founding could decide matters of fact and law for themselves, even when the entire legal power structure pushed for a conviction. The rights of citizens—as members of juries, and as individuals—to speak, petition, protest, and criticize those in power had to be built into the structure of constitutional rights and remedies for it to offer true protection against tyranny.

Race and Tyranny

Americans' fight against tyranny did not end with the Founding. Another form of tyranny continued in the form of slavery. Oppressive police tactics, including violent searches and seizures, enforced the inhumane conditions of enslaved people and tracked those who escaped.[26] Much as the American revolutionaries had their ideas criminalized to limit dissent, abolitionists were tracked, threatened, and policed in order to prevent them from traveling in the South to protest the continued injustices. These forms of arbitrary and tyrannical government surveillance were designed to maintain white supremacy and limit the mobility and freedom of Black Americans, both free and enslaved.

After the Civil War, Southern states granted private groups legal authority to maintain racial inequality by force. Slave patrols became local law enforcement.[27] Police and deputized white citizens physically enforced black codes that reified unequal labor relationships to maintain a form of economic peonage in the South.[28] The surveillance powers granted to these groups, which allowed for unbounded seizures of people and property, were quite like the dreaded general warrants and writs of assistance in their overbroad and arbitrary application. The Fourteenth Amendment was a response to these abusive and tyrannical actions.

Legal scholar Andrew Taslitz studied the Reconstruction era, drawing parallels between the early history of the Fourth Amendment and the history of the Fourteenth Amendment. In both time periods, the governmental threat necessitating constitutional change was arbitrary, overbroad—but lawful—surveillance that dramatically infringed on liberty and restricted dissent. As Professor Taslitz explains, "The Republicans who debated the Fourteenth Amendment understood the close connection among the kinds of rights that the Fourth Amendment protected, free speech and press, and the nature of free movement and privacy as central aspects of the expression of a message of equality."[29] Together, the Fourteenth Amendment's prohibition of unequal treatment and the Fourth Amendment's protection against arbitrary searches and seizures signify a rejection of this form of authorized tyranny. Whether it came in the form of British customs agents or white supremacists, tyranny required a structural response, and it does again today.

The Tyrant Test Today

Picture any brand-name authoritarian from history—or even your petty small-town mayor who cares more about personal grievances than governance. Picture a vindictive president or FBI director out of control. Do you want that person getting access to the data from your home? Your smartwatch? Your car? Your travels? Do you trust that a judge they appointed or socialize with is a sufficient check on their ability to invade your privacy? Would you be willing to trust the secrecy of your Google searches to the whims of corporate lawyers beholden to company shareholders? No, you wouldn't, and shouldn't be dumb enough to risk it all by trusting those in power.

So how do we minimize the dangers posed by today's potential tyrants? By taking a page out of the Founders' book and devising a structure that rebalances power and ensures that no one individual or group can amass too much of it. Like them, we need to worry as much about lawful grants of authority as individual abuses of power. Finally, we need to remember that the Founders were themselves violating the law (as were many who resisted slavery). As such, blind calls to law and order need to be nuanced with considerations of privacy, security, and liberty—even if that means allowing some lawbreaking. It is an underappreciated truth that the Founders put limits on the ability of governments to investigate wrongdoing in part because they were guilty of wrongdoing themselves.

The tyrant test borrows from the early history of the Fourth Amendment, which not only signified a distrust of power but also established methods to check that power, including judicial review, civil tort remedies, juries and grand juries, and substantive search limits. Viewed as a structural protection against arbitrary government power, the Fourth Amendment encodes distrust in government interests and demands procedural protections.

Part III considered in detail how judges, legislators, and individuals might respond to the threat posed by digital surveillance. But because the threat of tyranny can come from all branches of government—and even from the citizenry itself—the response to that threat must be holistic, ensuring that each locus of power is checked by the others. Here is what an ideal tyrant test response might look like.

Legislative Branch

One check on police surveillance power must be legislative. Before police could use a new surveillance technology or obtain personal data in a new way, they would need legislative approval.[30] Unlike the status quo, in which police can use new technologies until courts or legislatures decide otherwise, police power should require *ex ante* democratic authorization.[31] In practical terms, this means that before police decide to fly a drone to a crime scene, there must be a public law that explicitly authorizes police to use the drone, passed only after public debate about its costs and benefits.[32] The laws governing police access to data would be transparent and connected to a democratically accountable system. Legislatures could also add WALL warrant-like requirements to obtain certain kinds of data. The federal rules governing wiretaps offer a potential model: They are legislatively enacted and include a warrant requirement, plus minimization standards and other protections. It was a legislative choice to limit the ability of police to listen to phone calls in our homes. While legislative authorization does not eliminate concerns about abusive policing powers, it offers citizens clarity about what the police can and can't do and requires a case to be made that these powers are justified.

Executive Branch

Laws turn into policy. The legislative branch sets the rules, and the executive branch carries them out. But the mechanisms by which it does so must be constrained by transparent and enforceable rules. If the legislature gives a green light for drones, the executive branch must place strict limits on how they are used, by whom, when, and why. Before technologies are put to use, these ground rules need to be made clear via formal rulemaking processes.[33]

Any rules regarding the use of these technologies must also address risks, including the potential for disparate racial impacts in application and the erosion of civil liberties. To protect against the possibility of biased implementation, rules must make clear where, when, and against whom the technologies will be directed, and they must also study the results of that targeting and perform regular audits. Admittedly, policies written by the executive branch will not significantly constrain executive power, but in combination with other checks might provide some limits. If you must spell out in black and white how you are planning to use a technology and why it makes sense to use it in that way, you're forced to think through some of the potential problems. This is especially true if the policy is focused on avoiding foreseeable risks like disparate impacts on Black and Brown communities or religious minorities, or interfering with the right to protest.

Policies also need to address the police department's ability to acquire private data from private parties. There needs to be written rules spelling out what information can be obtained, when, and how. It should not be a given that police can access your pharmacy records simply because a digital trail of those visits exists in a database somewhere. There must be rules and procedures at a minimum—and ideally an open debate about whether data of this sort should be available to police at all.

Judicial Branch

The judicial branch has two important roles to play in the tyrant test—one procedural and one substantive. The first, procedural role is to oversee challenges to any legislative or executive overstepping. Without a strong judiciary, any structural limits will be ineffectual. If, for example, the police use a drone without authorization, or use it inappropriately, a court must be empowered to enjoin further use. In a system that requires democratic legislation to authorize the use of new technologies or the collection of private data, any breach of the authorization must result in shutting down the data collection and suppressing any inappropriately recovered evidence. In addition, this oversight role would require the judiciary to play a strong role in signing warrants or a "warrant-plus" document akin to those required under the Wiretap Act. If legislative rules impose heightened requirements to get a warrant, judges must uphold those requirements.

The second, more substantive role focuses on judicial interpretation and how to view the Fourth Amendment in a digital age. As I tell my students, the words of the Fourth Amendment have not changed since it was ratified in 1791, but we have. The work of judges is to interpret those words to make them relevant to a very different world. In the chapter on judicial responses, I offered thoughts about how to interpret the Fourth Amendment in a digital age. A Fourth Amendment respectful of informational security would expand the protection granted to our homes, papers, persons, and effects to their modern "smart" equivalents and the information they produce. Seeing the harms of persistent surveillance systems as different from those associated with traditional analog policing tools invites the former to be considered under a different analytical frame. The nature of digital policing tools, the type and amount of information they can obtain, and their ability to scale present new challenges that judges must acknowledge in their decisions. Viewing rummaging as a stand-alone Fourth Amendment harm opens up an entirely new way to address the dangers of everything-everywhere-all-at-once searches.

Judges must also consider placing limits on obtaining some kinds of data, no matter the law enforcement need. A substantive search limit would reflect the way the Founding generation understood the protection of papers. Theirs was an understanding shaped by a fear of tyranny. Those ideas written on papers were almost absolutely protected from interception because of the privacy harms inherent in their exposure. A tyrant test might then protect certain digital papers (especially those connected to the home, person, or private things) from law enforcement collection under any circumstances. Such protections would be strongest for papers and ideas related to religious freedom, dissent, protest, or freedom of association.

I once had the opportunity to address a room full of federal judges at the National Constitution Center. It was a workshop where judges came to learn about new technology and novel issues facing the judiciary. The conversation made apparent how hard questions of probable cause and warrant applications can be in a world of ever-evolving technology. Judges are generalists with thousands of different legal issues to master; they may not have given much thought to how the Fourth Amendment fits the problems of video analytics in Real-Time Crime Centers. Yet like the magistrate judge in the *Chatrie* case, they must make hard calls about whether to approve warrants related to these systems. These calls are made harder still because warrants are *ex parte* (meaning judges hear only from investigators) and require quick approval. This set of circumstances naturally leads judges to defer to police investigators and technology experts and sign the warrant. How can you push back on the nuances of some digital technology you do not fully understand?

My argument to those federal judges was that they should embrace their inner Founding Father (or Mother), cultivating a revolutionary skepticism about the power of government agents to surveil, track, and obtain personal information. The fact that data is available should be the beginning, not the end, of their analysis. When considering the constitutionality of surveilling someone's home for eighteen months, or obtaining someone's Amazon purchase history, or mapping a smart car's digital path, asking "What would James Otis do?" might be a good starting point. Starting from a position of distrust means that questions about the particularity of the warrant (or the scope and scale of the search, or the quantum of probable cause) become heightened. A judge might still ultimately sign off on the warrant, but it will be done in a considered way, rather than by default.

Individual Rights

As we've seen, there are many steps individuals can take to respond to the push to collect more of our data, some more effective than others. But there's something even more important than individual actions—individual rights. When legislatures authorize particular surveillance technologies and executive policy puts them into use, they should, as part of that process, make sure to enact enforceable rights that can be claimed when things go wrong. In other words, if the law says police need a warrant to obtain your smartphone data and police fail to get the warrant, but access your phone anyway, you should be able to sue the police for damages reflecting the cost to your privacy. Cases must be allowed to go forward without being stymied by claims of qualified immunity or procedural blocks. There must also be allowances for attorney's fees, as well as other incentives for individuals to bring cases to court. In a digital world that makes it easy for police to overstep the bounds of a search (whether by accident or on purpose), enforceable rights are critically important checks especially if the technology or data collection practices are racially discriminatory or unevenly implemented. Exposing the problem is insufficient. Individuals must be given legal tools to protect their data from government misuse.

Community Rights

Individuals should also have a collective say in what technologies are deployed in their communities. In fact, cities and smaller jurisdictions might be a better place to focus attention than the states or the federal government. After all, policing is fragmented, with decisions made at the local level, and attitudes around surveillance varying drastically from place to place. Different communities have different levels of comfort with police surveillance, even within the same city. Many of these differences reflect the history of capitalism, racism, and residential segregation that creates economic inequality, which means it can be challenging to channel community sentiment into a formal decision-making process. It is not easy to assess what "the community" thinks. Mechanisms for citizen participation must therefore be created to allow communities to decide on particular surveillance systems.

The tyrant test envisions building local institutions—akin to grand juries—to approve new policing technologies.[34] In simple form, before an ALPR system is deployed, or before a drone program is piloted, police would have to get community approval (in addition to legislative authorization). Some communities will welcome the technology, and some will not. The idea is to ensure the final decision rests in the hands of the people on whom that technology will be used.

This type of citizen participation has always been a part of the U.S. system. At the time of the drafting of the Fourth Amendment, grand juries functioned as decentralized checks on government power.[35] In addition to providing a local check on prosecutorial power, as they do today, grand juries also conducted investigations and assessed taxes.[36] They were bodies of active citizens who participated in the workings of government. While community oversight groups would not be actual grand juries, they could play the same role in the constitutional structure. Models like the Oakland Privacy Advisory Commission demonstrate how cities can turn to local community groups for advice and approval when considering new forms of surveillance.[37] The difference here would be to give that local entity the power to make final decisions about whether to adopt the technology and under what circumstances, rather than simply having them serve in an advisory role. If you cannot convince the community that surveillance is a good idea, it probably should not be used in that community.

Conclusion

The tyrant test offers a warning about the real future we face if we don't take action to confront the dangers of data-driven surveillance power on a structural level. But it also offers a starting point for considering what to do about the world we live in now—a digital world where everything is evidence that will be used against you. A technology passes the tyrant test only if proponents can show that the risks it presents have been mitigated. As such, the tyrant test reflects a societal commitment to legal and political supervision combining formal authorizing legislation with judicial oversight, executive branch limits, community-based institutional checks, and individual rights and remedies. Will there still be abuses of data-driven power? Of course. But establishing an intentional structural mitigation strategy is our best option for preventing these abuses. The threat of the tyrant is real, but it is a threat that the United States has lived with for years—and one that we can overcome if we plan now. A world where everything is evidence is a risky world, and who is at risk depends on who controls the levers of power. In a country divided by politics, values, and ideology, digital surveillance can be weaponized by either side. That is a danger both sides should be able to agree is worth addressing. Protecting our digital trails from the tyrant should be a shared goal—because one never knows who the next target will be.

NOTES

INTRODUCTION

1. Cleve R. Wootson Jr., *A Man Detailed His Escape from a Burning House. His Pacemaker Told Police a Different Story* WASH. POST, Feb. 8, 2017.
2. *See, e.g.*, Scott R. Peppet, *Regulating the Internet of Things: First Steps Toward Managing Discrimination, Privacy, Security, and Consent*, 93 TEX. L. REV. 85, 93 (2014).
3. *See* ANDREW GUTHRIE FERGUSON, THE RISE OF BIG DATA POLICING: SURVEILLANCE, RACE, AND THE FUTURE OF LAW ENFORCEMENT 190 (2017).
4. People v. Seymour, 536 P.3d 1260, 1273 (Colo. 2023).
5. *See* Alison Griswold, *Amazon Wants to Sell "Surveillance as a Service,"* QUARTZ (June 20, 2019), www.qz.com.
6. *See* FERGUSON, *supra* note 3.
7. *See* Alejandra Caraballo, Cynthia Conti-Cook, Yveka Pierre, Michelle McGrath & Hillary Aarons, *Extradition in Post-*Roe *America*, 26 CUNY L. REV. 1, 9 (2023).
8. *See* Paul Ohm, *Probably Probable Cause: The Diminishing Importance of Justification Standards*, 94 MINN. L. REV. 1514, 1515 (2010).
9. Cynthia Conti-Cook, *Surveilling the Digital Abortion Diary*, 50 U. BALT. L. REV. 1, 15 (2020).
10. Jennifer Daskal, *Notice and Standing in the Fourth Amendment: Searches of Personal Data*, 26 WM. & MARY BILL RTS. J. 437, 454 (2017).
11. *See* Aziz Z. Huq & Rebecca Wexler, *Digital Privacy for Reproductive Choice in the Post-*Roe *Era*, 98 N.Y.U. L. REV. 555, 574 (2023).
12. PAUL BUTLER, CHOKEHOLD: POLICING BLACK MEN 59–61 (2017).
13. *See generally* RUHA BENJAMIN, RACE AFTER TECHNOLOGY: ABOLITIONIST TOOLS FOR THE NEW JIM CODE (2019); ALEX S. VITALE, THE END OF POLICING (2017); POLICING THE BLACK MAN: ARREST, PROSECUTION, AND IMPRISONMENT (Angela J. Davis ed., 2017); MICHELLE ALEXANDER, THE NEW JIM CROW: MASS INCARCERATION IN THE AGE OF COLORBLINDNESS (2010).
14. *Id.*
15. BARRY FRIEDMAN, UNWARRANTED: POLICING WITHOUT PERMISSION 143–84 (2017).
16. Craig S. Lerner, *The Reasonableness of Probable Cause*, 81 TEX. L. REV. 951, 981–95 (2003).

17. Matt Ford, *When Your Judge Isn't a Lawyer*, THE ATLANTIC, Feb. 5, 2017.
18. *See generally* Andrew Guthrie Ferguson, *Why Digital Policing Is Different*, 83 OHIO ST. L.J. 817, 837 (2022).
19. Andrew Guthrie Ferguson, *Digital Habit Evidence*, 72 DUKE L.J. 723, 757 (2023).
20. *See generally* FERGUSON, *supra* note 3; Andrew Guthrie Ferguson, *Facial Recognition and the Fourth Amendment*, 105 MINN. L. REV. 1105, 1115 (2021).
21. *Id.*; *see also* Andrew Guthrie Ferguson, *Structural Sensor Surveillance*, 106 IOWA L. REV. 47, 57 (2020).
22. Andrew Guthrie Ferguson, *Persistent Surveillance*, 74 ALA. L. REV. 1, 5 (2022).
23. Zac Larkman, *The Quiet Rise of Real-Time Crime Centers*, WIRED, July 28, 2023; JAY STANLEY, ACLU, THE DAWN OF ROBOT SURVEILLANCE: AI, VIDEO ANALYTICS, AND PRIVACY 17–21 (2019).
24. Brandon Block, *Federal Aid Is Supercharging Local WA Police Surveillance Tech*, CROSSCUT (July 26, 2023), www.cascadepbs.org; Rachel Levinson-Waldman, *Private Eyes, They're Watching You: Law Enforcement's Monitoring of Social Media*, 71 OKLA. L. REV. 997, 998 (2019).
25. Jahd Khalil, *Real Time Crime Centers, Which Started in Bigger Cities, Spread Across the U.S.*, NPR (Aug. 16, 2023), www.npr.org; Jim McKay, *Crooks Can't Dodge the Real-Time Crime Center "Double Click,"* GOV'T TECH., Dec. 7, 2023.
26. Eva Ruth Moraveic, *Do Algorithms Have a Place in Policing*, THE ATLANTIC, (Sept. 5, 2019); Will D. Heaven, *Predictive Policing Is Still Racist—Whatever Data It Uses*, MASS. INST. TECH. TECH. REV., Feb. 5, 2021.
27. Andrew Guthrie Ferguson, *Surveillance and the Tyrant Test*, 110 GEO. L.J. 205, 208 (2021).
28. Kerry Abrams & Brandon L. Garrett, *DNA and Distrust*, 91 NOTRE DAME L. REV. 757, 758 (2015); Erin Murphy, *License, Registration, Cheek Swab: DNA Testing and the Divided Court*, 127 HARV. L. REV. 161, 180 (2013); Erin Murphy, *Relative Doubt: Familial Searches of DNA Databases*, 109 MICH. L. REV. 291, 294 (2010).
29. Mark Hansen, *Digital Detection Tracking Down the "Craigslist Killer,"* ABA J., June 2013, at 30.
30. Alec Karakatsanis, *Why "Crime" Isn't the Question and Police Aren't the Answer*, CURRENT AFFS., Aug. 10, 2020.
31. After all, even the Founding generation was involved in criminal activities like smuggling and tax evasion. Kiel Brennan-Marquez & Stephen E. Henderson, *Search and Seizure Budgets*, 13 U.C. IRVINE L. REV. 389, 404 (2023).

CHAPTER 1. OUR HOMES

1. Jon Fingas, *Florida Police Obtain Alexa Recordings in Murder Investigation*, ENGADGET, (Nov. 2, 2019), www.engadget.com.
2. Sidney Fussell, *Meet the Star Witness: Your Smart Speaker*, WIRED, Aug. 23, 2020.
3. *See How to Set Up and Get More from Your Echo Speaker*, WIRED, May 15, 2020.
4. Fingas, *supra* note 1; Fussell, *supra* note 2.
5. Muscolino v. State, 2020 Md. App. LEXIS 1184, at *2 (Md. Ct. Spec. App. 2020).

6. Tyler Lacoma, *How to Access Your Google Nest Cam or Doorbell from Any Device*, CNET (Apr. 5, 2024), www.cnet.com.
7. *Muscolino*, 2020 Md. App. LEXIS 1184 at *3.
8. *Id.*
9. *See generally*, Gabriel Bronshteyn, *Searching the Smart Home*, 72 STAN. L. REV. 455, 457 (2020).
10. Jonathan Levitt, *Smart Cities 101: What They Are and How to Build One*, FAST CO. (Mar. 9, 2023), www.fastco.com.
11. Thomas Brewster, *Smart Home Surveillance: Governments Tell Google's Nest to Hand Over Data 300 Times*, FORBES, Oct. 13, 2018.
12. Andrew Guthrie Ferguson, *The "Smart" Fourth Amendment*, 102 CORNELL L. REV. 547, 564 (2017).
13. Lorna Fox, *The Meaning of Home: A Chimerical Concept or a Legal Challenge?*, 29 J.L. & SOC'Y 580, 590–91 (2002); *see also* D. Benjamin Barros, *Home as a Legal Concept*, 46 SANTA CLARA L. REV. 255, 258 (2006).
14. Minnesota v. Carter, 525 U.S. 83, 107 (1998) (Ginsburg, J., dissenting) ("Our decisions indicate that people have a reasonable expectation of privacy in their homes in part because they have the prerogative to exclude others.").
15. *See* Miller v. United States, 357 U.S. 301, 307 (1958).
16. Bo Zhao, *Unraveling Home Protection in the IoT Age: Smart Living, Mixed Reality, and Home 2.0*, 21 COLUM. SCI. & TECH. L. REV. 1, 17 (2019).
17. RICHARD L. RUTLEDGE, AARON K. MASSEY, A. ANTÓN & PETER P. SWIRE, DEFINING THE INTERNET OF DEVICES: PRIVACY AND SECURITY IMPLICATIONS (2014).
18. Joshua McNichols, *A Smart Home Neighborhood: Residents Find It Enjoyably Convenient or a Bit Creepy*, NPR (Nov. 9, 2019), www.npr.org.
19. Matthew Tokson, *Inescapable Surveillance*, 106 CORNELL L. REV. 409, 432 (2021).
20. *See* Heather Kelly, *Parents Are Using AirTags to Track Kids and Give Them Freedom*, WASH. POST, July 26, 2023.
21. *See* Meagan Flynn, *Police Think Alexa May Have Witnessed a New Hampshire Double Homicide. Now They Want Amazon to Turn Her Over*, WASH. POST, Nov. 14, 2018.
22. Karen Dandurant, *Timothy Verrill Fights 2nd Double-Murder Trial After NH Police Errors Botched the First One*, FOSTER'S DAILY DEMOCRAT, Apr. 21, 2021.
23. State v. Timothy Verrill, Order on Motion to Search, No. 219–2017-CR-072 (N.H. Super. Ct., Strafford County, Nov. 5, 2018).
24. *Id.*; *see also* Dandurant, *supra* note 22.
25. Jack Morse, *How to Make Your Smart TV a Little Dumb (and Why You Should)*, MASHABLE, (Mar. 4, 2021), www.mashable.com.
26. *Id.*
27. Molly Price, *My Week with Sleep Sensing on Google's New Nest*, CNET (Apr. 12, 2021), www.cnet.com.

28. Minnesota v. Carter, 525 U.S. 83, 99 (1998) (Kennedy, J., concurring).
29. Florida v. Jardines, 569 U.S. 1, 6 (2013).
30. Payton v. New York, 445 U.S. 573, 589 (1980).
31. Stephanie M. Stern, *The Inviolate Home: Housing Exceptionalism in the Fourth Amendment*, 95 CORNELL L. REV. 101, 913–14 (2010).
32. Kyllo v. United States, 533 U.S. 27, 31 (2001) (internal citations omitted).
33. Eileen Guo, *A Roomba Recorded a Woman on the Toilet. How Did the Screenshots End Up on Facebook?*, TECH. REV., Dec. 19, 2022.
34. Stacy-Ann Elvy, *Commodifying Consumer Data in the Era of the Internet of Things*, 59 B.C. L. REV. 423, 433 (2018).
35. Andrew Guthrie Ferguson, *The Internet of Things and the Fourth Amendment of Effects*, 104 CAL. L. REV. 805, 835 (2016).
36. Kaitlin D. Corey, *How Far Will the Third Party Doctrine Extend?*, MD. B.J., July/August 2018, at 14, 15.
37. Kyllo v. United States, 533 U.S. 27, 29 (2001).
38. *Id.*
39. Naperville Smart Meter Awareness v. City of Naperville, 900 F.3d 521, 526 (7th Cir. 2018).
40. Erin Murphy, *The Case Against the Case for Third-Party Doctrine: A Response to Epstein and Kerr*, 24 BERKELEY TECH. L.J. 1239, 1240–41 (2009).
41. Dandurant, *supra* note 22.
42. Orin S. Kerr, *The Case for the Third-Party Doctrine*, 107 MICH. L. REV. 561, 563 (2009).
43. United States v. Miller, 425 U.S. 435, 440 (1976); Smith v. Maryland, 442 U.S. 735, 744 (1979).
44. *Miller*, 425 U.S. at 440.
45. Riley v. California, 573 U.S. 373, 403 (2014).
46. Elizabeth Weise, *Police Ask Alexa: Who Dunnit?*, USA TODAY, Dec. 29, 2016.
47. *Id.*
48. Complaint at 2–4, State v. Bates, No. CR20160370, 2016 WL 7587405 (Ark. Cir.).
49. *Id.*
50. Colin Dwyer, *Arkansas Prosecutors Drop Murder Case That Hinged on Amazon Echo*, NPR (Nov. 29, 2017), www.npr.org.
51. State of Arkansas v. James Andrew Bates, 2016 WL 7587405 (Ark. Cir.).
52. Deborah Becker, *ACLU Asks Supreme Court to Rule in Massachusetts Police Surveillance Case*, WBUR (Nov. 18, 2022), www.wbur.org.
53. United States v. Moore-Bush, 381 F. Supp. 3d 139, 149 (D. Mass. 2019), *as amended* (June 4, 2019), *rev'd and remanded*, 963 F.3d 29 (1st Cir. 2020), *reh'g en banc granted, opinion vacated*, 982 F.3d 50 (1st Cir. 2020), and *on reh'g en banc*, 36 F.4th 320 (1st Cir. 2022), and *rev'd and remanded*, 36 F.4th 320 (1st Cir. 2022).
54. 75 A.L.R. FED. 3d Art. 3 (2022) ("Pole cameras are video cameras commonly affixed to a utility pole or similar object.").
55. *Moore-Bush*, 381 F. Supp. 3d at 149.

56. United States v. Tuggle, 4 F.4th 505, 511 (7th Cir. 2021).
57. *Id.*
58. *Id.*
59. Andrew Guthrie Ferguson, *Persistent Surveillance*, 74 ALA. L. REV. 1, 13 (2022).
60. United States v. Romano, 388 F. Supp. 101, 104 n.4 (E.D. Pa. 1975).
61. Collins v. Virginia, 584 U.S. 586, 592 (2018).
62. Andrew Guthrie Ferguson, *Personal Curtilage: Fourth Amendment Security in Public*, 55 WM. & MARY L. REV. 1283, 1313 (2014).
63. California v. Ciraolo, 476 U.S. 207, 212–13 (1986).
64. United States v. Knotts, 460 U.S. 276, 285 (1983).
65. William J. Stuntz, *The Distribution of Fourth Amendment Privacy*, 67 GEO. WASH. L. REV. 1265, 1277 (1999).
66. Ferguson, *supra* note 62, at 1315.
67. California v. Ciraolo, 476 U.S. 207, 215 (1986).
68. Florida v. Riley, 488 U.S. 445, 448 (1989).
69. United States v. Knotts, 460 U.S. 276, 285 (1983).
70. Andrew Guthrie Ferguson, *Why Digital Policing Is Different*, 83 OHIO ST. L.J. 817, 819 (2022).
71. Ginia Bellafante, *The Landlord Wants Facial Recognition in Its Rent-Stabilized Buildings. Why?* N.Y. TIMES, Mar. 28, 2019.
72. Justin Wm. Moyer, *Lawsuit Alleges D.C. Housing's Cameras Could "Capture Intimate Details,"* WASH. POST, Dec. 30, 2022; Todd Feathers, *"Clearly Discrimination": How a City Uses Fusus to Spy on Its Poorest Residents*, GIZMODO (Feb. 11, 2025), www.gizmodo.com; *see also* Kate Weisburd, *The Carceral Home*, 103 B.U. L. REV. 1879, 1902 (2023).
73. *See* Douglass MacMillan, *Eyes on the Poor: Cameras, Facial Recognition Watch Over Public Housing*, WASH. POST, May 16, 2023.
74. Stoner v. California, 376 U.S. 483 (1964).
75. Monica Melton, *Lawmaker Who Challenged Facial Recognition in Majority Black Building Introduces New Bill for Public Housing*, FORBES, July 23, 2019.
76. Elizabeth Kim, *Brooklyn Landlord Does an About Face on Facial Recognition Plan*, GOTHAMIST (Nov. 21, 2019), www.gothamist.com.
77. *Id.*
78. Mutale Nkonde, *Automated Anti-Blackness: Facial Recognition in Brooklyn, New York*, HARV. KENNEDY SCH. J. AFR. AM. POL'Y, 2019–2020, at 30, 31, 34.
79. Lola Fadulu, *Facial Recognition Technology in Public Housing Prompts Backlash*, N.Y. TIMES, Sept. 24, 2019.
80. *Our Amenities*, 2100 HAMILTON, https://2100hamilton.com/amenities/ ("To that end, we have designed single-residence elevators that open directly to each unit using contactless facial recognition technology.").
81. Chris Gilliard, *The Rise of "Luxury Surveillance,"* THE ATLANTIC, Oct. 18, 2022.
82. *See Our Amenities*, *supra* note 80.

83. Emily West, *Amazon: Surveillance as a Service*, 17 SURVEILLANCE & SOC'Y 27 (2019).
84. *See* Matthew Guariglia, *Amazon's Ring Is a Perfect Storm of Privacy Threats*, ELEC. FRONTIER FOUND. (Aug. 8, 2019), www.eff.org.
85. Alec Karakatsanis, *The Punishment Bureaucracy: How to Think About "Criminal Justice Reform,"* 128 YALE L.J. FORUM 848, 853–54 (2019).
86. Alec Karakatsanis, *Why "Crime" Isn't the Question and Police Aren't the Answer*, CURRENT AFFS., Aug. 10, 2020.
87. John Herrman, *Who's Watching Your Porch?*, N.Y. TIMES, Jan. 20, 2020.
88. Alfred Ng, *The Privacy Loophole in Your Doorbell*, POLITICO (Mar. 7, 2023), www.politico.com.
89. POLICING PROJECT, RING & NEIGHBORS PUBLIC SAFETY SERVICE: A CIVIL RIGHTS AND CIVIL LIBERTIES AUDIT 13 (2022).
90. *See* David Priest, *Ring's Flying Security Cam Needs These 4 Features to Succeed*, CNET (June 2, 2021), www.cnet.com.
91. Rich Brown, *Nest Says Hello with a New Doorbell Camera*, CNET (Sept. 20, 2017), www.cnet.com; *Strategy Analytics: Amazon's Ring Remained atop the Video Doorbell Market in 2021*, BUS. WIRE (June 22, 2022), www.businesswire.com.
92. Siôn Geschwindt, *Intruders Beware: New Face-Detecting AI Security Cam Fires Paintballs and Teargas. Meet Eve—Every Criminal's Worst Nightmare*, THE NEXT WEB (Apr. 12, 2024), www.thenextweb.com.
93. Drew Harwell, *Doorbell-Camera Firm Ring Has Partnered with 400 Police Forces, Extending Surveillance Concerns*, WASH. POST, Aug. 28, 2019.
94. *See* POLICING PROJECT, *supra* note 89, at 12.
95. Louise Matsakis, *Cops Are Offering Ring Doorbell Cameras in Exchange for Info*, WIRED, Aug. 2, 2019.
96. POLICING PROJECT, *supra* note 89, at 13.
97. Emma McGowan, *Here's What Your Ring Doorbell Knows About You*, AVAST (Dec. 21, 2022), https://blog.avast.com.
98. Drew Harwell, *Ring and Nest Helped Normalize American Surveillance and Turned Us Into a Nation of Voyeurs*, WASH. POST, Feb. 18, 2020; Alfred Ng, *Amazon's Helping Police Build a Surveillance Network with Ring Doorbells*, CNET (June 5, 2019), www.cnet.com.
99. Ng, *supra* note 88.
100. Harwell, *supra* note 93.
101. POLICING PROJECT, *supra* note 89, at 17.
102. Matt Day, *Amazon's Ring to Stop Letting Police Request Doorbell Video from Users*, BLOOMBERG (Jan. 24, 2024), www.bloomberg.com.
103. Tyler Lacoma, *Amazon Ring No Longer Sharing Home Security Footage with Police, Company Says*, CNET (Jan 25, 2024), www.cnet.com.
104. David Priest, *Ring's Police Problem Never Went Away. Here's What You Still Need to Know*, CNET (Sept. 27, 2021), www.cnet.com.

105. *See* Sean Hollister, *Today I Learned Amazon Has a Form So Police Can Get My Data Without Permission or a Warrant*, THE VERGE (July 14, 2022), www.theverge.com.
106. Drew Harwell, *Police Can Keep Ring Camera Video Forever and Share with Whomever They'd Like, Amazon Tells Senator*, WASH. POST, Nov. 19, 2019.
107. Ng, *supra* note 88.
108. *Id.*
109. *Id.*
110. *See* Sarah Esther Lageson, *Do People Caught on Ring Cameras Have Privacy Rights?*, WIRED, May 19, 2022.
111. Caroline Haskins, *Amazon's Home Security Company Is Turning Everyone into Cops*, VICE (Feb. 7, 2019), www.vice.com.
112. Caroline Haskins, *How Ring Transmits Fear to American Suburbs*, MOTHERBOARD (Dec. 6, 2019), www.vice.com; Louise Matsakis, *The Ringification of Suburban Life*, WIRED, Sept. 26, 2019.
113. POLICING PROJECT, *supra* note 89, at 14.
114. Sara Ashley O'Brien, *Helicopters, a Patrol Car and Virtual Bodyguards: Inside Citizen's Scattered Push to Upend Public Safety*, CNN BUS. (June 3, 2021), www.cnn.com.
115. James Vincent, *Vigilante App Citizen Is Paying People to Livestream Crime Scenes and Emergencies*, THE VERGE (July 27, 2021), www.theverge.com.
116. Tom Jackman, *"Vigilante" Phone App Alerts New York Users to Crime, but Police Not Thrilled*, WASH. POST, Nov. 4, 2016.
117. *See, e.g.*, Sara Morrison, *How Citizen Sparked a $30,000 Manhunt for the Wrong Guy*, VOX (May 18, 2021), www.vox.com; Joseph Cox & Jason Koebler, *"FIND THIS FUCK": Inside Citizen's Dangerous Effort to Cash in on Vigilantism*, VICE (May 27, 2021), www.vice.com.
118. *See* Joseph Cox, *Leaked Emails Show Crime App Citizen Is Testing On-Demand Security Force*, VICE (May 21, 2021), www.vice.com.
119. *See* Joseph Cox, *Crime App Citizen Is Driving a Security Car Around L.A. and Won't Say Why*, VICE (May 21, 2021), www.vice.com.
120. Jackie Kent, *Civil Rights Group Calls Neighborhood License Plate Camera "Invasive,"* KOMO NEWS (Feb. 21, 2022), https://komonews.com.
121. FLOCK SAFETY, NEIGHBORHOOD SECURITY GUIDE (2023).
122. Georgia Gee, *License Plate Surveillance, Courtesy of Your Homeowners Association*, THE INTERCEPT (Mar. 22, 2023), www.theintercept.com.
123. Todd Feathers, *Civil Rights Groups Want Tech Sites to Stop Reviewing Amazon's Ring Cameras*, VICE (Mar. 24, 2021), www.vice.com.
124. *See, e.g.*, Annette Choi, *Record Number of Anti-LGBTQ Bills Have Been Introduced This Year*, CNN (Apr. 6, 2023), www.cnn.com; Melissa Block, *Bans on Medical Care for Trans Youth Are Moving Quickly Through State Legislatures*, NPR (Mar. 7, 2023), www.npr.org.
125. Bill Budington, *Ring Doorbell App Packed with Third-Party Trackers*, ELEC. FRONTIER FOUND. (Jan. 27, 2020), www.eff.org.

CHAPTER 2. OUR THINGS

1. United States v. Chatrie, 590 F. Supp. 3d 901, 918, n.26 (E.D. Va. 2022).
2. *Chatrie*, 590 F. Supp. 3d at 905.
3. *See* Michael Grothaus, *Google Tracks Your Movements Even If You've Turned Location History Off*, FAST CO. (Aug. 13, 2018), www.fastcompany.com.
4. *Chatrie*, 590 F. Supp. 3d at 914.
5. *Id.* at 906–07.
6. Shireen Allicott, *Car Auto-Dials 911 to Report Accident After Driver Allegedly Commits Hit-and-Run*, ABC7 (Dec. 4, 2015), https://abc7chicago.com.
7. Jenn Gidman, *Hit-and-Run Suspect Ratted Out by Her Own Ford Focus*, USA TODAY, Dec. 8, 2015.
8. *Ford Emergency Device Squeals on Florida Hit-and-Run Driver*, NPR (Dec. 14, 2015), www.npr.org.
9. Haley Tsukayama, *This Smart Car Seems to Have Tattled on Its Driver*, WASH. POST., Dec. 14, 2015.
10. *See* Alexander P. Carroll, *New Technology and the Right to Privacy: Do E-Scooters Implicate the Fourth Amendment?*, 40 J. NAT'L ASS'N ADMIN. L. JUDICIARY 27, 32–33 (2021).
11. *See* Andrew Guthrie Ferguson, *The Internet of Things and the Fourth Amendment of Effects*, 104 CAL. L. REV. 805, 813 (2016).
12. Kevin Ashton, *That "Internet of Things" Thing*, RFID J. (June 22, 2009), www.rfidjournal.com.
13. Scott R. Peppet, *Regulating the Internet of Things: First Steps Toward Managing Discrimination, Privacy, Security, and Consent*, 93 TEX. L. REV. 85, 98 (2014).
14. JEREMY RIFKIN, THE ZERO MARGINAL COST SOCIETY: THE INTERNET OF THINGS, THE COLLABORATIVE COMMONS, AND THE ECLIPSE OF CAPITALISM 11 (2014).
15. Andrew Guthrie Ferguson, *The "Smart" Fourth Amendment*, 102 CORNELL L. REV. 547, 560 (2017).
16. *See* Riley v. California, 573 U.S. 373, 395 (2014).
17. *Id.* at 385.
18. *See generally* Adam M. Gershowitz, *The Tesla Meets the Fourth Amendment*, 48 B.Y.U. L. REV. 1135, 1139 (2023).
19. *See* Jack Morse, *Your Car Knows Too Much About You. That Could Be a Privacy Nightmare*, MASHABLE (Sept. 18, 2021), www.mashable.com.
20. Michael Froomkin & Zak Colangelo, *Privacy as Safety*, 95 WASH. L. REV. 141, 200 (2020); Roland L. Trope & Thomas J. Smedinghoff, *Why Smart Car Safety Depends on Cybersecurity*, ABA SCITECH LAW., Summer 2018, at 8, 9.
21. Jen Caltrider, Misha Rykov & Zoë MacDonald, *It's Official: Cars Are the Worst Product Category We Have Ever Reviewed for Privacy*, MOZILLA (Sept. 6, 2023), www.mozilla.com; *"Privacy Nightmare on Wheels": Every Car Brand Reviewed by Mozilla—Including Ford, Volkswagen and Toyota—Flunks Privacy Test*, MOZILLA (Sept. 6, 2023), www.mozilla.com.

22. Com. v. Augustine, 4 N.E.3d 846, 853 (Mass. 2014).
23. Carpenter v. United States, 585 U.S. 296, 300–01 (2018).
24. *Id.*
25. Stephen E. Henderson, Carpenter v. United States *and the Fourth Amendment: The Best Way Forward*, 26 WM. & MARY BILL RTS. J. 495, 497 (2017).
26. *See* Paul Ohm, *The Many Revolutions of* Carpenter, 32 HARV. J.L. & TECH. 357, 369 (2019).
27. Cullen Seltzer, *Google Knows Where You've Been. Should It Tell the Police?*, SLATE (May 16, 2022), www.slate.com.
28. David Nield, *All the Ways Google Tracks You—and How to Stop It*, WIRED, May 27, 2019.
29. Ryan Nakashima, *Google Tracks Your Movements, Like It or Not*, ASSOCIATED PRESS (Aug. 13, 2018), www.ap.com; Ryan Nakashima, *Google Clarifies Location-Tracking Policy*, ASSOCIATED PRESS (Aug. 16, 2018), www.ap.com.
30. *See* John C. Ellis Jr., *Google Data and Geofence Warrant Process*, NAT'L LITIG. SUPPORT BLOG (June 6, 2022), https://nlsblog.org.
31. Brian L. Owsley, *The Best Offense Is a Good Defense: Fourth Amendment Implications of Geofence Warrants*, 50 HOFSTRA L. REV. 829, 834 (2022).
32. *Id.*
33. Zach Whittaker, *Google Moves to End Geofence Warrants, a Surveillance Problem It Largely Created*, TECHCRUNCH (Dec. 16, 2023), www.techcrunch.com.
34. Orin S. Kerr, *Did Google Just Defeat Every Geofence Warrant*? REASON, Dec. 13, 2023.
35. Commonwealth v. Ani, 293 A.3d 704, 731–32 (Pa. Super. Ct. 2023); *see also* Zak Doffman, *Google Will Track Your Location "Every 15 Minutes"—"Even with GPS Disabled"* FORBES, Oct. 5, 2024.
36. *Spies Use* Angry Birds *and Other Apps to Track People, Documents Show*, CBS NEWS (Jan. 27, 2014), www.cbsnews.com; *see also* Joseph Cox, Candy Crush, *Tinder, MyFitnessPal: See the Thousands of Apps Hijacked to Spy on Your Location*, WIRED, Jan. 9, 2025.
37. Sam Biddle, *Your Car Is Spying on You and a CBP Contract Shows the Risks*, THE INTERCEPT (May 3, 2021), www.theintercept.com; Jon Keegan & Alfred Ng, *Who Is Collecting Data from Your Car?*, THE MARKUP (July 27, 2022), www .themarkup.com.
38. Riley Beggin, *Questions Arise of Police Searches of Car Data Systems*, GOV'T TECH. Jan. 4. 2022.
39. Mobley v. State, 834 S.E.2d 785, 788 (Ga. 2019).
40. *Id.* at 788.
41. *Id.*
42. *Id.* at 800.
43. *Id.* at 792–93.
44. South Dakota v. Opperman, 428 U.S. 364, 376 (1976).
45. Matt Burgess, *How Your New Car Tracks You*, WIRED, June 21, 2023.

46. Anthony Gordon, *Every New Car Is a "Privacy Nightmare," Mozilla Researchers Conclude*, VICE (Sept. 6, 2023), www.vice.com.
47. Thomas Germain, *If You've Got a New Car, It's a Data Privacy Nightmare*, GIZMODO (Sept. 7, 2023), www.gizmodo.com.
48. Geoffrey Fowler, *My Car Was in a Hit-and-Run. Then I Learned It Recorded the Whole Thing*, WASH. POST, Feb. 27, 2020.
49. *Id.*
50. Steve Stecklow, Waylon Cunningham & Hyunjoo Jin, *Tesla Workers Shared Sensitive Images Recorded by Customer Cars*, REUTERS (Apr. 6, 2023), www.reuters.com.
51. Kate Fazzini & Lora Kolodny, *Tesla Cars Keep More Data Than You Think, Including This Video of a Crash That Totaled a Model 3*, CNBC (Mar. 29, 2019), www.cnbc.com.
52. *Advanced Driver Assistance Systems*, EXCHANGE AAA, https://exchange.aaa.com.
53. State v. Nunez, No. 2020AP176 CR, 2022 Wisc. App. LEXIS 708, at *2 (Wis. Ct. App. Aug. 9, 2022).
54. *Id.*
55. *Id.* at *3.
56. *Id.*
57. State v. Tate, 849 N.W.2d 798, 802 (Wis. 2014).
58. *Id.*
59. *Id.* at 803.
60. *Id.* at 804.
61. *Id.*
62. Audrey Conklin, Michael Ruiz, Rebecca Rosenberg & Stephanie Pagones, *Bryan Kohberger's Phone Pinged at Idaho Murder Scene Hours After Killings and 12 Times Prior: Investigators*, FOX5 ATLANTA (Jan. 5, 2023), www.fox5atlanta.com; Elizabeth Wolfe & John Miller, *Authorities Tracked the Idaho Students Killings Suspect Cross-Country to Pennsylvania, Sources Say*, CNN (Dec. 31, 2022), www.cnn.com.
63. Heather Tal Murphy, *How Police Actually Cracked the Idaho Killings Case*, SLATE (Jan. 10, 2023), www.slate.com.
64. U.S. CONST. amend. IV.
65. *See, e.g.*, Florida v. Riley, 488 U.S. 445, 462 (1989) (Brennan, J., dissenting); INS v. Delgado, 466 U.S. 210, 215 (1984).
66. United States v. Jones, 565 U.S. 400 (2012).
67. Carpenter v. United States, 585 U.S. 296, 301 (2018).
68. *Jones*, 565 U.S. at 402.
69. *Id.* at 403.
70. *Id.*
71. *Id.* at 404–05.
72. *See id.* at 413–16 (Sotomayor, J., concurring); *id.* at 429–31 (Alito, J., concurring in judgment).

73. *Id.* at 415–16 (2012) (citations omitted).
74. *Id.* at 416.
75. Carpenter v. United States, 585 U.S. 296, 300 (2018).
76. *Id.* at 310–13.
77. *Id.* at 311.
78. *Id.*
79. *Id.* at 315.
80. *Id.* at 312.
81. United States v. Chatrie, 590 F. Supp. 3d 901 (E.D. Va. 2022).
82. *Id.* at 906.
83. *Id.* at 918, n.26.
84. *See* Ramon Padilla & Javier Zarracina, *How Police Work with Google to Obtain Cellphone Location Data for Criminal Investigations*, USA TODAY, Sept. 8, 2022.
85. Brief of Amicus Curiae Google LLC in Support of Neither Party Concerning Defendant's Motion to Suppress Evidence from a "Geofence" General Warrant at 18, United States v. Chatrie, 590 F. Supp. 3d 901 (E.D. Va. 2022).
86. Interview with Richard Salgado (Mar. 23, 2023).
87. Declaration of Sarah Rodriguez ¶ 5, United States v. Chatrie, No. 19-cr-00130 (E.D. Va. Mar. 11, 2020), ECF No. 96–2.
88. *Chatrie*, 590 F. Supp. 3d at 927.
89. *See id.* at 917 (stating that David Bishop completed only a bachelor's degree and did not go to law school). https://www.nacdl.org/getattachment/20937630-8e79-4cf2-b1ce-cb9b82344033/210305-day-2-transcript.pdf.
90. *Id.* at 939–40.
91. *Id.* citing VA. CODE § 19.2–37.
92. Thomas v. Commonwealth, No. 0613-21-3, 2022 WL 3362920, at *37 (Va. Ct. App. Aug. 16, 2022).
93. *Id.* at *3–4.
94. *Id.* at *3–5.
95. *Id.* at *6.
96. *Id.* at *3–7.
97. *Id.* at *7.
98. Ned Oliver, *Virginia Police Routinely Use Secret GPS Pings to Track People's Cell Phones*, VA. MERCURY, Apr. 6, 2022.
99. *Id.*
100. Gilad Edelman, *Can the Government Buy Its Way Around the Fourth Amendment?*, WIRED, Feb. 11, 2020.
101. Byron Tau, *Treasury Watchdog Warns of Government's Use of Cellphone Data Without Warrants*, WALL ST. J., Feb. 22, 2021.
102. *See* Kashmir Hill, *Florida Man Sues G.M. and LexisNexis over Sale of His Cadillac Data*, N.Y. TIMES, Mar. 14, 2024.
103. *See* Press Release, *Senator Ron Wyden, Paul and Bipartisan Members of Congress Introduce the Fourth Amendment Is Not for Sale Act*, RON WYDEN (Apr. 21, 2021),

https://www.wyden.senate.gov/news/press-releases/wyden-paul-and-bipartisan-members-of-congress-introduce-the-fourth-amendment-is-not-for-sale-act-.

104. California Privacy Rights Act (CPRA) CAL. CIV. CODE §§ 1798.100 to .199.100. (Deering 2018).
105. Colorado Privacy Act (CPA) COLO. REV. STAT. §§ 6-1-1301 to -1313 (2023).
106. Connecticut Data Privacy Act (CDPA) 2022 CONN. ACTS NO. 22–15 (Reg. Sess.).
107. Utah Consumer Privacy Act (UCPA) UTAH CODE ANN. §§ 13-61-101 to -104 (LexisNexis 2022).
108. Virginia Consumer Data Protection Act (VCDPA) VA. CODE ANN. §§ 59.1–575 to 585 (2022).
109. *See* CAL. CIV. CODE § 1798.145(2); VA. CODE ANN. § 59.1–582(3) (2022); COLO. REV. STAT. §§ 6-1-1304 (3)(a)(III) (2022); 2022 CONN. ACTS NO. 22–15 §10(a)(3) (Reg. Sess.);UTAH CODE ANN. §13-61-304(1)(c) (LexisNexis 2022). *See also* Erin Murphy, *The Politics of Privacy in the Criminal Justice System: Information Disclosure, the Fourth Amendment, and Statutory Law Enforcement Exemptions*, 111 MICH. L. REV. 485, 496 (2013).
110. 740 ILL. COMP. STAT. 14/15(d)(4); TEX. BUS. & COM. CODE §503.001(c)(1)(D).
111. *See Cars & Consumer Data: On Unlawful Collection & Use*, FED. TRADE COMM'N BLOG (May 14, 2024), www.ftc.gov.
112. Benjamin Clubbs Coldron, Guido Noto La Diega, Tania Phipps-Rufus & Tabea Stolte, *Giving Surveillance Capitalism a Makeover: Wearable Technology in the Fashion Industry and the Challenges for Privacy and Data Protection Law*, in THE OXFORD HANDBOOK OF FASHION LAW (Irene Calboli & Eleonora Rosati eds., 2025).
113. Thomas Brewster, *The DEA Quietly Turned Apple's AirTag into a Surveillance Tool*, FORBES, Mar. 23, 2023; Mark Wilson, *Apple AirTags Could Enable Domestic Abuse in Terrifying Ways*, FAST CO. (Apr. 29, 2021), www.fastcompany.com.

CHAPTER 3. OUR BODIES

1. Marie-Helen Maras & Adam Scott Wandt, State of Ohio v. Ross Compton*: Internet-Enabled Medical Device Data Introduced as Evidence of Arson and Insurance Fraud*, 24 INT'L J. EVIDENCE & PROOF 321, 322 (2020).
2. Cleve R. Wootson Jr., *A Man Detailed His Escape from a Burning House. His Pacemaker Told Police a Different Story*, WASH. POST, Feb. 8, 2017; Deanna Paul, *Your Own Pacemaker Can Now Testify Against You in Court*, WIRED, July 29, 2017.
3. State v. Burch, 2021 WI 68, ¶ 4, 398 Wis. 2d 1 (2021), *cert. denied*, 142 S. Ct. 811, 211 L. Ed. 2d 503 (2022).
4. *Id.*
5. *Id.*
6. Adam D. Thierer, *The Internet of Things and Wearable Technology: Addressing Privacy and Security Concerns Without Derailing Innovation*, 21 RICH. J.L. & TECH. 1, 19 (2015).

7. Andrea M. Matwyshyn, *The Internet of Bodies*, 61 WM. & MARY L. REV. 77, 81 (2019).
8. Melanie Swan, *Sensor Mania! The Internet of Things, Wearable Computing, Objective Metrics, and the Quantified Self 2.0*, 1 J. SENSOR & ACTUATOR NETWORKS 217, 217–18 (2012).
9. *See* Halyna Kubiv, *How Many Apple Watches Has Apple Sold?*, MACWORLD (Feb. 12, 2021), www.macworld.com.
10. Matwyshyn, *supra* note 7, at 83.
11. Pam Belluck, *First Digital Pill Approved to Worries About Biomedical "Big Brother,"* N.Y. TIMES, Nov. 13, 2017; Celia Ford, *This Pill Tracks Your Vitals from the Inside*, WIRED, Dec. 7, 2023.
12. *See "Smart Bandage" Detects, May Prevent Infections*, US NAT'L SCI. FOUND. (Mar. 3, 2021), www.nsf.gov.
13. Christine Hauser, *In Connecticut Murder Case, a Fitbit Is a Silent Witness*, N.Y. TIMES, Apr. 27, 2017; Tracy Connor, *Fitbit Murder Case: Richard Dabate Pleads Not Guilty in Wife's Death*, NBC NEWS (Apr. 29, 2017), www.nbcnews .com.
14. Lydia X. Z. Brown, Center for Democracy and Technology, *Big Brother Meets Bedlam: Resisting Mental Health Surveillance Tech* (Feb. 2, 2023).
15. Scott R. Peppet, *Regulating the Internet of Things: First Steps Toward Managing Discrimination, Privacy, Security, and Consent*, 93 TEX. L. REV. 85, 93 (2014).
16. Valena E. Beety & Jennifer D. Oliva, *Policing Pregnancy "Crimes,"* 98 N.Y.U. L. REV. 29, 32 (2023); Aziz Z. Huq & Rebecca Wexler, *Digital Privacy for Reproductive Choice in the Post-*Roe *Era*, 98 N.Y.U. L. REV. 555, 570 (2023).
17. Flora Garamvolgyi, *Why US Women Are Deleting Their Period Tracking Apps*, THE GUARDIAN, June 28, 2022.
18. *Flo Ovulation & Period Tracker*, MOZILLA FOUND. (Aug. 9, 2022), www .mozillafoundation.org; Amina Kilpatrick, *Period Tracker App Flo Developing "Anonymous Mode" to Quell Post-*Roe *Privacy Concerns*, NPR (June 30, 2022), www.npr.org.
19. Julianne McShane, *Va. Republicans Shelve Bill to Protect Menstrual Data from Search Warrants*, NBC NEWS (Feb. 19, 2023), www.nbcnews.com.
20. Cynthia Conti-Cook, *Surveilling the Digital Abortion Diary*, 50 U. BALT. L. REV. 1, 36 (2020); *see also* Sarah Perez, *Consumers Swap Period Tracking Apps in Search of Increased Privacy Following* Roe v. Wade *Ruling*, TECHCRUNCH (June 27, 2022), www.techcrunch.com.
21. Thomas Germain, *Creepshow: FTC Fines Premom for Handing Period Data to Chinese Companies and Google*, GIZMODO (May 18, 2023), www.gizmodo.com.
22. *FTC Finalizes Order with Flo Health, a Fertility-Tracking App That Shared Sensitive Health Data with Facebook, Google, and Others*, FED. TRADE COMM'N (June 22, 2021), www.ftc.gov.
23. Carly Page, *Premom Fertility App Shared Sensitive Data with Chinese Analytics Firms, FTC Says*, TECHCRUNCH (May 18, 2023), www.techcrunch.com.

24. Katie Malone, *Eight Months Post-*Roe, *Reproductive Health Policy Is Still Messy*, ENGADGET (Mar. 3, 2023), www.engadget.com; Rebecca Pifer, *Period Tracker Flo Launches Anonymous Mode amid Post-*Roe *Privacy Concerns*, HEALTHCARE DIVE (Sept. 15, 2022), www.healthcaredive.com.
25. Ashley Gold & Oriana González, *Post-*Roe, *Prosecutors Can Seek Unprotected Reproductive Health Data*, AXIOS (Mar. 1, 2023), www.axios.com.
26. Yael Grauer, *What Big Tech Knows About Your Body*, THE ATLANTIC, Sept. 21, 2023.
27. Complaint, In the Matter of BetterHelp, Inc., No. 2023169 (2022), https://www.ftc.gov/system/files/ftc_gov/pdf/2023169-betterhelp-complaint_.pdf.
28. Andrew Blok, *BetterHelp Should Pay $7.8 Million for Sharing Sensitive Data, FTC Says*, CNET (Mar. 2, 2023), www.cnet.com.
29. Jen Caltrider, Misha Rykov & Zoë MacDonald, *Are Mental Health Apps Better or Worse at Privacy in 2023?*, MOZILLA (May 1, 2023), www.mozillafoundation.org.
30. Jess Weatherbed, *Therapy Apps Are Still Failing Their Privacy Checkups*, THE VERGE (May 4, 2023), www.theverge.com.
31. Colin Lecher & Jon Keegan, *Suicide Hotlines Promise Anonymity. Dozens of Their Websites Send Sensitive Data to Facebook*, THE MARKUP (June 13, 2023), www.themarkup.org.
32. *Law Enforcement Resources: Next Generation Identification (NGI)*, FED. BUREAU OF INVESTIGATION, https://le.fbi.gov/science-and-lab/biometrics-and-fingerprints/biometrics/next-generation-identification-ngi.
33. Ken Klippenstein, *FBI Hoovering Up DNA at a Pace That Rivals China, Holds 21 Million Samples and Counting*, THE INTERCEPT (Aug. 29, 2023), www.theintercept.com.
34. Stephen Mercer & Jessica D. Gabel, *Shadow Dwellers: The Underregulated World of State and Local DNA Databases*, 69 N.Y.U. ANN. SURV. AM. L. 639, 654 (2014).
35. Jordan Smith, *Orange County Prosecutors Operate "Vast" "Secretive" Genetic Surveillance Program*, THE INTERCEPT (July 3, 2021), www.theintercept.com.
36. Andrea Roth, *"Spit and Acquit": Prosecutors as Surveillance Entrepreneurs*, 107 CAL. L. REV. 405, 410 (2019).
37. Corin Faife, *NJ Police Used Baby DNA to Investigate Crimes, Lawsuit Claims*, THE VERGE (June 29, 2022), www.theverge.com.
38. Natalie Ram, *America's Hidden National DNA Database*, 100 TEX. L. REV. 1253, 1255 (2022).
39. Dana Difilippo, *Judge Orders State to Release Information about Police Use of Baby Blood Spots*, N.J. MONITOR, Jan. 4, 2023.
40. *Id.*
41. Natalie Ram, *Genetic Privacy After Carpenter*, 105 VA. L. REV. 1357, 1359, 1366 (2019).
42. Stephen Mayhew, *Pentagon to Test Rapid DNA Biometric Technology*, BIOMETRICUPDATE.COM (Oct. 17, 2012), www.biometricupdate.com.

43. Maura Dolan, *"Rapid DNA" Promises Breakthroughs in Solving Crimes. So Why Does It Face a Backlash?*, L.A. TIMES, Sept. 25, 2019.
44. CLARE GARVIE, GEO. L. CTR. ON PRIV. & TECH., A FORENSIC WITHOUT THE SCIENCE: FACE RECOGNITION IN U.S. CRIMINAL INVESTIGATIONS 1, 9–12 (2022).
45. People v. Reyes, 69 Misc. 3d 963 (N.Y. Sup. Ct. 2020).
46. *Id.*
47. Complaint at 2–4, Parks v. McCormack, No. PAS-L-003672–20, 2020 WL 7773857 (N.J. Sup. Ct. Law Div. filed Nov. 25, 2020); John General & Jon Sarlin, *A False Facial Recognition Match Sent This Innocent Black Man to Jail*, CNN BUS. (Apr. 29, 2021).
48. Kashmir Hill, *Another Arrest, and Jail Time, Due to a Bad Facial Recognition Match*, N.Y. TIMES, Dec. 29, 2020.
49. Kashmir Hill & Ryan Mac, *"Thousands of Dollars for Something I Didn't Do,"* N.Y. TIMES, Mar. 31, 2023; Kashmir Hill, *Another Arrest, and Jail Time, Due to a Bad Facial Recognition Match*, N.Y. TIMES, Dec. 29, 2020.
50. CLARE GARVIE, GEO. L. CTR. ON PRIV. & TECH., GARBAGE IN, GARBAGE OUT (May 16, 2019).
51. Khari Johnson, *The Hidden Role of Facial Recognition Tech in Many Arrests*, WIRED, Mar. 7, 2022; Andrew Guthrie Ferguson, *Facial Recognition and the Fourth Amendment*, 105 MINN. L. REV. 1105, 1127–28 (2021).
52. CLARE GARVIE & LAURA M. MOY, GEO. L. CTR. ON PRIV. & TECH., AMERICA UNDER WATCH-FACE SURVEILLANCE IN THE UNITED STATES (May 16, 2019).
53. GARVIE, *supra* note 44.
54. Joy Buolamwini, *Response: Racial and Gender Bias in Amazon Rekognition—Commercial AI System for Analyzing Faces*, MEDIUM (Jan. 25, 2019), www.medium.com; Joy Buolamwini, *Artificial Intelligence Has a Problem with Gender and Racial Bias. Here's How to Solve It*, TIME, Feb. 7, 2019.
55. Drew Harwell & Craig Timberg, *How America's Surveillance Networks Helped the FBI Catch the Capitol Mob*, WASH. POST, Apr. 2, 2021.
56. Judge Herbert B. Dixon Jr., *I Recognize Your Walk*, JUDGES' J., Spring 2008, at 45.
57. Ram, *supra* note 41, at 1366.
58. NAT'L ACADS. SCIS., ENG'G, & MED., FACIAL RECOGNITION TECHNOLOGY: CURRENT CAPABILITIES, FUTURE PROSPECTS, AND GOVERNANCE 26–27 (2024).
59. United States v. Dionisio, 410 U.S. 1, 14 (1973) (emphasis added).
60. Ferguson, *supra* note 51, *Facial Recognition* at 1127–28.
61. Andrew Guthrie Ferguson, *Video Analytics and Fourth Amendment Vision* 103 TEX. L. REV. 1253, 1256 (2025).
62. Ferguson, *supra* note 51, *Facial Recognition* at 1127–28.

63. Wayne A. Logan, *Government Retention and Use of Unlawfully Secured DNA Evidence*, 48 TEX. TECH L. REV. 269, 275 (2015); Maryland v. King, 133 S. Ct. 1958, 1971–72 (2013).
64. Schmerber v. California, 384 U.S. 757, 767 (1966).
65. Andrew Guthrie Ferguson, *The "Smart" Fourth Amendment*, 102 CORNELL L. REV. 547, 591–93 (2017).
66. Missouri v. McNeely, 569 U.S. 141, 148 (2013).
67. Skinner v. Ry. Lab. Executives' Ass'n, 489 U.S. 602, 614 (1989).
68. *See e.g.*, Tracey Maclin, *Government Analysis of Shed DNA Is a Search Under the Fourth Amendment*, 48 TEX. TECH L. REV. 287, 297 (2015).
69. Maryland v. King, 133 S. Ct. 1958, 1971–72 (2013).
70. Elizabeth E. Joh, *Reclaiming "Abandoned" DNA: The Fourth Amendment and Genetic Privacy*, 100 NW. U. L. REV. 857, 867 (2006).
71. Carten Cordell, *IARPA's New Pants Will Record Your Location*, NEXTGOV (Aug. 23, 2023), www.nextgov.com.
72. United States v. Jones, 565 U.S. 400, 404 (2012).
73. Grady v. North Carolina, 575 U.S. 306, 308 (2015).
74. *Id.* at 309.
75. Ferguson, *supra* note 65, at 591–93.
76. Jayla E. Harvey, *Commercialization of Your DNA Privacy Regulations Lagging for Companies Collecting Genetic Data*, N.J. LAW., August 2022, at 38, 39.
77. Jordan Smith, *Police Are Getting DNA Data from People Who Think They Opted Out*, THE INTERCEPT (Aug. 18, 2023), www.theintercept.com.
78. CLARE GARVIE, ALVARO BEDOYA & JONATHAN FRANKLE, GEO. L. CTR. ON PRIV. & TECH., THE PERPETUAL LINE-UP: UNREGULATED POLICE FACE RECOGNITION IN AMERICA (2016).
79. CLEARVIEW AI, www.clearview.ai; Kashmir Hill, *The Secretive Company That Might End Privacy as We Know It*, N.Y. TIMES, Jan. 18, 2020.
80. Kashmir Hill, YOUR FACE BELONGS TO US: A SECRETIVE STARTUP'S QUEST TO END PRIVACY AS WE KNOW IT 61 (2023).
81. *See, e.g.*, Roberson v. Clearview AI, Inc., No. 1:21-cv-00174 (N.D. Ill. 2021); Marron v. Clearview AI, Inc., No. 1:20-cv-02989 (N.D. Ill. 2020).
82. Rachel Metz, *Clearview AI Agrees to Restrict US Sales of Facial Recognition to Mostly Law Enforcement*, CNN BUS. (May 9, 2022), https://edition.cnn.com.
83. Sarah Wallace, *Face Recognition Tech Gets Girls Scout Mom Booted from Rockettes Show—Due to Where She Works*, CBSNEWS (Dec. 22, 2022), www.cbsnews.com
84. Irina Ivanova, *Madison Square Garden Uses Facial Recognition to Keep Out Enemy Lawyers. That May Be Illegal*, CBSNEWS (Jan. 23, 2023), www.cbsnews.com.
85. Georgia Gee, *Here Are the Stadiums Keeping Track of Your Face*, SLATE (March 14, 2023), www.slate.com.
86. *Id.*
87. Kaveh Waddell, *CSI: Walmart*, THE ATLANTIC, Apr. 3, 2017.

88. Peter Waldman & Lauren Etter, *How Target Got Cozy with the Cops, Turning Black Neighbors into Suspects*, BLOOMBERG: BUSINESSWEEK (Aug. 25, 2021), www.bloomberg.com.
89. *Rite Aid Banned from Using AI Facial Recognition After FTC Says Retailer Deployed Technology Without Reasonable Safeguards*, FED. TRADE COMM'N (May 14, 2024), www.ftc.gov.
90. David Oliver, *Facial Recognition Scanners Are Already at Some US Airports. Here's What to Know*, USA TODAY, Aug. 18, 2019.
91. Kate Albrecht, *Which Government Building Is Piloting Facial Recognition Technology?*, GOV'T TECH. (Dec. 5, 2018), www.govtech.com.
92. U.S. GOV'T ACCOUNTABILITY OFF., GAO-22–106100, TESTIMONY BEFORE THE SUBCOMMITTEE ON INVESTIGATIONS AND OVERSIGHT, COMMITTEE ON SCIENCE, SPACE, AND TECHNOLOGY, HOUSE OF REPRESENTATIVES, FACIAL RECOGNITION TECHNOLOGY: FEDERAL AGENCIES' USE AND RELATED PRIVACY PROTECTIONS (2022).
93. *Id.*
94. *Id.*
95. J. Brian Charles, *Baltimore Could See More Surveillance as Facial Recognition Technology Moratorium Ends*, BALTIMORE BEAT (Jan. 10, 2023).
96. Natalie Ram, *Investigative Genetic Genealogy and the Future of Genetic Privacy*, ABA SCITECH LAW., Summer 2020, at 18, 19.
97. Heather Tal Murphy, *How Police Actually Cracked the Idaho Killings Case*, SLATE (Jan. 10, 2023), www.slate.com; Ramon Antonio Vargas, *Idaho Student Killings Suspect Identified by DNA in Public Genealogy Database*, THE GUARDIAN, Jan. 3, 2023.
98. Roberta Estes, *STRs vs. SNPs, Multiple DNA Personalities*, DNAEXPLAINED (Feb. 10, 2014), www.dna-explained.com.
99. *Id.*
100. State v. Spinks, 842 S.E.2d 348 (N.C. Ct. App. 2020).
101. Estes, *supra* note 98.
102. Natalie Ram & Jessica L. Roberts, *Forensic Genealogy and the Power of Defaults*, 37 NATURE BIOTECHNOLOGY 707, 707 (2019).
103. Murphy, *supra* note 97.
104. Paige St. John, *The Untold Story of How the Golden State Killer Was Found: A Covert Operation and Private DNA*, L.A. TIMES, Dec. 8, 2020.
105. Paige St. John, *DNA Genealogical Databases Are a Gold Mine for Police, But with Few Rules and Little Transparency*, L.A. TIMES, Nov. 24, 2019; Avi Selk, *The Ingenious and "Dystopian" DNA Technique Police Used to Hunt the "Golden State Killer" Suspect*, WASH. POST, Apr. 28, 2018. *See also* Cary Aspinwall, *Some States Are Turning Stillbirths and Miscarriages into Criminal Cases Against Women*, MARSHALL PROJECT (Oct. 31, 2024), www.themarshallproject.org.

106. *GEDmatch: Privacy and Security*, GEDMATCH, https://www.gedmatch.com/privacy-security; *FamilyTreeDNA Privacy Statement*, FAMILYTREEDNA (Apr. 10, 2024), https://www.familytreedna.com/legal/privacy-statement.
107. *Ancestry Privacy Statement*, ANCESTRY (2023), https://www.ancestry.com/c/legal/privacystatement; *Ancestry Transparency Report*, ANCESTRY (Feb. 12, 2024), https://www.ancestry.com/c/transparency; *Privacy Statement*, 23ANDME (Oct. 4, 2023), https://www.23andme.com/legal/privacy/full-version; *Transparency Report*, 23ANDME (June 18, 2024), https://www.23andme.com/transparency-report.
108. Charlette Jee, *A Detective Has Been Given Access to an Entire Private DNA Database*, MIT TECH. REV., Nov. 6, 2019.
109. *Id.*
110. *Id.*
111. Heather Murphy, *Most White Americans' DNA Can Be Identified Through Genealogy Databases*, N.Y. TIMES, Oct. 11, 2018.
112. Jordan Smith, *Police Are Getting DNA Data from People Who Think They Opted Out*, THE INTERCEPT (Aug. 18, 2023), www.theintercept.com.
113. Virginia Hughes, *Two New Laws Restrict Police Use of DNA Search Method*, N.Y. TIMES, May 31, 2021; H.B. 240, 2021 Reg. Sess. (Md. 2021) (codified as MD. CODE, CRIM. PROC. § 17 (2022)), https://mgaleg.maryland.gov/2021RS/chapters_noln/Ch_681_hb0240E.pdf.
114. *Id.*
115. H.B. 602, 2021 Reg. Sess. (Mont. 2021), (codified as MONT. CODE § 44-6-104 (2022)); S.B. 156, 65th Leg., Gen. Sess. (Utah 2023), https://le.utah.gov/xcode/Title53/Chapter10/53-10-S403.7.html?v=C53-10-S403.7_2023050320230503.
116. U.S. DEP'T OF JUST., INTERIM POLICY: FORENSIC GENETIC GENEALOGICAL DNA ANALYSIS AND SEARCHING (Sept. 2, 2019), https://www.justice.gov/olp/page/file/1204386/dl.
117. Jocelyn Kaiser, *New Federal Rules Limit Searches of Family Tree DNA Databases*, SCIENCE (Sept. 29, 2019).
118. Antonio Regalado & Brian Alexander, *The Citizen Scientist Who Finds Killers from Her Couch*, MIT TECH. REV., June 22, 2018; *see also* DNA Justice Foundation, https://www.dnajustice.org/.
119. Emily Mullin, *A Nonprofit Wants Your DNA Data to Solve Crimes*, WIRED, Mar. 23, 2023.
120. Castelaz v. Estée Lauder Cos. Inc., No. 1:22-cv-05713 (N.D. Ill. Oct. 18, 2022); Theriot v. Louis Vuitton N. Am., Inc., No. 22-cv-2944, 2022 WL 17417261 (S.D.N.Y. 2022); Slater v. H&M, L.P., No. 1:22-CV-02944, 2018 WL 6921177 (Ill. Cir. Ct. 2018).
121. 740 ILL. COMP. STAT. ANN. 14/10.
122. 740 ILL. COMP. STAT. ANN. 14/15.
123. 740 ILL. COMP. STAT. ANN. 14/20.
124. *See e.g.*, *In re* Facebook Biometric Information Privacy Litigation, No. 21–15553, 2022 WL 822923 (9th Cir. Mar. 17, 2022); Figueroa v. Kronos, Inc., 454 F. Supp.3d

772, 778–79 (N.D. Ill. Apr. 13, 2020); Rivera v. Google Inc., 238 F. Supp. 3d 1088 (N.D. Ill. 2017); Norberg v. Shutterfly, Inc., 152 F. Supp. 3d 1103 (N.D. Ill. 2015).

CHAPTER 4. OUR CITIES

1. Michael Isaac Stein, *"Holy Cow": The Powerful Software Behind the City's Surveillance System*, THE LENS (Dec. 20, 2018), www.thelensnola.org.
2. *Police Unlock AI's Potential to Monitor, Surveil and Solve Crimes*, WALL ST. J.: VIDEO (May 30, 2019), www.wsj.com.
3. *Id.*
4. *Cape Cod Canal Bridges Program*, CAPE COD COMM'N, https://www.capecodcommission.org/our-work/cape-cod-canal-study-resources.
5. Commonwealth v. McCarthy, 142 N.E.3d 1090, 1096 (Mass. 2020).
6. *McCarthy*, 142 N.E.3d at 1095; David Maass & Beryl Lipton, *EFF and MuckRock Release Records and Data from 200 Law Enforcement Agencies' Automated License Plate Reader Programs*, ELEC. FRONTIER FOUND.: DEEPLINKS (Nov. 15, 2018), www.eff.org.
7. *McCarthy*, 142 N.E.3d at 1095–96.
8. *Id.* at 1096–97.
9. Andrew Guthrie Ferguson, *Structural Sensor Surveillance*, 106 IOWA L. REV. 47, 51–52 (2020).
10. Rob Kitchin, *The Real-Time City? Big Data and Smart Urbanism*, 79 GEOJOURNAL 1, 5–6 (2014); Jan Whittington, *Remembering the Public in the Race to Become Smart Cities*, 85 UMKC L. REV. 925, 927 (2017).
11. Andrew Guthrie Ferguson, *Video Analytics and Fourth Amendment Vision*, 103 TEX. L. REV. 1253, 1256 (2025).
12. PRIV. INT'L, SMART CITIES: UTOPIAN VISION, DYSTOPIAN REALITY 6–7 (Oct. 2017).
13. Paul Knox, *Telos and Techne*, 5 J. COMP. URB. L. & POL'Y 188, 196 (2022).
14. Chris Mellor, *Smart Cities? Tell It Like It Is, They're Surveillance Cities*, THE REGISTER (Sept. 7, 2017), www.theregister.com.
15. Alissa Walker, *A New Way to Track How the City Moves*, CURBED (Apr. 13, 2023), www.curbed.com.
16. Luis Gomez, *Thousands of San Diego Street Lights Are Equipped with Sensors and Cameras. Here's What They Record*, SAN DIEGO UNION-TRIB., Mar. 29, 2019.
17. Janine S. Hiller & Jordan M. Blanke, *Smart Cities, Big Data, and the Resilience of Privacy*, 68 HASTINGS L.J. 309, 317–18 (2017).
18. Jim Robbins, *Why the Luster on Once-Vaunted "Smart Cities" Is Fading*, YALE ENV'T 360 (Dec. 1, 2021).
19. Steven I. Friedland, *Drinking from the Fire Hose: How Massive Self-Surveillance from the Internet of Things Is Changing the Face of Privacy*, 119 W. VA. L. REV. 891, 897 (2017).
20. Natalie Ram et. al., *The Future of Wastewater Monitoring for the Public Health*, 56 U. RICH. L. REV. 911 (2022); Sara Castiglioni, et. al., *Identification and*

Measurement of Illicit Drugs and Their Metabolites in Urban Wastewater by Liquid Chromatography Tandem Mass Spectrometry, 78 ANALYTICAL CHEMISTRY 8421 (2006).

21. Shannon Mattern, *A City Is Not a Computer*, PLACES J. (Feb. 2017), https://placesjournal.org.
22. Paul McFedries, *The City as System [Technically Speaking]*, 51 IEEE SPECTRUM 36 (Apr. 2014).
23. Stephen Nessen, *MTA Installs Futuristic Cameras in Manhattan to Charge, Track Cars for Congestion Pricing*, GOTHAMIST (Feb. 28, 2024), https://gothamist.com.
24. Joseph Cox, *I Tracked an NYC Subway Rider's Movements with an MTA "Feature,"* 404 MEDIA (Aug. 30, 2023), www.404media.co.
25. *EFF, ACLU File Lawsuit to Stop Los Angeles from Collecting Real-Time Tracking Data on Citizens' Rental Scooters*, ELEC. FRONTIER FOUND. (June 8, 2020), www.eff.org.
26. Andrew Guthrie Ferguson, *Big Data Policing Is Coming to Small Towns. There's a Reason Big Cities Rejected It*, NEWS LEADER (Staunton, VA), Mar. 23, 2021.
27. Zac Larkham, *The Quiet Rise of Real-Time Crime Centers*, WIRED, July 10, 2023.
28. Brandon Block, *Federal Aid Is Supercharging Local WA Police Surveillance Tech*, CROSSCUT (July 26, 2023), www.cascadepbs.org.
29. Stanislava Ilic-Godfrey, *Artificial Intelligence: Taking on a Bigger Role in Our Future Security*, BLS: BEYOND THE NOS. (May 3, 2021), www.bls.gov.
30. Paul Bischoff, *Surveillance Camera Statistics: Which Are the Most Surveilled Cities?*, COMPARITECH (May 23, 2023), www.comparitech.com; *see also* Matthew Keegan, *Big Brother Is Watching: Chinese City with 2.6m Cameras Is World's Most Heavily Surveilled*, THE GUARDIAN, Dec. 2, 2019.
31. Timothy Williams, *Can 30,000 Cameras Help Solve Chicago's Crime Problem?*, N.Y. TIMES, May 26, 2018; JOHN S. HOLLYWOOD ET AL., RAND CORP., REAL-TIME CRIME CENTERS IN CHICAGO: EVALUATION OF THE CHICAGO POLICE DEPARTMENT'S STRATEGIC DECISION SUPPORT CENTERS 36, 38 (2019).
32. CITY OF N.Y. POLICE DEP'T, DOMAIN AWARENESS SYSTEM: IMPACT AND USE POLICY 3–4 (Apr. 11, 2021).
33. Sally Goldenberg & Joe Anuta, *"Big Brother Is Protecting You": Eric Adams Pledges Stronger Policing, More Technology in 2023*, POLITICO (Dec. 24, 2022), www.politico.com.
34. Michael Isaac Stein & Richard A. Webster, *Recently Settled Suit Highlights Growth of Surveillance-Based Police Stops in New Orleans, Advocates and Attorneys Say*, VERITE (Mar. 14, 2023), www.veritenews.com; Michael Isaac Stein, Caroline Sinders & Winnie Yoe, *The Toolbox: A List of the Police Surveillance Tools at the Disposal of the City of New Orleans*, THE LENS (Oct. 21, 2021), https://surveillance.thelensnola.org.
35. Verite News New Orleans, *Michael Celestine's Surveillance Footage*, YOUTUBE (Mar. 14, 2023), https://www.youtube.com/watch?v=m-DBvXlQgYQ&t=6s.

36. Michael Isaac Stein, Caroline Sinders & Winnie Yoe, *Neighborhoods Watched: The Rise of Urban Mass Surveillance*, THE LENS (Oct. 21, 2021), www.thelensnola.org.
37. Stein, *supra* note 1.
38. JAY STANLEY, ACLU, THE DAWN OF ROBOT SURVEILLANCE: AI, VIDEO ANALYTICS, AND PRIVACY, 3, 17–19 (2019); Erin Tracy, *Not Just Surveillance: Riverbank's New Cameras Recognize When You're Up to No Good*, MODESTO BEE, June 25, 2019.
39. *Search & Review Hours of Video in Minutes*, BRIEFCAM, https://www.briefcam.com/solutions/review-search/; *What Is Video Analytics?*, BRIEFCAM, https://www.briefcam.com/technology/video-analytics [https://perma.cc/2WCQ-UHWH].
40. BRIEFCAM V5.6.1 USER MANUAL 49–50, 56–58 (2020), https://www.documentcloud.org/documents/7218897-BriefCam20v5-6-120User20Manual201-Ontario.html#document.
41. Brenda Salinas, *High-End Stores Use Facial Recognition Tools to Spot VIPs*, NPR (July 21, 2013), www.npr.org; Chavie Lieber, *Your Favorite Store Could Be Tracking You with Facial Recognition*, RACKED (May 22, 2018), www.racked.com.
42. Jake Laperruque, *Preventing an Air Panopticon: A Proposal for Reasonable Legal Restrictions on Aerial Surveillance*, 51 U. RICH L. REV. 705, 717 (2017).
43. IPVM TEAM, VIDEO ANALYTICS FUNDAMENTALS GUIDE, IPVM (Mar. 4, 2021, 11:00 AM), https://ipvm.com/reports/analytics-fundamentals.
44. Noga Tarnopolsky, *The Israeli Technology That May Have Helped Identify the Alleged Boston Bombers*, THE WORLD: GLOBALPOST (July 30, 2016), www.theworld.org.
45. STANLEY, *supra* note 38, at 20.
46. *Hartford Police Make Smart City Changes with Video Technology*, BRIEFCAM, https://www.briefcam.com/resources/case-studies/helping-hartford-police-department-achieve-city-wide-change/.
47. Dave Maass & Matthew Guariglia, *Video Analytics User Manuals Are a Guide to Dystopia*, ELEC. FRONTIER FOUND. (Nov. 19, 2020), www.eff.org.
48. *See e.g.*, Mohammad Ibrahim Sarker et al., *Semi-Supervised Anomaly Detection in Video Surveillance Scenes in the Wild*, 21 SENSORS (Basel) 3993 (June 2021).
49. Erin Tracy, *Not Just Surveillance: Riverbank's New Cameras Recognize When You're Up to No Good*, MODESTO BEE, June 25, 2019.
50. Seth W. Stoughton, *Police Body-Worn Cameras*, 96 N.C. L. REV. 1363, 1371–73 (2018).
51. Elizabeth Joh & Thomas Joo, *The Harms of Police Surveillance Technology Monopolies*, 99 DENV. L. REV. FORUM 1, 11 (2022).
52. AXON: AXON EVIDENCE, https://www.axon.com/products/axon-evidence.
53. Stein et al., *supra* note 36.
54. Megan Cassidy, *S.F. Billionaire Sets Up Charity to Send $1 Million Gift to Police Department*, S.F. CHRON., June 11, 2024; *see also* Gilare Zada, *San Francisco to Deploy Mobile Surveillance Units in Latest Expansion of Police Tech*, KQED (Sept. 17, 2024) www.kqed.org.

55. Chris Baumohl, *Two Years in, COVID-19 Relief Money Fueling Rise of Police Surveillance*, EPIC (Mar. 9, 2023), www.epic.org.
56. Joseph Cox, *Is Your Local Police Department Using Fusus AI-Enabled Cameras? Find Out Here*, 404 MEDIA (Jan. 16, 2024), www.404media.co.
57. Avi Asher-Schapiro, *Privacy or Safety? U.S. Brings "Surveillance City to the Suburbs,"* THOMSON-REUTERS (May 11, 2023), www.reuters.com.
58. Jordan Pearson, *Bodycam Maker Axon Is on a Mission to Surveil America with AI*, VICE (Feb. 1, 2024), www.vice.com.
59. Patrick Sisson, *In (and Above) Beverly Hills, Police Are Watching*, BLOOMBERG (Jan. 19, 2023), www.bloomberg.com.
60. *Id.*
61. Patrick Sisson, *Welcome to Chula Vista, Where Police Drones Respond to 911 Calls*, MIT TECH. REV., Feb. 27, 2023.
62. Faine Greenwood, *The California City That Sends a Drone Almost Every Time Police Are Dispatched on a 911 Call*, SLATE (May 17, 2021), www.slate.com.
63. NAT'L CONF. OF STATE LEGS., CURRENT UNMANNED AIRCRAFT STATE LAW LANDSCAPE (Mar. 27, 2023); Dhruv Mehrota & Jesse Marx, *The Age of the Drone Police Is Here*, WIRED, June 5, 2024.
64. FEDERAL AVIATION ADMINISTRATION, FIRST RESPONDER TACTICAL BEYOND VISUAL LINE OF SIGHT (TBVLOS) 91.113 WAIVER GUIDE (2020); *see also id.* at 2.
65. Curt Fleming, *Remote Drone Dispatch: Law Enforcement's Future?*, POLICE CHIEF MAG. (2019).
66. Ryan McCauley, *Amazon Granted Patent for Police Shoulder Drones*, GOV'T TECH. (Oct. 20, 2016).
67. POLICING PROJECT, PRIVACY AUDIT & ASSESSMENT OF SHOTSPOTTER, INC.'S GUNSHOT DETECTION TECHNOLOGY 12 (2019) [hereinafter POLICING PROJECT].
68. Monte Reel, *Secret Cameras Record Baltimore's Every Move from Above*, BLOOMBERG BUSINESSWEEK (Aug. 23, 2016), www.bloomberg.com; Ethan McLeod, *Aerial Surveillance Planes to Begin Flying over Baltimore Friday*, BALT. BUS. J., Apr. 30, 2020.
69. ANDREW R. MORRAL ET AL., RAND CORP., EVALUATING BALTIMORE'S AERIAL INVESTIGATION RESEARCH PILOT PROGRAM: INTERIM REPORT 9 (2021).
70. Darlene Storm, *Baltimore Cops Using Private Company's Aerial Cameras to Conduct Secret Surveillance*, COMPUTERWORLD (Aug. 24, 2016), www.computerworld.com.
71. BENJAMIN H. SNYDER, SPY PLANE: INSIDE BALTIMORE'S SURVEILLANCE EXPERIMENT (2024).
72. *See id.*; *see also* MORRAL ET AL., *supra* note 69, at 9.
73. SNYDER, *supra* note 71.
74. Leaders of a Beautiful Struggle v. Balt. Police Dep't, 2 F.4th 330, 333 (4th Cir. 2021).

75. *Id.* at 346.
76. Maneka Sinha, *The Automated Fourth Amendment*, 73 EMORY L.J. 589, 595 (2024).
77. Dhruv Mehrotra & Joey Scott, *Here Are the Secret Locations of ShotSpotter Gunfire Sensors*, WIRED, Feb. 22, 2024.
78. *ShotSpotter Generated over 40,000 Dead-End Police Deployments in Chicago in 21 Months*, MACARTHUR JUST. CTR. (May 3, 2021), www.macarthurjustice.org.
79. POLICING PROJECT, *supra* note 67, at 12, 14.
80. CITY OF CHI. OFF. INSPECTOR GEN., THE CHICAGO POLICE DEPARTMENT'S USE OF SHOTSPOTTER TECHNOLOGY 4 (2021).
81. United States v. Rickmon, 952 F.3d 876, 884 (7th Cir. 2020).
82. Todd Feathers, *Gunshot-Detecting Tech Is Summoning Armed Police to Black Neighborhoods*, VICE (July 19, 2021), www.vice.com.
83. Yash Dattani, *Big Brother Is Scanning: The Widespread Implementation of ALPR Technology in America's Police Forces*, 24 VAND. J. ENT. & TECH. L. 749, 758 (2022).
84. JAMES M. ANDERSON ET AL., RAND CORP., LICENSE PLATE READERS FOR LAW ENFORCEMENT: OPPORTUNITIES AND OBSTACLES 1 (2014).
85. Randy L. Dryer & S. Shane Stroud, *Automatic License Plate Readers: An Effective Law Enforcement Tool or Big Brother's Latest Instrument of Mass Surveillance? Some Suggestions for Legislative Action*, 55 JURIMETRICS 226, 231–32 (2015).
86. Eric Markowitz, *Pay This Fee, or Go to Jail: How License Plate Scanner Vigilant Solutions Makes Money in Texas*, INT'L BUS. TIMES, Feb. 3, 2016.
87. *See* INTERNATIONAL ASSOCIATION OF CHIEFS OF POLICE, PRIVACY IMPACT ASSESSMENT REPORT FOR THE UTILIZATION OF LICENSE PLATE READERS 6 (Sept. 2009); Greg Buhl, *Analyzing LBPD's Use of License Plate Readers*, BEACHCOMBER (Aug. 8, 2020), https://beachcomber.news.
88. Lyndsay Winkley, *Is the El Cajon Police Department Sharing License Plate Data Illegally? Some Lawyers, Lawmakers Say Yes.*, SAN DIEGO UNION TRIB., Aug. 27, 2023.
89. *Id.*
90. Charlie Warzel, *When License-Plate Surveillance Goes Horribly Wrong*, N.Y. TIMES, Apr. 23, 2019.
91. Phil Goldstein, *What Are Fusion Centers and What Kind of Technology Do They Use?*, STATETECH (Dec. 22, 2020), https://statetechmagazine.com.
92. DEP'T OF HOMELAND SEC., 2021 NATIONAL NETWORK OF FUSION CENTERS ASSESSMENT: SUMMARY OF FINDINGS (2021); Michael German, Rachel Levinson-Waldman & Kaylana Mueller-Hsia, *Ending Fusion Center Abuses: A Roadmap for Robust Federal Oversight*, BRENNAN CTR. FOR JUST. (Dec. 15, 2022), www.brennancenter.org.
93. Thomas Brewster, *This AI Watches Millions of Cars Daily and Tells Cops If You're Driving Like a Criminal*, FORBES, Dec. 5, 2023.
94. *Id.*

95. Carpenter v. United States, 585 U.S. 296, 300 (2018); United States v. Jones, 565 U.S. 400, 415 (2012) (Sotomayor, J., concurring); *see also* Andrew Guthrie Ferguson, *Persistent Surveillance*, 74 Ala. L. Rev. 1, 48 (2022).
96. Kate Crawford, *Think Again: Big Data*, Foreign Pol'y, May 10, 2013; Omer Tene & Jules Polonetsky, *Taming the Golem: Challenges of Ethical Algorithmic Decision-Making*, 19 N.C. J. L. & Tech. 125, 128 (2017).
97. Matthew Guariglia & Dave Maass, *How Police Fund Surveillance Technology Is Part of the Problem*, Elec. Frontier Found. (Sept. 23, 2020), www.eff.org.
98. Catherine Crump, *Surveillance Policy Making by Procurement*, 91 Wash. L. Rev. 1595, 1595 (2016); Elizabeth E. Joh, *The Undue Influence of Surveillance Technology Companies on Policing*, 92 N.Y.U. L. Rev. Online 19, 20 (2017).
99. Andrew Guthrie Ferguson, The Rise of Big Data Policing: Surveillance, Race, and the Future of Law Enforcement 190 (2017).
100. *The Time Has Come to Defund the Police*, M4BL, https://m4bl.org/defund-the-police [https://perma.cc/ALX7-Q2XZ].
101. Jill Lepore, *The Invention of the Police*, New Yorker, July 20, 2020.
102. Peter Waldman & Lauren Etter, *How Target Got Cozy with the Cops, Turning Black Neighbors into Suspects*, Bloomberg Businessweek (Aug. 25, 2021), www.bloomberg.com.
103. Rocco Parascandola, *Details Are Hazy About NYPD's $3B Surveillance Costs*, Governing (Nov. 14, 2022), www.governing.com.
104. Andrew Guthrie Ferguson, *DOJ Funding Pipeline Subsidizes Questionable Big Data Surveillance Technologies*, The Conversation (Feb. 7, 2024), www.theconversation.com; Anastasia Valeeva, Weihua Li & Susie Cagle, *Rifles, Tasers and Jails: How Cities and States Spent Billions of COVID-19 Relief*, Marshall Project (Sept. 7, 2022), www.themarshallproject.org.
105. U.S. Dep't of Just., Bureau of Justice Assistance: Edward Byrne Memorial Justice Assistance Grant Program (2023), https://bja.ojp.gov/funding/fy23-state-jag-allocations.pdf; *List of Programs*, U.S. Dep't of Just., Bureau of Justice Assistance, https://bja.ojp.gov/program/list; *Homeland Security Grant Program*, Fed. Emergency Mgmt. Agency (2024), https://www.fema.gov/grants/preparedness/homeland-security#funding-totals.
106. Ese Olumhense, *The Tech at "Cop Con": Cigarette Carton Trackers, VR for School Shootings, and "Peacekeeper Batons,"* The Markup (Nov. 3, 2023), www.themarkup.org.
107. Emanuel Maiberg, *How the "Surveillance AI Pipeline" Literally Objectifies Human Beings*, 404 Media (Sept. 28, 2023), www.404media.co.
108. Asher-Schapiro, *supra* note 57.
109. Jordan McDonald, *What Cities Can Learn from Sidewalk and Toronto's Failed City of the Future*, Tech Brew (Sept. 21, 2022), wwwemergingtechbrew.com.
110. Josh O'Kane, *What Google's Sidewalk Labs Ignored About Building a City*, Next City (Oct. 31, 2022), https://nextcity.org.

111. *See* U.S. Dep't of Just., C.R. Div., Investigation of the Ferguson Police Department 2–3 (Mar. 4, 2015) [https://perma.cc/W7NS-9CSB]; U.S. Dep't of Just., C.R. Div., Investigation of the Baltimore City Police Department 24 (Aug. 10, 2016), [https://perma.cc/U4CT-49ZN].
112. Andrew Guthrie Ferguson, *The Exclusionary Rule in the Age of Blue Data*, 72 Vand. L. Rev. 561, 612 (2019).
113. *Id.*
114. *Id.*
115. *Id.*

CHAPTER 5. OUR PAPERS

1. Hiawatha Bray, *After Brian Walshe, Should Google Warn Police of an Impending Murder?*, Boston Globe, Jan. 22, 2023.
2. Abby Patkin, *"How Long Before a Body Starts to Smell": A List of Brian Walshe's Google Searches, According to Prosecutors*, Boston.com (Jan. 18, 2023), www.boston.com.
3. *Id.*
4. Sykes v. State, 253 Md. App. 78, 86–87 (2021).
5. *Id.* at 103.
6. *Id.*
7. *Id.* at 89.
8. Anna Lvovsky, *Fourth Amendment Moralism*, 166 U. Pa. L. Rev. 1189, 1213 (2018).
9. Boyd v. United States, 116 U.S. 616, 625–28 (1886).
10. *Id.*
11. Brendan J. Lyons, *FBI Sifts Mountain of Data in NXIVM's Seized Computers*, CT Insider (Sept. 24, 2018), www.timesunion.com.
12. *Id.*
13. Nina Pullano, *NXIVM Cult Boss Doubles Up Efforts to Overturn Conviction*, Courthouse News Serv. (May 3, 2022), www.courthousenews.com.
14. United States v. Raniere, 55 F.4th 354, 357 (2d Cir. 2022).
15. *Id.* at 358. *See also* Roberts v. New York State Bd. for Pro. Med. Conduct, 215 A.D.3d 1093, 1093, 187 N.Y.S.3d 370 (2023).
16. Steven Arango, *Cloudy with a Chance of Government Intrusion: The Third-Party Doctrine in the 21st Century*, 69 Cath. U. L. Rev. 723 (2020).
17. Production of Third-Party Records, THMC MA-CLE 17–1.
18. Dina Moussa, *Protecting Payment Privacy: Reconciling Financial Technology and the Fourth Amendment*, 1 Geo. L. Tech. Rev. 339 (2017).
19. Deborah Ahrens, *Methademic: Drug Panic in an Age of Ambivalence*, 37 Fla. St. U. L. Rev. 841, 865 (2010).
20. Brakkton Booker, Bill Chappell, David Schaper, Danielle Kurtzleben & Joseph Shapiro, *Violence Erupts as Outrage over George Floyd's Death Spills into a New Week*, NPR (June 1, 2020), www.npr.org.

21. Kelly Weill, *$10 Venmo Ensnares Utah Pol in America's Craziest Protest Case*, Daily Beast (Aug. 21, 2020), www.thedailybeast.com.
22. Pat Reavy, *Utah Sen. Derek Kitchen Accused of Helping Pay for Paint Used by Protesters*, Deseret News. Aug. 19, 2020.
23. Google Transparency Report, https://transparencyreport.google.com/userdata/overview?user_requests_report_period=authority:US&legal_process_breakdown=expanded:0&lu=legal_process_breakdown.
24. *Id.*
25. *Government Requests for User Data*, Meta Transparency Ctr., https://transparency.meta.com/reports/government-data-requests/country/US.
26. *Law Enforcement Requests Report*, Microsoft Corp. Resp., https://www.microsoft.com/en-us/corporate-responsibility/law-enforcement-requests-report.
27. Wayne Parham, *Three Tips for Investigators Using Cellphones as Evidence*, PoliceOne (Feb. 22, 2021), www.policemag.com.
28. Logan Koepke et al., *Mass Extraction: The Widespread Power of US Law Enforcement to Search Mobile Phones*, Upturn (Oct. 2020), www.upturn.org.
29. *See* Kai Mae Huessner, *Michigan Police Use Device to Download Cellphone Data; ACLU Objects*, ABC News (Apr. 21, 2011), www.abcnews.com.
30. Riley v. California, 573 U.S. 373, 393–94 (2014).
31. *Id.* 396–97.
32. *Id.* at 378.
33. *Id.* at 380.
34. *Fourth Amendment—Search and Seizure—Searching Cell Phones Incident to Arrest—Riley v. California*, 128 Harv. L. Rev. 251 (2014).
35. *See, e.g.*, Stephen E. Henderson, *Fourth Amendment Time Machines (and What They Might Say About Police Body Cameras)*, 18 U. Pa. J. Const. L. 933, 951 (2016).
36. *Riley*, 573 U.S. at 393–94, 401.
37. Maryam Mohsin, *10 Google Search Statistics You Need to Know in 2023*, Oberlo (Apr. 25, 2023), www.oberlo.com.
38. *Google Search History Helps Catch Would-Be Burglars*, Surrey Police UK (July 29, 2022), www.surrey.police.uk.
39. Vishwam Sankaran, *Two Alleged Capitol Rioters Arrested Based on Google Searches Afterwards: "Is It Illegal to Go into Capitol,"* The Independent (U.K.), Mar. 30, 2022.
40. People v. Seymour, 536 P.3d 1260, 1267 (Colo. 2023).
41. Thomas Brewster, *Government Secretly Orders Google to Identify Anyone Who Searched a Sexual Assault Victim's Name, Address or Telephone Number*, Forbes, Apr. 21, 2022.
42. Thomas Brewster, *Cops Demand Google Data on Anyone Who Searched a Person's Name . . . Across a Whole City*, Forbes, Mar. 20, 2017.
43. Kyla Pearce, *Reverse-Keyword Search Warrant Used to Identify Suspects in Deadly Arson Case Goes to Colorado Supreme Court*, Denv. Gazette, May 4, 2023; *Seymour*, 536 P.3d at 1267.

44. *Seymour*, 536 P.3d at 1267–69.
45. Motion to Suppress Evidence from a Keyword Warrant & Request for a Veracity Hearing at 3–4, People v. Seymour, 526 P.3d 954 (Colo. Jan. 17, 2023).
46. *Id.* at 2.
47. *Id.* at 3.
48. 18 U.S.C.A. § 2510 (West).
49. Orin S. Kerr, *A User's Guide to the Stored Communications Act, and a Legislator's Guide to Amending It*, 72 GEO. WASH. L. REV. 1208, 1218 (2004).
50. Deirdre K. Mulligan, *Reasonable Expectations in Electronic Communications: A Critical Perspective on the Electronic Communications Privacy Act*, 72 GEO. WASH. L. REV. 1557, 1564 (2004).
51. *Id.* at 1568–69.
52. *A Short History of the Web*, CERN, https://home.cern/science/computing/birth-web/short-history-web.
53. Samuel Mark Borowski, Aaron Midler & Pervin Taleyarkhan, *Evolving Technology & Privacy Law: Can the Fourth Amendment Catch Up?*, ABA SCITECH LAW., Spring 2012, at 14, 16.
54. Orin S. Kerr, *The Next Generation Communications Privacy Act*, 162 U. PA. L. REV. 373, 384 (2014).
55. KEVIN R. KOSAR & PAMELA A. HAIRSTON, CONG. RSCH. SERV., RS21562, NAMING POST OFFICES THROUGH LEGISLATION (2011).
56. Eric Schnapper, *Unreasonable Searches and Seizures of Papers*, 71 VA. L. REV. 869, 869–70 (1985).
57. Donald A. Dripps, *"Dearest Property": Digital Evidence and the History of Private "Papers" as Special Objects of Search and Seizure*, 103 J. CRIM. L. & CRIMINOLOGY 49, 61 (2013).
58. *Id.*
59. *Id.*
60. Wilkes v. Wood, 19 How. St. Tr. 1153, 1169–70 (C.P. 1763).
61. Entick v. Carrington, 19 How. St. Tr. 1029, 1029–31, 1066–67 (C.P. 1765).
62. Laura K. Donohue, *The Original Fourth Amendment*, 83 U. CHI. L. REV. 1181, 1196 (2016); *see also* Jeffrey Bellin, *Fourth Amendment Textualism*, 118 MICH. L. REV. 233, 255 (2019).
63. Stanford v. State of Tex., 379 U.S. 476, 483–84 (1965).
64. *Id.* at 483–84.
65. *Wilkes*, 19 How. St. Tr. at 1156.
66. *Stanford*, 379 U.S. at 483–84.
67. Richard A. Epstein, Entick v. Carrington *and* Boyd v. United States: *Keeping the Fourth and Fifth Amendments on Track*, 82 U. CHI. L. REV. 27, 28 (2015).
68. *Stanford*, 379 U.S. at 483–84.
69. *Entick*, 19 How. St. Tr. at 1066.
70. *See, e.g.*, United States v. Jones, 565 U.S. 400, 405 (2012).
71. Boyd v. United States, 116 U.S. 616, 627–28 (1886).

72. James Otis, *Against Writs of Assistance* (Feb. 24, 1761).
73. Donohue, *supra* note 63, at 1237–38.
74. *Id.* at 1208–14.
75. *Boyd*, 116 U.S. at 618.
76. The ruling—that the Fourth Amendment permitted searches and seizures only when the government had a superior claim of title to the items seized—became known as the "mere evidence rule."
77. Orin S. Kerr, *Digital Evidence and the New Criminal Procedure*, 105 COLUM. L. REV. 279, 291 (2005).
78. United States v. Jacobsen, 466 U.S. 109, 115–17 (1984); Walter v. United States, 447 U.S. 649, 657 (1980).
79. United States v. Wright, 838 F.3d 880, 885 (7th Cir. 2016); United States v. Morgan, 435 F.3d 660, 664 (6th Cir. 2006).
80. Riley v. California, 573 U.S. 373, 402 (2014).
81. Commonwealth v. Ani, 293 A.3d 704, 709 (Pa. Super. 2023).
82. *Id.* at 708.
83. State v. Tenold, 2020 MT 263, ¶ 7, 401 Mont. 532, 534–35, 474 P.3d 829, 831.
84. *Ani*, 293 A.3d at 732–33.
85. *Id.* at 714.
86. U.S. CONST. amend. IV. The court also decided the case on state constitutional grounds, *see* PA. CONST. art. I, § 8.
87. *Ani*, 293 A.3d at 712.
88. *See* Paul Ohm, *Massive Hard Drives, General Warrants, and the Power of Magistrate Judges*, 97 VA. L. REV. IN BRIEF 1, 10 (2011).
89. Rachel B. Doyle, *The Founding Fathers Encrypted Secret Messages, Too*, THE ATLANTIC, Mar. 30, 2017.
90. Rachel Kraus & Christianna Silva, *What Is Signal? The Basics of the Most Secure Messaging App*, MASHABLE (June 13, 2023), www.mashable.com.
91. Andy Greenberg, *Hacker Lexicon: What Is the Signal Encryption Protocol?*, WIRED, Nov. 29, 2020.
92. Jim Salter, *WhatsApp "End-to-End Encrypted" Messages Aren't That Private After All*, ARS TECHNICA (Sept. 8, 2021), www.arstechnica.com; Matt Burgess, *Switched to Telegram? You Need to Know This About Its Encryption*, WIRED, Jan. 27, 2021.
93. Attila Tomaschek & Moe Long, *What Is a VPN and How Does It Work?*, CNET (May 1, 2024), www.cnet.com.

CHAPTER 6. OUR LIKES

1. *See generally Raising Digital Natives: Technology and Our Kids*, NPR: SPECIAL SERIES (2013), https://www.npr.org/series/241605846/raising-digital-natives-technology-and-our-kids.
2. Rachel Levinson-Waldman, *Private Eyes, They're Watching You: Law Enforcement's Monitoring of Social Media*, 71 OKLA. L. REV. 997, 1007 (2019).

3. Ben Popper, *How the NYPD Is Using Social Media to Put Harlem Teens Behind Bars*, THE VERGE (Dec. 10, 2014), www.theverge.com; Sara Robinson, *When a Facebook Like Lands You in Jail*, BRENNAN CTR. FOR JUST. (July 6, 2018), www.brennancenter.org.
4. Meredith Broussard, *When Cops Check Facebook*, THE ATLANTIC, Apr. 19, 2015.
5. George Joseph, *Meet "Bob Smith," the Fake Facebook Profile Memphis Police Allegedly Used to Spy on Black Activists*, THE APPEAL (Aug. 2, 2018), www.theappeal.org; Daniel Jackson, *Judge Finds Memphis Illegally Spied on Activists*, COURTHOUSE NEWS SERV. (Oct. 29, 2018), www.courthousenews.com.
6. Antonia Noori Farzan, *Memphis Police Used Fake Facebook Account to Monitor Black Lives Matter, Trial Reveals*, WASH. POST, Aug. 23, 2018.
7. *See* Levinson-Waldman, *supra* note 2, at 999–1000.
8. Alvaro M. Bedoya, *The Color of Surveillance*, SLATE (Jan. 18, 2016), www.slate.com.
9. Isaiah Strong, *Surveillance of Black Lives as Injury-in-Fact*, 122 COLUM. L. REV. 1019, 1021 (2022).
10. *Social Media Fact Sheet*, PEW RSCH. CTR. (Jan. 31, 2024), www.pewresearch.org.
11. *Id.*
12. *Id.*
13. *Id.*
14. CONG. RSCH. CTR., LAW ENFORCEMENT AND TECHNOLOGY 3 (Jan. 11, 2022).
15. *Id.* at 1; *see also* Rachel Levinson-Waldman, *Directory of Police Department Social Media Policies*, BRENNAN CTR. FOR JUST. (Aug. 29, 2024), www.brennancenter.org.
16. *Id.* at 3.
17. *Chicago Authorities to Monitor Social Media amid Looting Threats, Lightfoot Says*, NBC CHICAGO (Aug. 14, 2020), www.nbcchicago.com.
18. Aaron Leibowitz & Sarah Karp, *Chicago Public Schools Monitored Social Media for Signs of Violence, Gang Membership*, PROPUBLICA (Feb. 11, 2019), www.propublica.org.
19. George Joseph, *How Police Are Watching You on Social Media*, BLOOMBERG CITYLAB (Dec. 14, 2016), www.bloomberg.com.
20. Kashmir Hill, *The Wildly Unregulated Practice of Undercover Cops Friending People on Facebook*, THE ROOT (Oct. 23, 2018), www.theroot.com.
21. *Id.*
22. RYAN J REILLY, SEDITION HUNTERS: HOW JANUARY 6TH BROKE THE JUSTICE SYSTEM (2023).
23. Michael Isaac Stein, *"Holy Cow": The Powerful Software Behind the City's Surveillance System*, THE LENS (Dec. 20, 2018), https://thelensnola.org.
24. *See* Aric Toler, Christiaan Triebert, Haley Willis, Malachy Browne, Michael Schwirtz & Riley Mellen, *The Airman Who Gave Gamers a Real Taste of War*, N.Y. TIMES, Apr. 13, 2023; Joseph Cox, *The Powerful AI Tool That Cops (or*

Stalkers) Can Use to Geolocate Photos in Seconds*, 404 MEDIA (Jan. 20, 2025), www.404media.co.

25. Dean Takashashi, *ZeroEyes Uses AI and Security Cameras to Detect Guns in Public and Private Spaces*, VENTURE BEAT (July 31, 2023), https://venturebeat.com; *Enhancing Security with Object Recognition Technology*, KEYLABS (May 13, 2024), https://keylabs.ai.
26. Opeyemi Bamigbade, John Sheppard & Mark Scanlon, *Computer Vision for Multimedia Geolocation in Human Trafficking Investigation: A Systematic Literature Review*, https://arxiv.org/html/2402.15448v1.
27. Tom Simonite, *How Facial Recognition Is Fighting Child Sex Trafficking*, WIRED, June 19, 2019; *PhotoDNA*, MICROSOFT, https://www.microsoft.com/en-us/photodna.
28. United States v. Tutis, 216 F. Supp. 3d 467, 483 (D.N.J. 2016).
29. Facebook, Inc. v. State, 254 N.J. 329, 342–43 (2023).
30. *See, e.g.*, M. Jackson Jones, *Shady Trick or Legitimate Tactic—Can Law Enforcement Officials Use Fictitious Social Media Accounts to Interact with Suspects?*, 40 AM. J. TRIAL ADVOC. 69, 71–72 (2016).
31. Chris Gelardi, *The State Police Sent You a Friend Request*, N. Y. FOCUS (June 13, 2022).
32. *Id.*
33. *Id.*
34. Steve Karnowski, *Report Calls Out Abuse of Social Media by Minneapolis Police*, ASSOCIATED PRESS (May 2, 2022), https://apnews.com.
35. *Id.*
36. Marco Poggio, *LAPD Case Sheds Light on LAPD Social Media Monitoring*, LAW360 (Jan. 9, 2022), www.law360.com.
37. Margaret Hu, *Horizontal Cybersurveillance Through Sentiment Analysis*, 26 WM. & MARY BILL RTS. J. 361, 372–73 (2017).
38. *LAPD Social Media Monitoring Documents*, BRENNAN CTR. FOR JUST. (Dec. 15, 2021), https://www.brennancenter.org/our-work/research-reports/lapd-social-media-monitoring-documents.
39. Adi Robertson, *Secret Service Bought Access to Cellphone Location Data*, THE VERGE (Aug. 17, 2020), www.theverge.com; *see also* Joseph Cox, *The IRS Is Being Investigated for Using Location Data Without a Warrant*, VICE: MOTHERBOARD (Oct. 6, 2020), www.vice.com.
40. Scott Ikeda, *FBI Investing Heavily in Social Media Tracking: "Predictive" Surveillance Software Raises Civil Liberties Concerns*, CPO MAG. (Apr. 11, 2022), www.cpomagazine.com.
41. Poggio, *supra* note 36; Chris Gelardi, *Congress Has a Chance to Rein in Police Use of Surveillance Tech*, THE INTERCEPT (Apr. 2, 2024), www.theintercept.com.
42. Sam Biddle, *Police Surveilled George Floyd Protests with Help from Twitter-Affiliated Startup Dataminr*, THE INTERCEPT (July 9, 2020), www.theintercept.com.

43. Mary Pat Dwyer & José Guillermo Gutiérrez, *Documents Reveal LAPD Collected Millions of Tweets from Users Nationwide*, BRENNAN CTR. FOR JUST. (Dec. 15, 2021), www.brennancenter.org.
44. Nicole Ozer, *Police Use of Social Media Surveillance Software Is Escalating, and Activists Are in the Digital Crosshairs*, ACLU (Sept. 22, 2016), www.aclu.org.
45. Leibowitz & Karp, *supra* note 18; Tom Simonite, *Schools Are Mining Students' Social Media Posts for Signs of Trouble*, WIRED, Aug. 20, 2018.
46. *See* Todd Feathers, *Schools Spy on Kids to Prevent Shootings, but There Is No Evidence It Works*, MOTHERBOARD: TECH BY VICE (Dec. 4, 2019), www.vice .com; Cat Ansar, *Nashville Schools Implement AI Monitoring Service "Bark" to Shield Students from Cyber Threats*, HOODLINE (Apr. 13, 2024), https://hoodline.com.
47. Aaron Leibowitz, *Could Monitoring Students on Social Media Stop the Next School Shooting?*, N.Y. TIMES, Sept. 6, 2018; Joel Rose & Brakkton Booker, *Parkland Shooting Suspect: A Story of Red Flags, Ignored*, NPR (Mar. 1, 2018), www.npr.org.
48. Rachel Levinson-Waldman, *School Social Media Monitoring Won't Stop the Next Mass Shooting*, BRENNAN CENT. FOR JUST. (June 22, 2022), www .brennancenter.org.
49. Leibowitz, *supra* note 47.
50. Arijit D. Sen & Derêka K. Bennett, *Tracked: How Colleges Use AI to Monitor Student Protests*, DALL. MORNING NEWS, Sept. 20, 2022.
51. Lizzie O'Leary, *Monitoring Has Failed to Protect Schools*, SLATE (June 4, 2022), www.slate.com.
52. Benjamin Herold, *Schools Are Deploying Massive Digital Surveillance Systems. The Results Are Alarming*, EDU. WEEK (May 30, 2019), www.edweekorg.
53. Sen & Bennett, *supra* note 50.
54. Zach Rounceville, *UNC Schools Used AI Program to Surveil Students' Social Media Accounts*, CAROLINA J. (Sept. 26, 2022), www.carolinajournal.com.
55. Everett v. State, 186 A.3d 1224, 1229 (Del. 2018).
56. Stored Communications Act ("SCA"), 18 U.S.C. § 2701 et seq.
57. United States v. Warshak, 631 F.3d 266, 284 (6th Cir. 2010).
58. Hoffa v. United States, 385 U.S. 293, 302 (1966).
59. Commonwealth v. Carrasquillo, 489 Mass. 107, 110, 179 N.E.3d 1104, 1110 (2022).
60. *Id. See generally* Tonja Jacobi & Dustin Stonecipher, *A Solution for the Third-Party Doctrine in a Time of Data Sharing, Contact Tracing, and Mass Surveillance*, 97 NOTRE DAME L. REV. 823, 844 (2022).
61. CONG. RSCH. CTR., *supra* note 14, at 3.
62. Thomas Brewster, *Your Deleted TikTok Content Can Still Be Used Against You by the FBI*, FORBES, June 15, 2022.
63. *Id.*
64. *What Does It Mean to "Like" Something on Facebook?*, FACEBOOK, https://www .facebook.com/help/110920455663362.
65. Social Media Privacy, ELEC. PRIV. INFO. CTR., https://epic.org/issues /consumer-privacy/social-media-privacy/.

66. Janice C. Sipior, Burke T. Ward & Ruben A. Mendoza, *Online Privacy Concerns Associated with Cookies, Flash Cookies, and Web Beacons*, 10 J. INTERNET COM. 1, 1 (2011); Harry Guinness, *Cookies Are Going Away, But Internet Tracking May Still Be Here to Stay*, POPULAR SCI. (Apr. 21, 2022), www.popsci.com.
67. *Data Brokerage, the Sale of Individuals' Data, and Risks to Americans' Privacy, Personal Safety, and National Security, Hearing Before the H. Comm. on Energy and Commerce, Subcomm. on Oversight and Investigations*, 118th Cong. (2023) (testimony of Justin Sherman Senior Fellow and Research Lead for Data Brokerage Project, Duke University Sanford School of Public Policy).
68. Justin Sherman, *How Shady Companies Guess Your Religion, Sexual Orientation, and Mental Health*, SLATE (April 26, 2023), www.slate.com.
69. *Id.*; *Data Brokers*, ELEC. PRIV. INFO. CTR., https://epic.org/issues /consumer-privacy/data-brokers/#:~:text=There%20is%20no%20federal%20 law,regulates%20the%20data%20broker%20industry (last visited May 1, 2023).
70. *FTC Enforcement Action to Bar GoodRx from Sharing Consumers' Sensitive Health Info for Advertising*, FED. TRADE COMM'N (Feb. 1, 2023), www.ftc.gov.
71. *Id.*
72. Sharon Bradford Franklin, Greg Nojeim & Dhanaraj Thakur, *Legal Loopholes and Data for Dollars: How Law Enforcement and Intelligence Agencies Are Buying Your Data from Brokers*, CTR. FOR DEMOCRACY & TECH. 13–14 (Dec. 2021), www .cdt.org.
73. JOANNE KIM, DUKE SANFORD CYBER POL'Y PROGRAM, DATA BROKERS AND THE SALE OF AMERICANS' MENTAL HEALTH DATA (2023).
74. Emily A. Vogels & Colleen McClain, *Key Findings About Online Dating in the U.S.*, PEW RSCH. CTR. (Feb. 2, 2023), www.pewresearch.org.
75. Rebecca Heilweil, *Tinder May Not Get You a Date. It Will Get Your Data*, VOX (Feb. 14, 2020), www.vox.com.
76. Anna Lovine, *How Do All the Best Dating App Algorithms Work?*, MASHABLE (Oct. 9, 2021), www.mashable.com.
77. Chris Fox, *Gay Dating Apps Still Leaking Location Data*, BBC (Aug. 8, 2019), www .bbc.com.
78. Ahmed Shihab-Eldin, *How Egyptian Police Hunt LGBT People on Dating Apps*, BBC (Jan. 30, 2023), www.bbc.com.
79. Jen Caltrider, Misha Rykov & Zoë MacDonald, *Data-Hungry Dating Apps Are Worse Than Ever for Your Privacy*, MOZILLA (Apr. 23, 2024), www .mozillafoundation.org; Joseph Cox, *More Muslim Apps Worked with X-Mode, Which Sold Data to Military Contractors*, VICE (Jan. 28, 2021), www.vice.com.
80. *Grindr Facing U.K. Lawsuit over Alleged Data Protection Breaches*, REUTERS (Apr. 22, 2024), www.reuters.com.
81. Jon Keegan & Joel Eastwood, *From "Heavy Purchasers" of Pregnancy Tests to the Depression-Prone: We Found 650,000 Ways Advertisers Label You*, THE MARKUP (June 8, 2023), https://themarkup.org.
82. *Id.*

83. René Kladzyk, *Policing Gender: How Surveillance Tech Aids Enforcement of Anti-Trans Laws*, PROJECT ON GOV'T OVERSIGHT (June 28, 2023), www.pogo.org.
84. Michael Kwet, *ShadowDragon: Inside the Social Media Surveillance Software That Can Watch Your Every Move*, THE INTERCEPT (Sept. 21, 2021), www.theintercept.com.
85. *Id.*
86. Dan Goodin, *Meta Sues "Scraping-for-Hire" Business That Sells User Data to Law Enforcement*, ARSTECHNICA (Jan. 13. 2023), https://arstechnica.com.
87. Rachel Levinson-Waldman & Gabriella Sanchez, *Meta Sues Surveillance Firm that Worked with Police*, BRENNAN CTR. FOR JUST. (Jan. 26, 2023), www.brennancenter.org.
88. *Id.*
89. Joseph Cox, *The DEA Bought Customer Data from Rogue Employees Instead of Getting a Warrant*, VICE (Mar. 29, 2023), www.vice.com.
90. *Id.* (citing https://oig.justice.gov/reports/2016/a1633.pdf).
91. *Id.*
92. Fourth Amendment Is Not for Sale Act, S. 2576, 118th Cong. § 2 (2023).
93. Bennett Cyphers & Gennie Gebhart, *Behind the One-Way Mirror: A Deep Dive into the Technology of Corporate Surveillance*, ELEC. FRONTIER FOUND. (Dec. 2, 2019), www.eff.org.
94. Sara Morrison, *A Surprising Number of Government Agencies Buy Cellphone Location Data. Lawmakers Want to Know Why*, VOX (Dec. 2, 2020), www.vox.com.
95. Garance Burke & Jason Dearen, *Tech Tool Offers Police "Mass Surveillance on a Budget,"* ASSOCIATED PRESS (Sept. 2, 2022), www.apnews.com; *see also* Joseph Cox, *Location Data Firm Offers to Help Cops Track Targets via Doctor Visits*, 404 MEDIA (Dec. 10, 2024), www.404media.co.
96. *Id.*
97. Stuart A. Thompson & Charlie Warzel, *Twelve Million Phones, One Dataset, Zero Privacy*, N.Y. TIMES Dec. 19, 2019.
98. Bennett Cyphers, *Inside Fog Data Science, the Secretive Company Selling Mass Surveillance to Local Police*, ELEC. FRONTIER FOUND. (Aug. 31, 2022), www.eff.org.
99. Burke & Dearen, *supra* note 95.
100. *3 Arrested for Running Down Employee While Stealing $10K Bike in Chino*, CBS NEWS (Mar. 20, 2019), www.cbsnews.com; Chino Police Department, *Memos to Request and Recommend Purchase of Fog Subscription* 2 (2019), https://www.documentcloud.org/documents/22187494-chino_2019-20_attachments/.
101. *Id.*; *Chino Memos* at 2.
102. *Id.*
103. *Data Brokers: A Call for Transparency and Accountability: A Report of the Federal Trade Commission*, FED. TRADE COMM'N (May 2014), www.ftc.gov.
104. *FTC Sues Kochava for Selling Data That Tracks People at Reproductive Health Clinics, Places of Worship, and Other Sensitive Locations*, FED. TRADE COMM'N

(Aug. 29, 2022), www.ftc.gov; Joseph Cox, *FTC Bans Location Data Company That Powers the Surveillance Ecosystem*, 404 MEDIA (Dec. 3, 2024), www.404media.co.

105. Tonya Riley, *FTC Moves to Ban Location Data Sales Raise New Broker Duties*, BLOOMBERG L. (Feb. 1, 2024), www.bloomberglaw.com; *FTC Order Will Ban InMarket from Selling Precise Consumer Location Data*, FED. TRADE COMM'N (Jan. 18, 2024), www.ftc.gov.
106. *FTC Sues Kochava*, *supra* note 104.
107. William Chalk, *Landmark Laws: Data Brokers and the Future of US Privacy Regulation*, CSO (Mar. 6, 2019), www.csoonline.com; *Data Broker Registry*, CAL. DEP'T JUST., OFF. ATT'Y GEN., https://www.oag.ca.gov/data-brokers?combine=flock+safety.
108. Colorado Privacy Act (CPA), COLO. REV. STAT. § 6-1-1303(16); California Privacy Rights Act (CPRA), CAL. CIV. CODE § 1798.140(ae)(1)(C).
109. *See generally* JULIA ANGWIN, DRAGNET NATION: A QUEST FOR PRIVACY, SECURITY, AND FREEDOM IN A WORLD OF RELENTLESS SURVEILLANCE 3 (2014); SHOSHANA ZUBOFF, THE AGE OF SURVEILLANCE CAPITALISM: THE FIGHT FOR A HUMAN FUTURE AT THE FRONTIER OF POWER (2019).
110. *See generally* RUHA BENJAMIN, RACE AFTER TECHNOLOGY: ABOLITIONIST TOOLS FOR THE NEW JIM CODE (2019); MEREDITH BROUSSARD, ARTIFICIAL UNINTELLIGENCE: HOW COMPUTERS MISUNDERSTAND THE WORLD (2018); SAFIYA UMOJA NOBLE, ALGORITHMS OF OPPRESSION: HOW SEARCH ENGINES REINFORCE RACISM (2018); VIRGINIA EUBANKS, AUTOMATING INEQUALITY: HOW HIGH-TECH TOOLS PROFILE, POLICE, AND PUNISH THE POOR (2017); FRANK PASQUALE, THE BLACK BOX SOCIETY: THE SECRET ALGORITHMS THAT CONTROL MONEY AND INFORMATION (2015).
111. Commonwealth v. Dilworth, No. 1884CR00453, 2019 WL 469356, at *2 (Mass. Super. Jan. 18, 2019), *aff'd*, 147 N.E.3d 445 (Mass. 2020).
112. *See* Abrar Al-Heeti, *Beyond Tinder: How Muslim Millennials Are Looking for Love*, CNET (Apr. 10, 2019), www.cnet.com; Joseph Cox, *More Muslim Apps Worked with X-Mode, Which Sold Data to Military Contractors*, VICE (Jan. 28, 2021), www.vice.com.
113. Joseph Cox, *How the U.S. Military Buys Location Data from Ordinary Apps*, VICE (Nov. 16, 2020), www.vice.com.
114. Corey G. Johnson & Byard Duncan, *Gun Lobbyists and Cambridge Analytica Weaponized Gun Owners' Private Details for Political Gain*, PROPUBLICA (Feb. 5, 2025), www.propublica.org.

CHAPTER 7. POWER PROBLEMS

1. *See* Jill Lepore, *The Invention of the Police*, NEW YORKER, July 20, 2020.
2. Alec Karakatsanis, *The Punishment Bureaucracy: How to Think About "Criminal Justice Reform,"* 128 YALE L.J. F. 848, 854–56 (2019).

3. *See* Andrew Guthrie Ferguson, *Why Digital Policing Is Different*, 83 Ohio St. L.J. 817, 837 (2022); Andrew Guthrie Ferguson, *Persistent Surveillance*, 74 Ala. L. Rev. 1, 14 (2022).
4. BriefCam, https://www.briefcam.com/ (last visited Nov. 29, 2024).
5. *See* Ferguson, *supra* note 3, *Persistent Surveillance* at 16.
6. *See* Ferguson, *supra* note 3, *Why Digital Policing Is Different* at 847–50.
7. *See* Brandon Block, *Federal Aid Is Supercharging Local WA Police Surveillance Tech*, Cascade PBS (July 26, 2023), www.cascasdepbs.org; Joseph Cox, *AI Cameras Took Over One Small American Town. Now They're Everywhere*, 404 Media (Nov. 2, 2023), www.404media.co.
8. *See* Ferguson, *supra* note 3, *Persistent Surveillance* at 30–32.
9. *See* Erik Luna, *Principled Enforcement of Penal Codes*, 4 Buff. Crim. L. Rev. 515, 594–608 (2000); Wayne R. LaFave, *Controlling Discretion by Administrative Regulations: The Use, Misuse, and Nonuse of Police Rules and Policies in Fourth Amendment Adjudication*, 89 Mich. L. Rev. 442, 449–51 (1990).
10. Kim Forde-Mazrui, *Ruling Out the Rule of Law*, 60 Vand. L. Rev. 1497, 1503 (2007).
11. *See* Alex Vitale, The End of Policing 34 (2017).
12. Kiara Alfonseca, *Map: Where Gender-Affirming Care Is Being Targeted in the US*, ABC News (May 22, 2023), https://abcnews.go.com.
13. Brian Klosterboer, *Texas' Attempt to Tear Parents and Trans Youth Apart, One Year Later*, ACLU Blog (Feb. 23, 2023) www.aclu.org.
14. *See generally* Angela J. Davis, Arbitrary Justice: The Power of the American Prosecutor 4–7 (2007); Michelle Alexander, The New Jim Crow 17 (2012).
15. I. Bennett Capers, *Race, Policing, and Technology*, 95 N.C. L. Rev. 1241, 1288–89 (2017).
16. *See generally* Ruha Benjamin, Race After Technology: Abolitionist Tools for the New Jim Code 184 (2019); *see also* Larry Redmond, *Why We Need Community Control of the Police*, 21 Loy. Pub. Int. L. Rep. 226, 227 (2016).
17. *See* Simone Brown, Dark Matters: On the Surveillance of Blackness 12–17 (2015).
18. Craig Timberg, *New Surveillance Technology Can Track Everyone in an Area for Several Hours at a Time*, Wash. Post, Feb. 5, 2014; *see also* Katie Hawkinson, *In Every Reported Case Where Police Mistakenly Arrested Someone Using Facial Recognition, That Person Has Been Black*, Bus. Insider (Aug. 6, 2023), www.businessinsider.com.
19. Ben Austen, *Public Enemies: Social Media Is Fueling Gang Wars in Chicago*, Wired, Sept. 17, 2013.
20. Todd Feathers, *Gunshot-Detecting Tech Is Summoning Armed Police to Black Neighborhoods*, Vice (July 19, 2021), www.vice.com.
21. Dhruv Mehrotra, Surya Mattu, Annie Gilbertson & Aaron Sankin, *How We Determined Crime Prediction Software Disproportionately Targeted Low-Income,*

Black, and Latino Neighborhoods, THE MARKUP (Dec. 2, 2021), www.themarkup.org.

22. Scholars such as Alex Vitale, Alec Karakatsanis, and Amna Akbar have made similar arguments.
23. Paul Butler, *The System Is Working the Way It Is Supposed to: The Limits of Criminal Justice Reform*, 104 GEO. L.J. 1419, 1425 (2016).
24. VITALE, *supra* note 11, at 31–54.
25. *See* BROWN, *supra* note 17.
26. Sarah Brayne, Sarah Lageson & Karen Levy, *Surveillance Deputies: When Ordinary People Surveil for the State*, 57 LAW & SOC'Y REV. 462, 463 (2023).
27. Mark Harris, *How Peter Thiel's Secretive Data Company Pushed into Policing*, WIRED, Aug. 9, 2017.
28. *Gotham*, PALANTIR, https://www.palantir.com/platforms/gotham/ (last visited Nov. 29, 2024); Michael Posner, *How Palantir Falls Short of Responsible Corporate Conduct*, FORBES, Sept. 12, 2019.
29. *See generally* SARAH BRAYNE, PREDICT AND SURVEIL: DATA, DISCRETION, AND THE FUTURE OF POLICING (2021).
30. Sarah Brayne, *Big Data Surveillance: The Case of Policing*, 82 AM. SOC. REV. 977, 987 (2017).
31. *Id.*
32. Michael Rosenberg, *The Price of Privacy: How Access to Digital Privacy Is Slowly Becoming Divided by Class*, 20 UCLA J. L. & TECH. 1, 4, 19–20 (2016).
33. Haleluya Hadero, *Ring Will No Longer Allow Police to Request Doorbell Camera Footage from Users*, ASSOCIATED PRESS (Jan. 24, 2024), www.apnews.com.
34. Matthew Guariglia, *What Is Fog Data Science? Why Is the Surveillance Company So Dangerous?*, ELEC. FRONTIER FOUND. (Aug. 31, 2022), www.eff.org.
35. David Murakami Wood & Torin Monahan, Editorial, *Platform Surveillance*, 17 SURVEILLANCE & SOC'Y 1 (2019).
36. Eric Savitz, *Razor-and-Blades Pricing Strategies in the Digital Age*, FORBES, Dec. 19, 2012.
37. AXON, https://www.axon.com/products/axon-evidence (last visited Nov. 29, 2024).
38. *Axon Records*, AXON, https://www.axon.com/products/axon-records (last visited Nov. 29, 2024).
39. *Axon Respond*, AXON, https://www.axon.com/products/respond (last visited Nov. 29, 2024).
40. *Axon Standards*, AXON, https://www.axon.com/products/axon-standards (last visited Nov. 29, 2024).
41. *Resource Router*, SOUNDTHINKING, https://www.soundthinking.com/law-enforcement/resource-deployment-resourcerouter/ (last visited Nov. 29, 2024).
42. SoundThinking, *SafetySmart Platform Overview*, YOUTUBE (Apr. 10, 2023), https://www.youtube.com/watch?v=SW9KUPw5UPE; *CrimeTracer*,

SoundThinking, https://www.soundthinking.com/law-enforcement/crime-analysis-crimetracer/ (last visited Nov. 29, 2024).

43. *CaseBuilder*, SoundThinking, https://www.soundthinking.com/law-enforcement/investigation-management-casebuilder/ (last visited Nov. 29, 2024).
44. N.Y. Police Dep't, Domain Awareness System: Impact and Use Policy 1, 3 (2021), https://www.nyc.gov/assets/nypd/downloads/pdf/public_information/post-final/domain-awareness-system-das-nypd-impact-and-use-policy_4.9.21_final.pdf.
45. David Lidsky, *Mark43*, Fast Co. (Feb. 9, 2015), www.fastcompany.com.
46. Amy Feldman, *How Mark43's Scott Crouch, 25, Built Software to Help Police Departments Keep Cops on the Streets*, Forbes, Jan. 22, 2017.

CHAPTER 8. PRIVACY PROBLEMS

1. Aziz Z. Huq & Rebecca Wexler, *Digital Privacy for Reproductive Choice in the Post-*Roe *Era*, 98 N.Y.U. L. Rev. 555, 634–35 (2023).
2. United States v. Miller, 425 U.S. 435, 443 (1976).
3. Jennifer Stisa Granick, *If the Government Had Its Way, Everything Could Be Wiretapped*, ACLU (Feb. 19, 2019), www.aclu.org.
4. *See, e.g.*, Zoe Richards, *Special Counsel Sought Trump's Tweets and Direct Messages in Search Warrant*, NBC News (Aug. 15, 2023), www.nbcnews.com.
5. Daniel J. Solove, *A Taxonomy of Privacy*, 154 U. Pa. L. Rev. 477, 484 (2006).
6. *See, e.g.*, Danielle Keats Citron, *Sexual Privacy*, 128 Yale L.J. 1870, 1918 (2019); Ann Cavoukian, *Privacy by Design: The 7 Foundational Principles: Implementation and Mapping of Fair Information Practices* 1, 4 (2009); Julie E. Cohen, *Examined Lives: Informational Privacy and the Subject as Object*, 52 Stan. L. Rev. 1373, 1403–05 (2000); Neil M. Richards, *Intellectual Privacy*, 87 Tex. L. Rev. 387, 389 (2008); Helen Nissenbaum, Privacy in Context: Technology, Policy, and the Integrity of Social Life 4 (2010).
7. *See* Andrew Guthrie Ferguson, *Why Digital Policing Is Different*, 83 Ohio St. L.J. 817, 821 (2022).
8. Katz v. United States, 389 U.S. 347, 361 (1967) (Harlan, J. concurring).
9. California v. Ciraolo, 476 U.S. 207, 211 (1986).
10. Matthew Tokson, *Automation and the Fourth Amendment*, 96 Iowa L. Rev. 581, 585–86 (2011).
11. United States v. Jones, 565 U.S. 400, 418 (2012) (Sotomayor, J., concurring); Daniel J. Solove, *Digital Dossiers and the Dissipation of Fourth Amendment Privacy*, 75 S. Cal. L. 1083, 1138 (2002).
12. *See* Alice Marwick, *Privacy Without Power: What Privacy Research Can Learn from Surveillance Studies*, 20 Surveillance & Soc'y 397, 398 (2022).
13. Rakas v. Illinois, 439 U.S. 128, 139 (1978).
14. *Id.*
15. Scott Michelman, *Who Can Sue over Government Surveillance?*, 57 UCLA L. Rev. 71, 79 (2009).

16. *See* Christopher Slobogin, *Standing and Covert Surveillance*, 42 PEPP. L. REV. 517, 521 (2015).
17. Clapper v. Amnesty Int'l USA, 568 U.S. 398, 402 (2013).
18. *Id.*
19. FISA Amendments Act of 2008, Pub. L. No. 110–261, § 702(a), 122 Stat. 2438 (codified as amended at 50 U.S.C. § 1881a(a)).
20. David Gray, *A Collective Right to Be Secure from Unreasonable Tracking*, 48 TEX. TECH L. REV. 189, 191, 199 (2015).
21. Andrew Guthrie Ferguson, *Digital Rummaging*, 101 WASH. U. L. REV. 1473, 1484 (2024).
22. *See* Woodrow Hartzog, Evan Selinger & Johanna Gunawan, *Privacy Nicks: How the Law Normalizes Surveillance*, 101 WASH. U. L. REV. 717, 782 (2024).
23. 740 ILL. COMP. STAT. 14/5 (d) (2020).
24. California Consumer Privacy Act of 2018, CAL. CIV. CODE §§ 1798.100–199 (West 2018).
25. *See US State Privacy Legislation Tracker*, INT'L ASS'N PRIV. PROFS. (Dec. 16, 2024), https://iapp.org/resources/article/us-state-privacy-legislation-tracker/.

CHAPTER 9. PRAXIS PROBLEMS

1. *See* Aaron Sankin & Surya Mattu, *Predictive Policing Software Terrible at Predicting Crimes*, THE MARKUP (Oct. 2, 2023), www.themarkup.org; Aaron Sankin, Dhruv Mehrota, Surya Mattu & Annie Gilbertson, *Crime Prediction Software Promised to Be Free of Biases. New Data Shows It Perpetuates Them*, THE MARKUP (Dec. 21, 2021), www.themarkup.org.
2. *See generally* ANDREW GUTHRIE FERGUSON, THE RISE OF BIG DATA POLICING: SURVEILLANCE, RACE, AND THE FUTURE OF LAW ENFORCEMENT (2017).
3. Andrew Guthrie Ferguson, *DOJ Funding Pipeline Subsidizes Questionable Big Data Surveillance Technologies*, THE CONVERSATION (Feb. 7, 2024), https://theconversation.com.
4. *See* U.S. DEP'T OF JUST., BUREAU OF JUSTICE ASSISTANCE, FACT SHEET: EDWARD BYRNE MEMORIAL JUSTICE ASSISTANCE GRANT PROGRAM (2023), https://bja.ojp.gov/funding/fy23-state-jag-allocations.pdf.
5. Emily Opilo, *Texas Philanthropists Say They're Backing Out of Financing Surveillance Plane Technology That Flew over Baltimore*, BALT. SUN, Jan. 26, 2021.
6. Craig Wall, *Chicago Given $10M to Expand Predictive Policing, Officer Training*, ABC7 NEWS (Apr. 11, 2018), [https://perma.cc/B62D-CDKC].
7. *See* Joel Handley, Jennifer Helsby & Freddy Martinez, *Inside the Chicago Police Department's Secret Budget*, CHI. READER (Sept. 29, 2016), https://chicagoreader.com/news/inside-the-chicago-police-departments-secret-budget/; Dana Rubinstein, *Security Robots. DigiDog. GPS Launchers. Welcome to New York*, N.Y. TIMES, Apr. 11, 2023; Sidney Fussell, *The NYPD Had a Secret Fund for Surveillance Tools*, WIRED, Aug. 10, 2021.

8. *See generally* Shoshana Zuboff, The Age of Surveillance Capitalism: The Fight for a Human Future at the New Frontier of Power (2019).
9. *See Applying CBA to Public Safety*, Policing Project, https://www.policingproject.org/cba (last visited Oct. 22, 2024).
10. Matt Stroud, Thin Blue Lie: The Failure of High-Tech Policing 91–128 (2019).
11. *See, e.g.*, Drew Harwell, *Taser Maker Proposed Shock Drones for Schools. What Could Go Wrong?*, Wash. Post, June 6, 2022.
12. James Vincent & Russell Brandom, *Axon Launches AI Ethics Board to Study the Dangers of Facial Recognition*, The Verge (Apr. 26, 2018), www.theverge.com; Chaim Gartenberg, *Axon (Formerly Taser) Says Facial Recognition on Police Body Cams Is Unethical*, The Verge (June 27, 2019), www.theverge.com.
13. Khari Johnson, *Axon Taser-Drone Plans Prompt AI Ethics Board Resignations*, Wired, June 6, 2022; *Statement of Resigning Axon AI Ethics Board Members*, Policing Project (June 6, 2022), https://www.policingproject.org/statement-of-resigning-axon-ai-ethics-board-members.
14. *Axon Halts Its Plans for a Taser Drone as 9 on Ethics Board Resign over the Project*, NPR (June 6, 2022), www.npr.org.
15. IPVM Team, Video Analytics Fundamentals Guide (Mar. 4, 2021).
16. *See* Jay Stanley, ACLU, The Dawn of Robot Surveillance: AI, Video Analytics, and Privacy 3–9 (2019).
17. Maheshkumar H. Kolekar, Intelligent Video Surveillance Systems: An Algorithmic Approach 75 (2018).
18. *See* Jody Booth, Werner Metz, Anahit Tarkhanyan & Sunil Cheruvu, Demystifying Intelligent Multimode Security Systems: An Edge-To-Cloud Cybersecurity Solutions Guide 74 (2023).
19. Bobby Allyn, *"The Computer Got It Wrong": How Facial Recognition Led to False Arrest of Black Man*, NPR (June 24, 2020), www.npr.org.
20. Nicolás Rivero, *The Little-Known AI Firms Whose Facial Recognition Tech Led to a False Arrest*, Quartz (June 26, 2020), https://qz.com.
21. Dave Maass & Matthew Guariglia, *Video Analytics User Manuals Are a Guide to Dystopia*, Elec. Frontier Found. (Nov. 19, 2020), www.eff.org; Concerned Researchers, *On Recent Research Auditing Commercial Facial Analysis Technology*, Medium (Mar. 26, 2019), https://medium.com/@bu64dcjrytwitb8/on-recent-research-auditing-commercial-facial-analysis-technology-19148bda1832.
22. *See generally id.*
23. Paul Scharre, Four Battlegrounds: Power in the Age of Artificial Intelligence (2023).
24. Matthew Humphries, *US Marines Use Cardboard Box to Defeat DARPA Robot Trained to Detect Humans*, PC Mag. (Jan. 19, 2023), www.pcmag.com.
25. *Id.*

26. Brinegar v. United States, 338 U.S. 160, 175 (1949); Hill v. California, 401 U.S. 797, 804 (1971).
27. *See* Max Minzner, *Putting Probability Back into Probable Cause*, 87 TEX. L. REV. 913, 915 (2009).
28. Ronald J. Bacigal, *Making the Right Gamble: The Odds on Probable Cause*, 74 MISS. L.J. 279, 338–39 (2004); Daniel A. Crane, *Rethinking Merger Efficiencies*, 110 MICH. L. REV. 347, 356 (2011).
29. Dhruv Mehrotra, *An Anti-Porn App Put Him in Jail and His Family Under Surveillance*, WIRED, June 12, 2023.
30. *Id.*
31. *Id.*
32. *Id.*
33. *See generally* Maneka Sinha, *Radically Reimagining Forensic Evidence*, 73 ALA. L. REV. 879, 904 (2022).
34. BRANDON L. GARRETT, AUTOPSY OF A CRIME LAB: EXPOSING THE FLAWS IN FORENSICS 5–9, 20, 52 (2021); Valena E. Beety & Jennifer D. Oliva, *Evidence on Fire*, 97 N.C. L. REV. 483, 487–88 (2019); Michael J. Saks et al., *Forensic Bitemark Identification: Weak Foundations, Exaggerated Claims*, 3 J.L. & BIOSCIENCES 538, 540 (2016).
35. *See* COMM. ON IDENTIFYING THE NEEDS OF THE FORENSIC SCI. CMTY., NAT'L RSCH. COUNCIL, STRENGTHENING FORENSIC SCIENCE IN THE UNITED STATES: A PATH FORWARD 85–110 (2009); PRESIDENT'S COUNCIL OF ADVISORS ON SCI. & TECH., FORENSIC SCIENCE IN CRIMINAL COURTS: ENSURING SCIENTIFIC VALIDITY OF FEATURE-COMPARISON METHODS 1, 87–88 (2016).
36. *See* Nina Sunde & Itiel E. Dror, *A Hierarchy of Expert Performance (HEP) Applied to Digital Forensic: Reliability and Biasability in Digital Forensic Decision Making*, 37 FORENSIC SCI. INT'L: DIGIT. INVESTIGATION 1 (2021).
37. *Id.*
38. *See* Garance Burke & Michael Tarm, *Lawsuit: Chicago Police Misused ShotSpotter in Murder Case*, AP NEWS (July 21, 2022).
39. *Id.*
40. *Id.*
41. Garance Burke, Martha Mendoza, Juliet Linderman & Michael Tarm, *How AI-Powered Tech Landed Man in Jail with Scant Evidence*, AP NEWS (Mar. 5, 2022), https://apnews.com; Garance Burke & Michael Tarm, *Lawsuit: Chicago Police Misused ShotSpotter in Murder Case*, AP NEWS (July 21, 2022), https://apnews.com; Garance Burke & Michael Tarm, *Confidential Document Reveals Key Human Role in Gunshot Tech*, AP NEWS (Jan. 20, 2023), https://apnews.com.
42. Burke et al., *supra* note 41, *AI-Powered Tech Landed Man*.
43. *ShotSpotter Files $300 Million Defamation Suit Against Vice Media*, CBS NEWS (Oct. 12, 2021), www.cbsnews.com.

44. *News Outlet Walks Back ShotSpotter Data Manipulation Claim*, Gov't Tech., (Aug. 4, 2022).
45. 18 U.S.C. §§ 2701–12.
46. Rebecca Wexler, *Privacy Asymmetries: Access to Data in Criminal Defense Investigations*, 68 UCLA L. Rev. 212, 242–43 (2021).
47. Rebecca Wexler, *Life, Liberty, and Trade Secrets: Intellectual Property in the Criminal Justice System*, 70 Stan. L. Rev. 1343, 1365–66 (2018).
48. Clare Garvie, Alvaro Bedoya & Jonathan Frankle, *The Perpetual Line-Up: Unregulated Police Face Recognition in America*, Geo. L. Ctr. on Priv. & Tech. (Oct. 18, 2016), https://www.perpetuallineup.org/.
49. Jagdish Chandra Joshi & K. K. Gupta, *Face Recognition Technology: A Review*, 8 IUP J. Telecomms. 53, 54 (2016).
50. Elizabeth E. Joh, *The New Surveillance Discretion: Automated Suspicion, Big Data, and Policing*, 10 Harv. L. & Pol'y Rev. 15, 15 (2016).
51. Lafler v. Cooper, 566 U.S. 156, 170 (2012).
52. Missouri v. Frye, 566 U.S. 134, 143 (2012).
53. D.C. Code § 22–4132.
54. Safia Umoja Noble, Algorithms of Oppression: How Search Engines Reinforce Racism (2018).
55. Ruha Benjamin, Race After Technology: Abolitionist Tools for the New Jim Code (2019).
56. Meredith Broussard, More than a Glitch: Confronting Race, Gender, and Ability Bias in Tech (2023).
57. *IIP & Manhattan DA's Office Host Symposium on Intelligence-Driven Prosecution*, John Jay C. Crim. Just. (June 7, 2016), https://www.jjay.cuny.edu/news-events/news/iip-manhattan-das-office-host-symposium-intelligence-driven-prosecution.
58. Kerry Chicon, *Intelligence-Driven Prosecution: Promoting Collaboration*, N.Y. Cnty. Dist. Att'y Off. 1 (2010), https://perma.cc/ZA37-A8RD.
59. *David O'Keefe, Head of the Manhattan District Attorney's Crime Strategies Unit*, Ctr. for Just. Innovation (Sept. 2013), www.innovatingjustice.org; Heather Mac Donald, *Op-Ed: First Came Data-Driven Policing. Now Comes Data-Driven Prosecutions*, L.A. Times, Aug. 8, 2014.
60. Jennifer A. Tallon, Dana Kralstein, Erin J. Farley & Michael Rempel, *The Intelligence-Driven Prosecution Model: A Case Study in the New York County District Attorney's Office*, Ctr. for Ct. Innovation (2016), www.innovatingjustice.org.
61. James C. McKinley Jr., *In Unusual Collaboration, Police and Prosecutors Team Up to Reduce Crime*, N.Y. Times, June 4, 2014.
62. Manhattan Dis. Att'y's Off., Models for Innovation: The Manhattan District Attorney's Office 2010–2018, at 1, 9, 14 (2018).
63. Andrew Guthrie Ferguson, *Big Data Prosecution and* Brady, 67 UCLA L. Rev. 180, 184 (2020); Andrew Guthrie Ferguson, *Predictive Prosecution*, 51 Wake Forest L. Rev. 705, 716 (2016).

64. Brady v. Maryland, 373 U.S. 83, 87 (1963).
65. *Id.*
66. *See* Kyles v. Whitley, 514 U.S. 419, 441–45 (1995).
67. *See* Giglio v. United States, 405 U.S. 150, 154–55 (1972).
68. Chicon, *supra* note 59, at 1, 7.
69. *Id.* at 21, 24.
70. *How Technology Powers Real Time Crime Centers*, POLICE, (Sept. 27, 2023).
71. Andrew Guthrie Ferguson, *Facial Recognition and the Fourth Amendment*, 105 MINN. L. REV. 1105, 1111 (2021).
72. CLARE GARVIE, GEO. L. CTR. ON PRIV. & TECH., A FORENSIC WITHOUT THE SCIENCE: FACE RECOGNITION IN U.S. CRIMINAL INVESTIGATIONS 1, 7, 9–10 (2022).

CHAPTER 10. JUDICIAL RESPONSES

1. *See* Andrew Guthrie Ferguson, *Implied Artistic License: The Distorted Lines of* Florida v. Jardines, in PAINTING CONSTITUTIONAL LAW (M. C. Mirow & Howard M. Wasserman eds., 2021).
2. Much of the argument in this section comes from Andrew Guthrie Ferguson, *Why Digital Policing Is Different*, 83 OHIO ST. L.J. 817, 820 (2022).
3. Katz v. United States, 389 U.S. 347, 353 (1967).
4. This argument builds on arguments discussed in Andrew Guthrie Ferguson, *Persistent Surveillance*, 74 ALA. L. REV. 1, 13–21 (2022).
5. *Id.*
6. Riley v. California, 573 U.S. 373, 403 (2014).
7. Carpenter v. United States, 585 U.S. 296, 301 (2018).
8. *Id.*
9. *Id.* at 321–23 (Kennedy, J., dissenting).
10. This future-proofing argument is something I have developed in a series of articles. *See* Ferguson, *supra* note 4, at 13–21; Andrew Guthrie Ferguson, *Facial Recognition and the Fourth Amendment*, 105 MINN. L. REV. 1105, 1108 (2021); Andrew Guthrie Ferguson, *Structural Sensor Surveillance*, 106 IOWA L. REV. 47, 49 (2020).
11. Leaders of a Beautiful Struggle v. Balt. Police Dep't, 456 F. Supp. 3d 699, 702 (Md. 2020), *aff'd*, 979 F.3d 219 (4th Cir. 2020), *rev'd en banc*, 2 F.4th 330 (4th Cir. 2021).
12. Leaders of a Beautiful Struggle v. Balt. Police Dep't, 2 F.4th 330, 347–48 (4th Cir. 2021).
13. This question and my answers are discussed in more depth in two articles. *See* Andrew Guthrie Ferguson, *The "Smart" Fourth Amendment*, 102 CORNELL L. REV. 547, 551 (2017); Andrew Guthrie Ferguson, *The Internet of Things and the Fourth Amendment of Effects*, 104 CALIF. L. REV. 805, 808, 823 (2016).
14. The theory of informational security is more fully developed in Ferguson, *supra* note 13, *"Smart" Fourth Amendment* at 604.
15. *Id.* at 606.

16. *Id.* at 604–14.
17. *See* California v. Acevedo, 500 U.S. 565, 580 (1991).
18. *See., e.g.*, Ferguson, *supra* note 3, at 13–21; Ferguson, *supra* note 10, *Facial Recognition* at 1108; Ferguson, *supra* note 10, *Structural Sensor Surveillance* at 49.
19. *See id.*, discussing my "future-proofing theory" as applied to these questions. The origin of the future-proofing theory can be found at Andrew Guthrie Ferguson, *Future-Proofing the Fourth Amendment*, HARV. L. REV. BLOG (June 25, 2018), https://harvardlawreview.org/blog/2018/06/future-proofing-the-fourth-amendment/.
20. *Id.*
21. Stephen E. Henderson, *Fourth Amendment Time Machines (and What They Might Say About Police Body Cameras)*, 18 U. PA. J. CONST. L. 933, 954–60 (2016).
22. Carpenter v. United States, 585 U.S. 296, 305 (2018); United States v. Jones, 565 U.S. 400, 416–17 (2012) (Sotomayor, J., concurring).
23. *See* Ferguson, *supra* note 4, at 34–37; Ferguson, *supra* note 10, *Facial Recognition* at 1135–36, 1137–39; Ferguson, *supra* note 10, *Structural Sensor Surveillance* at 76–77.
24. *Id.*
25. *See* Ferguson, *supra* note 10, *Facial Recognition* at 1135–39.
26. *See* Ferguson, *supra* note 10, *Structural Sensor Surveillance* at 76–77.
27. *See* Andrew Guthrie Ferguson, *Digital Rummaging*, 101 WASH. U.L. REV. 1473, 1509 (2024).
28. *Id.*
29. Barry Friedman & Cynthia Benin Stein, *Redefining What's "Reasonable": The Protections for Policing*, 84 GEO. WASH. L. REV. 281, 316 (2016).
30. *See* Laura K. Donohue, *The Original Fourth Amendment*, 83 U. CHI. L. REV. 1181, 1196 (2016).
31. Riley v. California, 573 U.S. 373, 403 (2014) (emphasis added).
32. U.S. CONST. amend. IV; Andresen v. Maryland, 427 U.S. 463, 480 (1976). *See* Thomas K. Clancy, *The Fourth Amendment Aspects of Computer Searches and Seizures: A Perspective and a Primer*, 75 MISS. L.J. 193, 258 (2005).
33. *See, e.g.*, Chimel v. California, 395 U.S. 752, 767–68 (1969).
34. *Id.* at 767–68 (1969) (quoting United States v. Kirschenblatt, 16 F.2d 202 (2d Cir. 1926)).
35. Florida v. Wells, 495 U.S. 1, 4 (1990); Coolidge v. New Hampshire, 403 U.S. 443, 467 (1971).
36. *See* Ferguson, *supra* note 27, at 1525.
37. Donald A. Dripps, *"Dearest Property": Digital Evidence and the History of Private "Papers" as Special Objects of Search and Seizure*, 103 J. CRIM. L. & CRIMINOLOGY 49, 70–71 (2013).
38. Craig M. Bradley, *Constitutional Protection for Private Papers*, 16 HARV. C.R.-C.L. L. REV. 461, 480–81 (1981).
39. *Formalism, Legal Realism, and Constitutionally Protected Privacy Under the Fourth and Fifth Amendments*, 90 HARV. L. REV. 945, 986 (1977).

40. Warden, Md. Penitentiary v. Hayden, 387 U.S. 294, 323–24 (1967) (Douglas, J. dissenting).
41. *See* Dripps, *supra* note 37, at 61.
42. Morgan Cloud, *Property Is Privacy: Locke and Brandeis in the Twenty-First Century*, 55 AM. CRIM. L. REV. 37, 45 (2018).
43. *Id.* at 44.
44. *Id.* at 45–46 ("Locke's broad theory of property included a man's *person*, his *labor*, and the *products* of that labor. . . . A man's property includes his own person, his labor, and the products of that labor. When the products of his labor incorporate external objects, they are transformed into his property as well. These products of his labor are not merely things that he now owns. They are extensions of his being, expressions of his very personhood.").
45. *Id.* at 48 ("Madison's definition of property is similar to Locke's. If anything, Madison expresses the Lockean theories of property—both broad and narrow—more clearly than had Locke.").
46. *Id.*
47. *Id.* at 55 ("Papers are expressive property. A written document is a tangible thing, but typically its value depends upon its contents. The contents, whether prepared for personal or business purposes, are the physical manifestation of the author's ideas. This insight comports with Locke's broad theory of property. If a person's property includes the products of her labor, then her expressive writings are expressions of her being that deserve protection as property.").
48. *Id.* at 49.
49. United States v. Bennett, 409 F.2d 888 (2d Cir.1969).
50. Wilkes v. Wood, 19 How. St. Tr. 1153, 1154 (C.P. 1763).
51. *See* Ferguson, *supra* note 27, at 1513.

CHAPTER 11. LEGISLATIVE RESPONSES

1. *See* BRIAN HOCHMAN, THE LISTENERS: A HISTORY OF WIRETAPPING IN THE UNITED STATES 194–98 (2022).
2. *See* Electronic Communications Privacy Act of 1986, Pub. L. No. 99–508, 100 Stat. 1848 (1986) (codified as amended in scattered sections of 18 U.S.C. §§2510–23, §§ 3121–327); Orin S. Kerr, *The Next Generation Communications Privacy Act*, 162 U. PA. L. REV. 373, 378–83 (2014).
3. Health Insurance Portability and Accountability Act of 1996 § 262 et seq., 42 U.S.C.A. § 1320d et seq.; Genetic Information Nondiscrimination Act of 2008, Pub. L. No. 110–233, 122 Stat. 881 (2008).
4. Ben Wolford, *What Is the GDPR, the EU's New Data Protection Law?*, GDPR, https://gdpr.eu/what-is-gdpr/.
5. *See US State Privacy Legislation Tracker*, INT'L ASS'N PRIV. PROFS. (July 22, 2024), https://iapp.org/resources/article/us-state-privacy-legislation-tracker/.

6. *See* Avi Asher-Schapiro & Anastasia Moloney, *My Body, My Data: US Fight for Abortion Access Turns Digital*, Thompson Reuters (June 22, 2023), www.reuters.com.
7. 18 U.S.C.A. §§ 2514–19 (West); 18 U.S.C. §§ 2510–23.
8. *See generally* Brian Hochman, The Listeners: A History of Wiretapping in the United States 190–95 (2022).
9. *Id.*, at 195–200.
10. *See* 18 U.S.C. § 2516; 18 U.S.C. § 2517; 18 U.S.C. § 2518; 18 U.S.C. § 2519.
11. 18 U.S.C. § 2516–19.
12. 18 U.S.C. § 2518(1)(c).
13. 18 U.S.C. § 2518(1).
14. 18 U.S.C. § 2518(1)(e).
15. 18 U.S.C. § 2518(1)(b).
16. *Id.*
17. 18 U.S.C. § 2518(3).
18. 18 U.S.C. § 2519.
19. *Wiretap Reports*, U.S. Courts, https://www.uscourts.gov/statistics-reports/analysis-reports/wiretap-reports (last visited Sept. 16, 2024).
20. Jennifer D. Oliva, *Prescription-Drug Policing: The Right to Health-Information Privacy Pre- and Post-*Carpenter, 69 Duke L.J. 775, 780 (2020).
21. 18 U.S.C. § 2518(1)(c).
22. 18 U.S.C. § 2518(1)(b).
23. U.S. Courts, Wiretap Report 2021 (2021), https://www.uscourts.gov/statistics-reports/wiretap-report-2021.
24. Rachel A. Harmon, *Federal Programs and the Real Costs of Policing*, 90 N.Y.U. L. Rev. 870, 872 (2015).
25. Clare Garvie, Alvaro Bedoya & Jonathan Frankle, *The Perpetual Line-Up: Unregulated Police Face Recognition in America*, Geo. L. Ctr. on Priv. & Tech. (Oct. 18, 2016), www.perpetuallineup.org.
26. *See* Commonwealth v. McCarthy, 142 N.E.3d 1090, 1095 (Mass. 2020).
27. *See* Nirja Chokshi, *How Surveillance Cameras Could Be Weaponized with A.I.*, N.Y. Times, June 13, 2019.
28. *See* Barry Friedman & Maria Ponomarenko, *Democratic Policing*, 90 N.Y.U. L. Rev. 1827, 1874–75 (2015).
29. *See generally* Catherine Crump, *Surveillance Policy Making by Procurement*, 91 Wash. L. Rev. 1595, 1595 (2016); Elizabeth E. Joh, *The Undue Influence of Surveillance Technology Companies on Policing*, 92 N.Y.U. L. Rev. Online 19, 20 (2017).
30. Barry Friedman & Elizabeth G. Jánszky, *Policing's Information Problem*, 99 Tex. L. Rev. 1, 30 (2020).
31. *See Community Control Over Police Surveillance: (CCOPS)*, ACLU, https://www.aclu.org/issues/privacy-technology/surveillance

-technologies/community-control-over-police-surveillance [https://perma.cc/6XVJ-4WYC].

32. Orin S. Kerr, *Searches and Seizures in a Digital World*, 119 HARV. L. REV. 531, 581 (2005).
33. *See, e.g.*, FED. R. EVID. 501.
34. *See* Jerry Kang, Katie Shilton, Deborah Estrin, Jeff Burke & Mark Hansen, *Self-Surveillance Privacy*, 97 IOWA L. REV. 809, 835 (2012).
35. United States v. Hubbell, 530 U.S. 27, 34 (2000).
36. Pennsylvania v. Muniz, 496 U.S. 582, 588–89 (1990).
37. *Digital Dragnets: Examining The Government's Access to Your Personal Data*, 117th Cong. (2022) (statement of Rebecca Wexler, Faculty Co-director, Berkeley Center for Law & Technology and Assistant Professor of Law, University of California, Berkeley, School of Law).
38. Aziz Z. Huq & Rebecca Wexler, *Digital Privacy for Reproductive Choice in the Post-*Roe *Era*, 98 N.Y.U. L. REV. 555, 637 (2023).
39. *Id.*
40. *Id.* at 638.
41. Similarly, Jerry Kang and others proposed a "self-surveillance privilege" that focused on data stored in a "personal data vault." Jerry Kang et al., *supra* note 34, at 835.
42. *See US State Legislation Tracker*, *supra* note 5.
43. Biometric Information Privacy Act, 740 ILL. COMP. STAT. 14/1–99 (2008).
44. *See, e.g., FTC Order Prohibits Data Broker X-Mode Social and Outlogic from Selling Sensitive Location Data*, FED. TRADE COMM'N (Jan. 9, 2024), www.ftc.gov.
45. Facial Recognition and Biometric Technology Moratorium Act of 2023, S. 681, 118th Cong. (as reported by the S. Comm. on the Judiciary, Mar. 3, 2023).
46. Justice in Forensic Algorithms Act of 2019, H.R. 4368, 116th Cong. § 2(c) (as reported by the H.R. Comm. on Judiciary, Oct. 2, 2019).

CHAPTER 12. INDIVIDUAL RESPONSES

1. *Smart Cups*, PERSON CENTRED SOFTWARE, https://personcentredsoftware.com/products/digital-care-system/key-features/smart-cups.
2. Alex Hern, *Fitness Tracking App Strava Gives Away Location of Secret Location of US Army Bases*, THE GUARDIAN, Jan. 28, 2018.
3. *See* Chapter 4.
4. Tate Ryan-Mosley, *The Movement to Limit Face Recognition Tech Might Finally Get a Win*, MIT TECH. REV., July 20, 2023.
5. *See generally* OUR DATA BODIES, https://www.odbproject.org/ [https://perma.cc/68K7-VGYT].
6. Freddy Martinez & Lucy Parsons Labs, *Op-Ed: End the City's ShotSpotter Contract*, SOUTH SIDE WEEKLY, Apr. 28, 2021.

7. *See* Rosalind Brazel, *City of Seattle Hires Ginger Armbruster as Chief Privacy Officer*, SEATTLE TECH TALK (July 11, 2017), https://techtalk.seattle.gov/2017/07/11/city-of-seattle-hires-ginger-armbruster-as-chief-privacy-officer/; *see also* Ira S. Rubinstein, *Privacy Localism*, 93 WASH. L. REV. 1961, 1997 (2018).
8. Darwin BondGraham, *Oakland Privacy Commission Approves Surveillance Transparency and Oversight Law*, E. BAY EXPRESS, Jan. 6, 2017.
9. *See generally* STOP LAPD SPYING COAL., BEFORE THE BULLET HITS THE BODY: DISMANTLING PREDICTIVE POLICING IN LOS ANGELES 5, 29–31 (2018); OFF. OF THE INSPECTOR GEN., L.A. POLICE COMM'N, REVIEW OF SELECTED LOS ANGELES POLICE DEPARTMENT DATA-DRIVEN POLICING STRATEGIES 3 (2019).
10. *See Atlas of Surveillance*, ELEC. FRONTIER FOUND., https://atlasofsurveillance.org/ [https://perma.cc/TKR7-DRUR].
11. *See* ELEC. FRONTIER FOUND., https://www.eff.org/.
12. ALGORITHMIC JUST. LEAGUE, https://www.ajl.org/.
13. Joy Buolamwini, UNMASKING AI: MY MISSION TO PROTECT WHAT IS HUMAN IN A WORLD OF MACHINES 94–97 (2023).
14. Joy Buolamwini & Timnit Gebru, *Gender Shades: Intersectional Accuracy Disparities in Commercial Gender Classification*, 18 PROC. MACH. LEARNING RSCH. 1 (2018).
15. *See* POET OF CODE, https://www.poetofcode.com/.
16. CODED BIAS (Netflix 2020), https://www.netflix.com/title/81328723.
17. *Facial Recognition Technology (Part I): Its Impact on Our Civil Rights and Liberties: Hearing Before the H. Comm. on Oversight and Reform*, 116th Cong. 2 (2019) (statement of Joy Buolamwini, Founder, Algorithmic Justice League).
18. *See, e.g.*, Justin Jouvenal, *The New Way Police Are Surveilling You: Calculating Your Threat "Score,"* WASH. POST, Jan. 10, 2016); Geoffrey Fowler, *What Does Your Car Know About You? We Hacked a Chevy to Find Out*, WASH. POST, Dec. 17, 2019; Drew Harwell, *Colleges Are Turning Students' Phones into Surveillance Machines, Tracking the Locations of Hundreds of Thousands*, WASH. POST, Dec. 24, 2019.
19. *See generally* 404 MEDIA, https://www.404media.co/.
20. *See, e.g.*, Jon Schuppe, *How Facial Recognition Became a Routine Policing Tool in America*, NBC NEWS (May 11, 2019), www.nbcnews.com; Cyrus Farivar & Olivia Solon, *FBI Trawled Facebook to Arrest Protestors for Inciting Riots, Court Records Show*, NBC NEWS (June 19, 2020), www.nbcnews.com.
21. Dell Cameron, *The FBI Just Admitted It Bought US Location Data*, WIRED, Mar. 8, 2023.
22. Garance Burke, Martha Mendoza, Juliet Linderman & Michael Tarm, *How AI-Powered Tech Landed a Chicago Grandfather in Jail for Nearly a Year with Scant Evidence*, CHI. TRIB., June 17, 2022.
23. Avi Asher-Schapiro, *Privacy or Safety? U.S. Brings "Surveillance City to the Suburbs,"* REUTERS (May 11, 2023),www.reuters.com.

24. Kashmir Hill, *The Secretive Company That Might End Privacy as We Know It*, N.Y. Times, Nov. 2, 2021.
25. Jennifer Valentino-DeVries, Natasha Singer, Michael H. Keller & Aaron Krolik, *Your Apps Know Where You Were Last Night, and They're Not Keeping It Secret*, N.Y. Times, Dec. 10, 2018.
26. Caroline Haskins, *New Map Reveals That at Least 231 Cities Have Partnered with Ring*, Vice (Aug. 8, 2019), www.vice.com; Alfred Ng, *Amazon's Helping Police Build a Surveillance Network with Ring Doorbells*, CNET (Jun. 5, 2019), www.cnet.com.
27. Ali Winston, *Palantir Has Secretly Been Using New Orleans to Test Its Predictive Policing Technology*, The Verge (Feb. 27, 2018), www.theverge.com.
28. Sidney Fussell, *The New Tech That Could Turn Police Body Cams into Nightmare Surveillance Tools*, Gizmodo (Mar. 9, 2017), https://gizmodo.com.
29. Dhruv Mehrotra, Surya Mattu, Annie Gilbertson & Aaron Sankin, *How We Determined Crime Prediction Software Disproportionately Targeted Low-Income, Black, and Latino Neighborhoods*, The Markup (Dec. 2, 2021), www.themarkup.org.
30. Aaron Sankin, Dhruv Mehrota, Surya Mattu & Annie Gilbertson, *Crime Prediction Software Promised to Be Free of Biases. New Data Shows It Perpetuates Them*, The Markup (Dec. 21, 2021), www.themarkup.org.
31. Kathleen McGrory & Neil Bedi, *Targeted*, Tampa Bay Times, Sept. 3, 2020.
32. Stacy-Ann Elvy, *Paying for Privacy and the Personal Data Economy*, 117 Colum. L. Rev. 1369, 1401 (2017).
33. *See Tech, Internet and Cybersecurity*, Ron Wyden, https://www.wyden.senate.gov/issues/tech-internet-and-cybersecurity.
34. *Facial Recognition Technology (Part I): Its Impact on Our Civil Rights and Liberties: Hearing Before the H. Comm. on Oversight and Reform*, 116th Cong. 2 (2019) (statement of Andrew Guthrie Ferguson, Professor of Law).

CONCLUSION

1. *See generally* Paul Mozur, *Inside China's Dystopian Dreams, A.I., Shame, and Lots of Cameras*, N.Y. Times, July 8, 2018; Paul Mozur, *One Month, 500,000 Face Scans: How China Is Using A.I. to Profile a Minority*, N.Y. Times, Apr. 14, 2019; Simon Denyer, *China's Watchful Eye: Beijing Bets on Facial Recognition in a Big Drive for Total Surveillance*, Wash. Post, Jan. 7, 2018.
2. Andrew Guthrie Ferguson, *Surveillance and the Tyrant Test*, 110 Geo. L.J. 205, 213 (2021).
3. *Id.* Much of this chapter is inspired by my article *Surveillance and the Tyrant Test.*
4. Timothy Snyder, On Tyranny: Twenty Lessons from the Twentieth Century 10 (2017).
5. Stephen F. Rohde, *Presidential Power vs. Free Press*, L.A. Law., Oct. 2017, at 26.
6. *See* Stanford v. Texas, 379 U.S. 476, 481 (1965).

7. *Cf.* Rachel Moran, *In Police We Trust*, 62 VILL. L. REV. 953, 958 (2017).
8. ANDREW E. TASLITZ, RECONSTRUCTING THE FOURTH AMENDMENT: A HISTORY OF SEARCH AND SEIZURE, 1789–1868, at 256 (2006); Andrew E. Taslitz, *Slaves No More! The Implications of the Informed Citizen Ideal for Discovery Before Fourth Amendment Suppression Hearings*, 15 GA. ST. U. L. REV. 709, 748 (1999).
9. SIMONE BROWNE, DARK MATTERS: ON THE SURVEILLANCE OF BLACKNESS 12–17 (2015); RUHA BENJAMIN, RACE AFTER TECHNOLOGY: ABOLITIONIST TOOLS FOR THE NEW JIM CODE 184 (2019); Chris Gilliard, *The Rise of "Luxury Surveillance,"* THE ATLANTIC, Oct. 18, 2022.
10. Alvaro M. Bedoya, *The Color of Surveillance*, SLATE (Jan. 18, 2016), www.slate.com; Dorothy Roberts & Jeffrey Vagle, Opinion, *Racial Surveillance Has a Long History*, THE HILL (Jan. 4, 2016), https://thehill.com.
11. Potter Stewart, *The Road to* Mapp v. Ohio *and Beyond: The Origins, Development, and Future of the Exclusionary Rule in Search and-Seizure Cases*, 83 COLUM. L. REV. 1365, 1371 (1983).
12. Laura K. Donohue, *The Original Fourth Amendment*, 83 U. CHI. L. REV. 1181, 1240 (2016).
13. Payton v. New York, 445 U.S. 573, 583 (1980).
14. Riley v. California, 573 U.S. 373, 403 (2014).
15. James Otis, *Against Writs of Assistance* (Feb. 24, 1761).
16. Thomas K. Clancy, *The Framers' Intent: John Adams, His Era, and the Fourth Amendment*, 86 IND. L.J. 979, 983–84 (2011).
17. James J. Tomkovicz, California v. Acevedo: *The Walls Close in on the Warrant Requirement*, 29 AM. CRIM. L. REV. 1103, 1134 (1992).
18. David A. Sklansky, *The Fourth Amendment and Common Law*, 100 COLUM. L. REV. 1739, 1792 (2000).
19. Steven I. Friedland, *Of Clouds and Clocks: Police Location Tracking in the Digital Age*, 48 TEX. TECH L. REV. 165, 172 (2015).
20. Donohue, *supra* note 12, at 1322.
21. Thomas Y. Davies, *Recovering the Original Fourth Amendment*, 98 MICH. L. REV. 547, 590 (1999).
22. Moran, *supra* note 7, at 959.
23. Albert W. Alschuler & Andrew G. Deiss, *A Brief History of Criminal Jury in the United States*, 61 U. CHI. L. REV. 867, 871 (1994).
24. Raymond Shih Ray Ku, *Privacy Is the Problem*, 19 WIDENER L.J. 873, 886 (2010).
25. *Id.*
26. Taslitz, *supra* note 8, *Slaves No More!* at 738.
27. Seth W. Stoughton, *The Blurred Blue Line: Reform in an Era of Public & Private Policing*, 44 AM. J. CRIM. L. 117, 123 (2017).
28. Taslitz, *supra* note 8, *Slaves No More!* at 746.
29. *Id.* at 748.

30. Barry Friedman & Maria Ponomarenko, *Democratic Policing*, 90 N.Y.U. L. Rev. 1827, 1874–75 (2015); Maria Ponomarenko, *Rethinking Police Rulemaking*, 114 Nw. U. L. Rev. 1, 51–56 (2019).
31. Mailyn Fidler, *Local Police Surveillance and the Administrative Fourth Amendment*, 36 Santa Clara High Tech. L.J. 481, 555 (2020).
32. Barry Friedman, *Lawless Surveillance*, 97 N.Y.U. L. Rev. 1143, 1166 (2022).
33. Christopher Slobogin, *Policing as Administration*, 165 U. Pa. L. Rev. 91, 120–21 (2016).
34. Ferguson, *supra* note 2, at 279.
35. Roger A. Fairfax Jr., *Grand Jury Innovation: Toward a Functional Makeover of the Ancient Bulwark of Liberty*, 19 Wm. & Mary Bill Rts. J. 339, 354 (2010).
36. *Id.*
37. *Privacy Advisory Commission*, City of Oakland, https://www.oaklandca.gov/boards-commissions/privacy-advisory-board#page-documents [https://perma.cc/R28N-9T75].

INDEX

ABOUT THE AUTHOR

Andrew Guthrie Ferguson is Professor of Law at the George Washington University Law School. He is a national expert on new surveillance technologies, policing, and criminal justice. He is the author of the 2018 PROSE Award–winning book *The Rise of Big Data Policing: Surveillance, Race, and the Future of Law Enforcement.*

www.ingramcontent.com/pod-product-compliance
Lightning Source LLC
Chambersburg PA
CBHW020031060426
42338CB00071B/1818/J

* 9 7 8 1 4 7 9 8 3 8 2 8 8 *